Test Bank

to accompany

Social Psychology

Sixth Edition

David G. Myers
Hope College

Prepared by
Julia Zuwerink Jacks
University of North Carolina–Greensboro

 **McGraw-Hill College**

**Boston   Burr Ridge, IL   Dubuque, IA   Madison, WI   New York   San Francisco   St. Louis
Bangkok   Bogotá   Caracas   Lisbon   London   Madrid
Mexico City   Milan   New Delhi   Seoul   Singapore   Sydney   Taipei   Toronto**

McGraw-Hill College

A Division of The McGraw·Hill Companies

Test Bank to accompany SOCIAL PSYCHOLOGY, SIXTH EDITION

2 3 4 5 6 7 8 9 0 QPD/QPD 9 0 9 8

ISBN 0-07-2902213

www.mhhe.com

CONTENTS

This test bank retains 70% of the multiple choice questions that appeared in Dr. Martin Bolt's *Fifth Edition* test bank. My debt to Dr. Bolt is obvious and immense. I have selectively replaced 30% of the multiple choice questions, being particularly sensitive to cover material that is new or revised in Myers' *Social Psychology, Sixth Edition*. I have also added 5 "critical thinking questions" per chapter. These questions are designed to encourage both integrative and creative thinking. As always, test banks benefit enormously from the feedback and comments of classroom teachers who use them. Please continue to share your suggestions for improving the items in this test bank.

Guide to Using the Test Bank

For each chapter in David G. Myers' *Social Psychology, Sixth Edition*, this test bank provides the instructor with 100 multiple-choice items to use in composing tests. Although some critical thinking questions may be used for chapter tests, the instructor may prefer to use them as a basis for classroom discussion and/or short written assignments. The multiple choice items do not contain page references as in previous editions. However, the items generally follow the order of the text. As in previous editions, each item contains the following information:

Answer: The correct answer for the item.

Type: The type of understanding the item is intended to test:

DEF = Definition items require recognition of the key terms and basic concepts of the discipline.

FAC = Factual items require knowledge of information that is explicitly presented in the textbook. They test knowledge of research findings, methods, and important people and events.

CON = Conceptual items require analysis, synthesis, or application of information presented in the textbook. Designed to promote critical thinking, these items often require deduction from key principles or application to everyday life.

Test Composition

In this Test Bank you will occasionally find that several items address the same or similar knowledge. In such cases it is best to select only one of the items for inclusion in a test. Further, you may find that the wording of some items provides clues for answering other items. Be sensitive to this possibility so you do not inadvertently choose items that, in combination with others, render certain questions useless or redundant.

Items 86 to 100 in each chapter of this test bank are specifically drawn from the *Study Guide to Accompany Myers' Social Psychology, Fifth Edition*, by Dr. Martin Bolt. To encourage students' use of this study guide and mastery of the text material, you may want to announce that a limited number of test items will come directly from it.

<u>Micro Test III</u>

The questions in the Test Bank are available on MicroTest III, a powerful but easy-to-use test-generating program by Chariot Software Group. MicroTest is available for Windows and Macintosh personal computers. With MicroTest, you can easily select the questions from the Test Bank and print a test and answer key. You can customize questions, headings, and instructions; add or import questions of your own; and print the test in a choice of fonts if your printer supports them. You can obtain a copy of MicroTest III by contacting your McGraw-Hill sales representative.

Julia Zuwerink Jacks
Department of Psychology
University of North Carolina-Greensboro
P.O. Box 26164
Greensboro, NC 27402-6164
jrjacks@goodall.uncg.edu

CHAPTER ONE
INTRODUCING SOCIAL PSYCHOLOGY

Multiple Choice Questions

1. Which of the following questions is not likely to be addressed by social psychologists?
   A. Are our social beliefs self-fulfilling?
   B. In what ways do other people influence our attitudes and actions?
   C. What situations trigger people to be helpful or greedy?
   D. Is human development a continuous process or does it proceed through a series of stages?
   Answer D, Type FAC

2. The examples cited in your text as phenomena of particular interest to social psychology are similar to each other because they all
   A. deal with how people view and affect one another.
   B. show the influence of personality on behavior.
   C. represent various forms of groups and organizations.
   D. show the power of internal influences on human action.
   Answer A, Type FAC

3. Social psychology is the scientific study of
   A. how people think about, influence, and relate to one another.
   B. how people perceive, think about, and communicate with one another.
   C. how people observe, predict, and control one another.
   D. social groups, organizations, and institutions.
   Answer A, Type DEF

4. Cindarella's Prince had trouble recognizing her in her home, as opposed to the ballroom where they met. This observation reflects
   A. the power of the situation.
   B. the importance of cognition.
   C. the power of the person.
   D. common sense psychology.
   Answer A, Type CON

5. Contemporary social psychology emphasizes the importance of cognition because
   A. emotions are unimportant to social psychological theory.
   B. social reality is something we subjectively construct.
   C. people all think alike.
   d. social thinking is objective.
   Answer B, Type FAC

6. Contemporary social psychology emphasizes the
   A. power of the situation.
   B. power of the person.
   C. importance of cognition.
   D. All of the above.
   Answer D, Type FAC

7. Sociologists study the structure and function of

A.   relationships.
B.   societies.
C.   groups.
D.   cultures.
Answer C, Type DEF

8.   The social psychologist is usually interested in studying the
A.   group.
B.   individual.
C.   institution.
D.   community.
Answer B, Type DEF

9.   Social psychology is to _____ as sociology is to _____.
A.   cognition; influence
B.   manipulation; control
C.   individuals; groups
D.   social theory; social problems
Answer C, Type CON

10.   The first social psychology experiments were reported
A.   just two centuries ago.
B.   just a century ago.
C.   just 75 years ago.
D.   just after World War I.
Answer B, Type FAC

11.   Which of the following examples is a question a social psychologist would be most likely to
study?
A.   How have divorce rates changed over time?
B.   What accounts for racial differences in intelligence?
C.   In deciding how they will vote in an election, are individuals more influenced by one
persuasive medium than by another?
D.   In what ways do children learn differently than do adults?
Answer C, Type CON

12.   Of the following studies, which is the most likely to be conducted by a social psychologist?
A.   An experimenter watches to see whether hungry game players use a more aggressive
strategy than players who are not hungry.
B.   An interviewer does a case study of a physically disabled veteran.
C.   An archival researcher examines records of divorce rates across cultures.
D.   A test administrator measures the skills of an adolescent whose class performance has
been poor.
Answer A, Type CON

13.   Social psychologists rely more heavily than sociologists on studies in which they
A.   conduct naturalistic observations of real-world events.
B.   manipulate a factor to see what effect it has on behavior.
C.   consult records of past events and statistics to identify important trends in the data.
D.   focus their efforts on analyzing and sometimes solving social problems.
Answer B, Type FAC

14.   The factors that sociologists study, such as economic class, are typically
A.   difficult or unethical to manipulate.

B.   easy to translate into experimental research.

C.   better understood with the research methods preferred by social psychologists.

D.   identical to those examined by social psychologists.

Answer A, Type FAC

15.   Although sociologists and social psychologists are often interested in similar topics, social psychologists are more likely to investigate the topic through the use of

A.   experiments.

B.   surveys.

C.   case studies.

D.   face-to-face interviews.

Answer A, Type FAC

16.   Personality psychologists are more interested in _____, while social psychologists more likely focus on _____.

A.   normal personality; disordered or abnormal behavior

B.   individual differences; our common humanity

C.   situational influences; internal motivations

D.   cognition; emotion

Answer B, Type FAC

17.   Compared to personality psychologists, most social psychologists are

A.   well known even to laypersons.

B.   people who worked in the late nineteenth and early twentieth centuries.

C.   best known for having developed grand theories of human behavior.

D.   alive today and making smaller-scale contributions to theory.

Answer D, Type FAC

18.   Compared to personality psychology, social psychology

A.   has a shorter history.

B.   is more likely to focus on the individual.

C.   is more likely to use the case study in research.

D.   places greater emphasis on the value of correlational research.

Answer A, Type FAC

19.   The various disciplines that study human beings

A.   often offer different levels of explanation that are all valuable.

B.   typically offer conflicting perspectives that have to be sorted out.

C.   are usually free of value judgments.

D.   can be useful only to the extent that they employ the scientific method.

Answer A, Type FAC

20.   Which of the following statements best summarizes the relationship among different "levels of explanation?"

A.   They compete with each other.

B.   They discredit each other.

C.   Higher-level explanations replace lower-level ones.

D.   They complement each other.

Answer D, Type FAC

21.   Social psychological explanations of human behavior are less integrative than _____, but more integrative than _____.

A.   biology; theology

B.   theology; biology

C.   biology; chemistry
D.   chemistry; physics
Answer B, Type FAC

22.   How do values obviously enter the picture in social psychology?
       A.   Values influence researchers' choice of topics.
       B.   Values affect the types of people attracted to various disciplines.
       C.   Values are frequently the object of social psychological analysis.
       D.   All of the above.
    Answer D, Type FAC

23.   Values can subtly influence science by guiding
       A.   scientists' assumptions and preconceptions.
       B.   the labels scientists use for their concepts.
       C.   scientists' thoughts about what ought to be.
       D.   All of the above.
    Answer D, Type FAC

24.   Which of the following statements about values and social psychology is true?
       A.   Research trends are usually out of step with the social concerns of their times.
       B.   The fact that human thinking always involves interpretation is precisely why we need scientific analysis.
       C.   Research into how values form, change, and influence one another helps us identify which of them are right.
       D.   All of the above are true.
    Answer B, Type FAC

25.   Contrary to popular opinion, scientists investigate nature
       A.   from a position of pure objectivity, with no personal motives or social agenda.
       B.   by interpreting it according to their own mental categories.
       C.   for its aesthetic value with little or no regard for the artificial value of objectivity.
       D.   with no preconceptions.
    Answer B, Type FAC

26.   Common assumptions often go unchallenged among a group of scholars who share the same
       A.   area of interest.
       B.   method of inquiry.
       C.   level of intelligence.
       D.   culture.
    Answer D, Type FAC

27.   In the 1950s, Hastorf and Cantril asked rival students at Princeton and Dartmouth to evaluate a film of a recent football game between their schools' teams. Which of the following summarizes their judgments?
       A.   The Princeton students saw twice as many Princeton violations as the Dartmouth students saw.
       B.   The Dartmouth students saw the Princeton players as "victims" of unfair infractions and fighting.
       C.   Each school's students agreed that the opposing team was responsible for the rough play.
       D.   When asked to be objective, each school's students seemed able to put aside their biases.
    Answer C, Type FAC

28.   We tend to take for granted the shared beliefs that European social psychologists call our _____, our most important but least debated convictions.

A. social representations
B. symbolic interactions
C. hindsights
D. naturalistic truths
Answer A, Type DEF

29. Which of the following psychological terms reflects a disguised value judgment?
A. well-adjusted
B. mentally ill
C. self-actualized
D. All of the above.
Answer D, Type FAC

30. Which of the following labels implies a judgment based on subjective values?
A. freedom fighter
B. terrorist
C. patriot
D. All of the above.
Answer D, Type CON

31. "The way things are is the way they ought to be." This statement reflects the
A. hindsight bias.
B. social representation bias.
C. naturalistic fallacy.
D. correlation-causality bias.
Answer C, Type DEF

32. A cross-cultural researcher finds that across the world most legislators are male. He concludes that political office in his own country should be closed to women. The researcher is most clearly guilty of
A. the naturalistic fallacy.
B. the hindsight bias.
C. illusory correlation.
D. false consensus effect.
Answer A, Type CON

33. Which of the following countries compose psychology's first world?
A. United States and Great Britain
B. Great Britain and Germany
C. United States and Canada
D. United States and Russia
Answer C, Type FAC

34. In comparison to social psychologists elsewhere, those in third-world countries are
A. more likely to use questionnaires in their research.
B. more likely to explore issues related to poverty and conflict.
C. more likely to give attention to the personal and interpersonal levels of explanation.
D. more likely to explore the basics of human nature.
Answer B, Type FAC

35. European social psychologists question the emphasis that social psychologists in the United States place on
A. social issues.
B. individualism.

C.   the natural observation of behavior.

D.   the intergroup level of explanation.

Answer B, Type FAC

36.   Two contradictory criticisms faced by social psychology are that its findings are obvious and that

A.   its findings are trivial.

B.   its findings are false.

C.   its findings could be used to manipulate people.

D.   its findings are contradictory.

Answer C, Type FAC

37.   The hindsight bias contributes to the idea that

A.   psychological experiments lack mundane realism.

B.   social psychology is potentially dangerous.

C.   the results of psychological experiments are mere common sense.

D.   psychological experiments lack experimental realism.

Answer C, Type FAC

38.   The day after Ronald Reagan defeated Jimmy Carter in the 1980 presidential election, survey respondents claimed that just before the election they would have predicted

A.   a slim Reagan victory.

B.   a landslide Reagan victory.

C.   a slim Carter victory.

D.   a landslide Carter victory.

Answer B, Type FAC

39.   The hindsight bias affects the way we view decision makers, making us more likely to

A.   see their decisions as surprisingly insightful and correct.

B.   blame them for making obviously bad choices.

C.   forgive them for making understandable mistakes in crises.

D.   admire them for handling well those choices we ourselves cannot make.

Answer B, Type FAC

40.   Amy reads a research article and feels like it didn't tell her anything she didn't already know. However, when asked to guess the results of another experiment before reading it, she cannot. Amy's experience illustrates the

A.   hindsight bias.

B.   foresight bias.

C.   confirmation bias.

D.   correspondence bias.

Answer A, Type CON

41.   When researcher Karl Teigen gave students the actual proverb "fear is stronger than love," most rated it as true. When he gave others the reverse form, "love is stronger than fear,"

A.   most rated it as false.

B.   most rated it as true.

C.   half as many rated it as true.

D.   only 1% rated it as true.

Answer B, Type FAC

42.   The I-knew-it-all-along phenomenon can often lead students of social psychology

A.   to over-prepare for an exam.

B.   to study just the right amount for an exam.

C.   to under-prepare for an exam.

D.   None of the above.
Answer C, Type CON

43.   An integrated set of principles that explain and predict observed events is called
    A.   a test.
    B.   an hypothesis.
    C.   a proof.
    D.   a theory.
Answer D, Type DEF

44.   A good theory will make clear predictions that
    A.   confirm or modify the theory.
    B.   generate new exploration.
    C.   suggest practical application.
    D.   All of the above.
Answer D, Type FAC

45.   A research hypothesis is a
    A.   testable prediction.
    B.   theory.
    C.   collection of empirical observations.
    D.   technique for analyzing data.
Answer A, Type DEF

46.   Hypotheses implied by a theory allow researchers to
    A.   learn about the theory.
    B.   test the theory.
    C.   confirm the theory.
    D.   disconfirm the theory.
Answer B, Type FAC

47.   Social psychologist Kurt Lewin has aptly commented, "There is nothing so practical as a good
    _____."
    A.   experiment
    B.   theory
    C.   laboratory
    D.   guess
Answer B, Type FAC

48.   When theories are discarded, it is usually because they
    A.   have been falsified.
    B.   have been displaced by newer, better theories.
    C.   attempted to summarize too large a body of data.
    D.   generated too many testable hypotheses.
Answer B, Type FAC

49.   Research done in natural, real-life settings outside the laboratory is called
    A.   case study research.
    B.   field research.
    C.   correlational research.
    D.   experimental research.
Answer B, Type DEF

50.   A researcher is interested in learning whether young people whose fathers are absent from the
    home are more likely to engage in delinquent behavior. She compares the arrest rates of boys

whose fathers are absent with those of boys whose fathers are present in the home. This is an example of

A.   a correlational study.
B.   an experimental study.
C.   a field experiment.
D.   a self-report study.

Answer A, Type CON

51.   A naturally occurring relationship among variables is known as
A.   a correlation.
B.   a coefficient.
C.   an attribution.
D.   a causal link.

Answer A, Type DEF

52.   Variable X is correlated with Variable Y. Which of the following could explain this correlation?
A.   X causes Y.
B.   Y causes X.
C.   A third variable causes or influences both X and Y.
D.   All of the above.

Answer D, Type FAC

53.   Cause-effect relationships are studied using
A.   experimental research methods.
B.   correlational research methods.
C.   field research methods.
D.   survey research methods.

Answer A, Type FAC

54.   In a study of Minnesota students, Maruyama and colleagues concluded that self-esteem and achievement are positively correlated because
A.   higher self-esteem boosts achievement.
B.   achievement produces higher self-esteem.
C.   both self-esteem and achievement are linked to underlying intelligence and family social status.
D.   both self-esteem and achievement are linked to healthy physical and psychological adjustment.

Answer C, Type FAC

55.   Research has shown that tall grave markers (a status symbol) are
A.   the cause of longevity.
B.   unrelated to longevity.
C.   positively correlated with longevity.
D.   negatively correlated with longevity.

Answer C, Type FAC

56.   The great strength of correlational survey research is that it
A.   brings important factors into the laboratory.
B.   studies factors in real-world settings that cannot be manipulated in the laboratory.
C.   establishes clear cause-effect connections among variables.
D.   maintains high mundane realism and thus increases generalizability.

Answer B, Type FAC

57.   Which of the following statements about correlational research is true?

A.　It enables prediction of one variable given knowledge of the other.
B.　It specifies the cause-effect relationship among variables.
C.　It can only be carried out in controlled laboratory settings.
D.　All of the above.
Answer A, Type FAC

58.　A researcher finds that higher social status is associated with greater health. What could explain this positive correlation?
A.　Having a high social status leads to better health.
B.　Being in good health allows one to achieve higher social status.
C.　Other facts like family background may contribute to a greater likelihood of having good health and high status.
D.　All of the above.
Answer D, Type CON

59.　The great disadvantage of correlational research is that
A.　it does not allow us to examine factors like race and social status.
B.　knowing that two variables change together does not allow us to predict one when we know the other.
C.　it rules out consideration of confounding variables.
D.　it does not specify cause and effect.
Answer D, Type FAC

60.　In selecting a random sample from a population, a researcher must
A.　allow chance to determine the size of the sample.
B.　sacrifice control by disregarding information about the population.
C.　make sure every member of the population has an equal chance of being chosen for the sample.
D.　select most sample members from the middle of any ordered listing.
Answer C, Type FAC

61.　In conducting your research, you make sure that every person in the population has an equal chance of participating in your survey. This procedure is known as
A.　random sampling.
B.　random assignment.
C.　naturalistic observation.
D.　equal sampling.
Answer A, Type FAC

62.　Surveying about _____ will enable a survey researcher to be 95 percent confident of describing the entire population, with only a 3 percent margin of error.
A.　12,000 randomly assigned participants
B.　1200 randomly selected participants
C.　one-third of the total population
D.　one-twelfth of the total population
Answer B, Type FAC

63.　A news reporter wants to survey voters about their candidate preferences in an upcoming national election. In order to be 95 percent confident of her results, and have only a 3 percent margin of error, she should make sure the sample has at least _____ individuals.
A.　200
B.　1200
C.　15,000

D.   55,000
Answer B, Type CON

64.   In 1936, the news magazine <u>Literary Digest</u> got the opinions of over two million Americans regarding the presidential election. The results suggested that Landon would win in a landslide over Franklin D. Roosevelt. Weeks later, FDR won in a landslide. This survey was plagued by
    A.   lack of random assignment.
    B.   sampling bias.
    C.   confounded variables.
    D.   lack of experimental control.
    Answer B, Type FAC

65.   Opinion polls and surveys
    A.   describe public opinion at the moment they are taken.
    B.   predict respondents' immediate behavior.
    C.   predict respondents' long-range behavior.
    D.   are too biased to be meaningful.
    Answer A, Type FAC

66.   Ann Landers' 1984 survey of women readers' opinions about romantic affection and sex was probably
    A.   not valid because it did not include men.
    B.   flawed because it was not representative of the population.
    C.   worthless because the sample size was too small.
    D.   as valid and informative as other, more "scientific" surveys.
    Answer B, Type FAC

67.   The answers respondents give to surveys may be influenced by biases from which of the following sources?
    A.   the order in which questions are asked
    B.   the wording of the questions themselves
    C.   the response options
    D.   All of the above.
    Answer D, Type FAC

68.   Research on the wording of survey questions suggests that
    A.   how questions are framed influence how they are answered.
    B.   how questions are framed have very little influence on how they are answered.
    C.   wording is an unimportant element of survey research.
    D.   framing the questions differently will not influence apparent public opinion.
    Answer A, Type FAC

69.   Which research method have social psychologists used in about three-fourths of their studies?
    A.   correlational
    B.   experimental
    C.   survey
    D.   naturalistic observation
    Answer B, Type FAC

70.   The experimental factor that a researcher manipulates in an experiment is the
    A.   independent variable.
    B.   dependent variable.
    C.   control group.
    D.   hypothesis.

Answer A, Type DEF

71. An experimenter exposes participants to different temperature levels to determine its effect on aggression. Temperature is the
   A.   independent variable.
   B.   dependent variable.
   C.   control variable.
   D.   confounding variable.
   Answer A, Type CON

72. In an experimental study of the effects of fear on the desire to affiliate, fear would be the _____ variable.
   A.   experimental
   B.   independent
   C.   control
   D.   dependent
   Answer B, Type CON

73. Snyder and Haugen found that when men were asked to evaluate a woman whom they presumed was obese, she
   A.   spoke less warmly and less happily.
   B.   spoke with more humor and laughter.
   C.   tried to compensate with more intelligent conversation.
   D.   showed greater interest in politics and sports.
   Answer A, Type FAC

74. In a psychological experiment, the factor being measured is called the _____ variable.
   A.   independent
   B.   experimental
   C.   dependent
   D.   controlled
   Answer C, Type DEF

75. The two essential ingredients of a social psychological experiment are
   A.   random assignment and correlation.
   B.   control and random sampling.
   C.   control and random assignment.
   D.   random sampling and random assignment.
   Answer C, Type FAC

76. An experimenter exposes participants to different temperature levels to determine its effect on aggression. Aggression is the
   A.   independent variable.
   B.   dependent variable.
   C.   control variable.
   D.   confounding variable.
   Answer B, Type CON

77. Manipulating one or two factors while holding others constant is the essence of
   A.   independent variables.
   B.   dependent variables.
   C.   experimental control.
   D.   random sampling.
   Answer C, Type FAC

78. Putting participants in one of two conditions by flipping a coin illustrates
    A. random sampling.
    B. sampling bias.
    C. random assignment.
    D. representative sampling.
    Answer C, Type FAC

79. An experimenter studying the overjustification effect wants to compare the behavior of students who are rewarded for doing an enjoyable task with that of students who are not rewarded. For each student she decides which condition they will be in by flipping a coin. This procedure
    A. ensures that each student has an equal chance of being in either condition.
    B. does not ensure that a random sample of participants will be selected.
    C. helps to rule out initial group differences as a potential cause of the experimental effects.
    D. All of the above.
    Answer D, Type CON

80. When the laboratory experiment is superficially similar to everyday situations, the experiment is said to be high in
    A. mundane realism.
    B. experimental realism.
    C. quality control.
    D. situational validity.
    Answer A, Type DEF

81. When the laboratory experiment deeply absorbs and involves participants, the experiment has
    A. field quality.
    B. experimental realism.
    C. situational validity.
    D. mundane realism.
    Answer B, Type DEF

82. For a social psychological experiment to be useful and conclusive, it must have
    A. experimental realism.
    B. demand characteristics.
    C. low generalizability.
    D. low control.
    Answer A, Type FAC

83. Deception of participants is employed when necessary to maintain
    A. experimenter authority.
    B. situational validity.
    C. experimental realism.
    D. demand characteristics.
    Answer C, Type FAC

84. Cues in the experiment that tell the participant what behavior is expected are called
    A. hidden values.
    B. demand characteristics.
    C. naturalistic fallacies.
    D. coefficients.
    Answer B, Type DEF

85. American Psychological Association ethical principles dictate that potential research participants should be told enough about the experiment to

A. make inaccurate guesses about its true purpose.
B. accurately perceive demand characteristics.
C. be able to give their informed consent.
D. detect the researcher's hidden values.
Answer C, Type FAC

The following items also appear in the study guide:

86. Social psychology began to emerge as the vibrant field it is today during
    A. the Depression of the early 1930s when researchers examined the effects of deprivation
    on aggression and altruism.
    B. World War I, when psychologists conducted studies of social conflict and cooperation.
    C. World War II, when researchers performed studies of persuasion and soldier morale.
    D. the Korean War, when psychologists examined the effects of brainwashing on prisoners
    of war.
    Answer C, Type FAC

87. In comparison to the sociologist, the social psychologist
    A. is more likely to study the social causes of behavior.
    B. is more likely to study individuals than groups.
    C. gives less attention to our internal functioning.
    D. relies more heavily on correlational research.
    Answer B, Type FAC

88. The text states that as a scientific discipline, social psychology
    A. is superior to those disciplines which assume a more subjective approach to the study of
    human nature.
    B. can assist in explaining the meaning of life.
    C. is one perspective from which we can view and better understand human nature.
    D. offers explanations for human nature that often contradict the claims of other disciplines.
    Answer C, Type FAC

89. Which of the following distinguishes the correlational method from experimentation?
    A. The correlational method uses a smaller group of participants.
    B. The correlational method enables researchers to study social attitudes.
    C. No attempt is made to systematically manipulate one or more factors with the
    correlational method.
    D. The findings from the correlational method are more likely to be contaminated by the
    experimenter's values.
    Answer C, Type FAC

90. To determine whether changing one variable (like education) will produce changes in another
    (like income), we need to conduct _____ research.
    A. survey
    B. correlational
    C. experimental
    D. statistical
    Answer C, Type FAC

91. According to the text, _____ tends to make people overconfident about the validity
    of their judgments and predictions.
    A. the fundamental attribution error
    B. illusory correlation
    C. the naturalistic fallacy

13

D.   the hindsight bias
Answer D, Type FAC

92.   In comparison to North American social psychologists, European social psychologists tend to give more attention to the _____ levels of explanation.
A.   intrapersonal and interpersonal
B.   intergroup and societal
C.   interpersonal and intergroup
D.   intrapersonal and societal
Answer B, Type FAC

93.   Who among the following would be most likely to study how the political attitudes of middle-class people differ from those of lower-class people?
A.   a personality psychologist
B.   a social psychologist
C.   a social biologist
D.   a sociologist
Answer D, Type CON

94.   You would like to know the relationship between the number of psychology courses people take and their interpersonal sensitivity. You survey college students to determine how much psychology they have taken and then have them complete a test of social sensitivity. Finally you plot the relationship. This is an example of
A.   a laboratory experiment.
B.   a field experiment.
C.   a correlational study.
D.   participant observation.
Answer C, Type CON

95.   A research psychologist manipulates the level of fear in human participants in the laboratory and then examines what effect the different levels of fear have on the participants' reaction times. In this study, reaction time is the _____ variable.
A.   dependent
B.   correlational
C.   independent
D.   experimental
Answer A, Type CON

96.   In conducting a study of conformity, the experimenters decide to tape-record the instructions that are to be presented to all participants. Their decision is most likely an attempt to minimize the effect of
A.   hindsight bias.
B.   mundane realism.
C.   naturalistic fallacy.
D   demand characteristics.
Answer D, Type CON

97.   A researcher finds that Americans bathe on the average of once a day. He concludes that an educational program is necessary to encourage more frequent bathing by those who bathe less often than once a day. The researcher is probably guilty of
A.   hindsight bias.
B.   the "I knew it all along" phenomenon.
C   illusory correlation.

D.   the naturalistic fallacy.
Answer D, Type CON

98.   Which of the following research methods would be most effective in demonstrating that the presence of others improves our performance of a task?
A.   an experiment
B.   a correlational study
C.   a survey
D.   a field study
Answer A, Type CON

99.   Which of the following techniques would be the most effective way of investigating the relationship between the political preferences and the age of American citizens?
A.   an experiment
B.   a case study
C.   a correlational study
D.   participant observation
Answer C, Type CON

100.   In a research study investigating the effects of stress on the desire to affiliate, half the participants complete an easy test of mental ability and half complete a difficult test. What technique should the investigators use to ensure that any posttest differences in the group's desire to affiliate actually result from the differences in test difficulty?
A.   random sampling
B.   random assignment
C.   replication
D.   correlational measurement
Answer B, Type CON

Critical Thinking Questions

101.   Illustrate the power of the situation using an example from your own life (e.g., describe a time when others failed to recognize you because the situation was different from usual, or describe a time when the situation influenced you to act contrary to your beliefs).

102.   "Social psychology reflects social history." Keeping in mind the social psychologist's interest in the individual, can you predict the topics that will interest social psychologists as we approach the turn of the millenium?

103.   Describe the hindsight bias and explain how it could influence how much the typical student prepares for a social psychology exam.

104.   Design an experiment to test the hypothesis that students who have knowledge of the hindsight bias do better on exams than students who have no knowledge of this bias.

105.   Debate the pros and cons of deception in social psychological experimentation.

CHAPTER TWO
THE SELF IN A SOCIAL WORLD

Multiple Choice Questions

1. The most researched topic in psychology today is
   A. the self.
   B. attitudes.
   C. cultural influence.
   D. problem solving.
   Answer A, Type FAC

2. How you answer the question "Who am I?" defines your
   A. self-esteem.
   B. possible self.
   C. self-concept.
   D. social identity.
   Answer C, Type DEF

3. The beliefs about self that organize and guide the processing of self-relevant information are called
   A. self-references.
   B. possible selves.
   C. social comparisons.
   D. self-schemas.
   Answer D, Type DEF

4. Your perception of yourself as athletic, smart, too short, and shy is part of your
   A. self-esteem.
   B. self-schema.
   C. self-efficacy.
   D. self-references.
   Answer B, Type CON

5. The tendency to process efficiently and remember well information related to oneself is called the _____ effect.
   A. self-handicapping
   B. self-actualization
   C. false uniqueness
   D. self-reference
   Answer D, Type DEF

6. The self-reference effect illustrates that
   A. our sense of self is at the center of our world.
   B. self-efficacy promotes achievement.
   C. individualism leads to social isolation.
   D. most of us suffer from a negative self-image.
   Answer A, Type FAC

7. The images of what we dream of or dread becoming in the future constitute our _____ selves.

17

A.   unlikely
B.   imaginary
C.   future
D.   possible
Answer D, Type DEF

8.   Psychologists would consider your dream of becoming a famous politician and your recurrent fear of being unemployed to be part of your
A.   self-esteem.
B.   possible self.
C.   anticipatory self.
D.   unlikely self.
Answer B, Type CON

9.   A person's overall self-evaluation or sense of self worth constitutes his or her
A.   self-efficacy.
B.   self-awareness.
C.   possible self.
D.   self-esteem.
Answer D, Type DEF

10.   The top-down view of self-esteem holds that
A.   people with generally high self-esteem are more likely to accept their specific attributes.
B.   people with positive specific attributes are more likely to have high self-esteem.
C.   people with low self-esteem are more likely to accept their specific attributes.
D.   people with positive specific attributes are more likely to struggle with low self-esteem.
Answer A, Type FAC

11.   Our self-concept is often shaped by
A.   the roles we play.
B.   our successes and failures.
C.   other people's judgments.
D.   All of the above.
Answer D, Type FAC

12.   That aspect of our self-concept that comes from our group memberships is called
A.   collective efficacy.
B.   social identity.
C.   personal identity.
D.   social comparison.
Answer B, Type DEF

13.   We are more likely to be conscious of our social identity when our social group
A.   is in the majority.
B.   is in the minority.
C.   is esteemed by others
D.   is threatened.
Answer B, Type CON

14.   Imagine that John is a white man attending a multi-racial support group for stay-at-home-parents. There are 40% Whites, 30% Blacks, and 30% Hispanics attending. Ninety percent of the group are mothers. John is most likely to be conscious of his identity as
A.   a parent.
B.   a White person.

C.   a man.

D.   an unemployed person.

Answer C, Type CON

15.   We come to know ourselves in part by looking at others and evaluating our abilities and opinions in light of those others. This process is known as

A.   social comparison.

B.   social identity.

C.   the self-reference effect.

D.   self-esteem.

Answer A, Type DEF

16.   Cooley (1902) argued that we come to know ourselves by seeing our reflection in how we appear to others. Other people's judgments, then, help to shape what he called

A.   the social self.

B.   the perceived self.

C.   the looking-glass self.

D.   self-appraisal.

Answer C, Type FAC

17.   Compared to Japanese, Americans have been shown to compliment one another

A.   much less often.

B.   equally often.

C.   much more often.

D.   None of the above.

Answer C, Type FAC

18.   Books and movies that celebrate those who do their social duty, even if it means personal sacrifice, are more likely to be found in

A.   individualistic cultures.

B.   collectivistic cultures.

C.   independent cultures.

D.   Western cultures.

Answer B, Type FAC

19.   A magazine ad for a hair-care product says, "She's got a style all her own." This ad is most likely to appear in

A.   Korea.

B.   Japan.

C.   America.

D.   None of the above.

Answer C, Type CON

20.   Nisbett and Schacter gave students a series of increasingly intense electric shocks. Some were given a fake pill and told it would produce symptoms similar to those of experiencing shock. Results indicated that, compared to students who did not receive the pill, those students who took the pill

A.   were not able to withstand as much shock.

B.   were able to withstand about the same amount of shock but firmly believed that their tolerance for shock had increased.

C.   withstood more shock but denied the pill had any influence.

D.   withstood more shock and maintained that the pill had helped them.

Answer C, Type FAC

21. In some studies, people have been asked to record their moods daily for 3 months along with those factors they believe have influenced their moods. Then they rate how important those factors are in affecting their daily moods. Results demonstrate that people
    A.   are very good at predicting their moods.
    B.   are very good at understanding the factors that affect their moods.
    C.   are not very good at recording their moods.
    D.   are not very good at understanding the factors that affect their moods.
    Answer D, Type FAC

22. Nisbett and Wilson had students rate a film while a noisy power saw was operated nearby. Results indicated that most felt the noise
    A.   affected their ratings, but it didn't.
    B.   affected their ratings, as it had.
    C.   had not affected their ratings, though it had.
    D.   had not affected their ratings, and they were correct.
    Answer A, Type FAC

23. The best advice for predicting your own behavior is to
    A.   ask an expert.
    B.   analyze your current mood.
    C.   consider your past behavior in similar situations.
    D.   ask your closest friend.
    Answer C, Type FAC

24. Research suggests that if the cause is not obvious, we are
    A.   very good at predicting our behavior and our feelings.
    B.   not very good at predicting our behavior or our feelings.
    C.   very good at predicting our behavior.
    D.   very good at predicting our feelings.
    Answer B, Type FAC

25. Studies of perception and memory show that we are
    A.   more aware of the process than the results of our thinking.
    B.   more aware of the results than the process of our thinking.
    C.   equally well aware of the process and the results of our thinking.
    D.   oblivious to both the process and the results of our thinking.
    Answer B, Type FAC

26. Research suggests that drawing people's attention to _____ diminishes the usefulness of attitude reports in predicting behaviors driven by _____.
    A.   values underlying their behavior; self-esteem
    B.   reasons for their behavior; feelings
    C.   feelings underlying their behavior; physical safety
    D.   reasons for their behavior; cognitions
    Answer B, Type FAC

27. Which of the following is a practical implication of findings discussed in the chapter on the self?
    A.   The sincerity with which people report their experience is one useful indicator of their testimony's accuracy.
    B.   Self-reports are less erroneous and more trustworthy than the reports of external observers.
    C.   The persuasiveness of personal testimonies is highly predictive of their accuracy.
    D.   Introspective self-reports are often untrustworthy.

28. Western cultures are to _____ as Asian cultures are to _____.
    A. the actual self; the possible self
    B. self-forgetfulness; self-esteem
    C. the independent self; the interdependent self
    D. self-denial; self-acceptance
    Answer C, Type CON

29. Japanese are more likely than Americans to complete the sentence "I am ..." with their
    A. personal traits.
    B. group identities.
    C. negative rather than their positive characteristics.
    D. physical rather than their psychological characteristics.
    Answer B, Type FAC

30. The sense that one is competent and effective constitutes one's
    A. self-esteem.
    B. independent self.
    C. learned helpfulness.
    D. self-efficacy.
    Answer D, Type DEF

31. People with strong feelings of self-efficacy are likely to be more
    A. persistent.
    B. prone to stress.
    C. socially sensitive.
    D. anxious.
    Answer A, Type FAC

32. The extent to which people perceive their lives as internally controllable by their own efforts and actions or as externally controlled by chance or outside forces constitutes their
    A. interdependent-independent self.
    B. intrinsic-extrinsic motivation.
    C. controllability quotient.
    D. locus of control.
    Answer D, Type DEF

33. "Sometimes I feel that I can't do anything about the direction my life is taking." This statement reflects
    A. an external locus of control.
    B. an internal locus of control.
    C. an interdependent self.
    D. high self-efficacy.
    Answer A, Type CON

34. If you believe your fate is determined by _____, you probably have an _____ locus of control.
    A. your own abilities; external
    B. personal motivation; external
    C. fate or luck; internal
    D. None of the above.
    Answer D, Type FAC

35. Sally believes that she will be highly successful in medical school if she works hard and carefully manages her time. Her belief most clearly illustrates

A.   integrative ability.
B.   an internal locus of control.
C.   an interdependent self.
D.   the self-reference effect.
Answer B, Type CON

36.   Bandura is to _____ as Seligman is to _____ .
A.   self-efficacy; learned helplessness
B.   internal locus of control; external locus of control
C.   self-esteem; self-concept
D.   the self-reference effect; depression
Answer A, Type CON

37.   Martin Seligman notes a basic similarity between learned helplessness in dogs and _____ in people.
A.   conformity
B.   collective efficacy
C.   schizophrenia
D.   depression
Answer A, Type FAC

38.   The experience of repeated uncontrollable bad events contributes to
A.   an internal locus of control.
B.   an interdependent self.
C.   learned helplessness.
D.   self-efficacy.
Answer C, Type FAC

39.   After moving into a nursing home and experiencing little control over his daily schedule, Mr. Roark became apathetic, stopped eating, and even seemed to lose the will to live. Mr. Roark's reaction most clearly illustrates
A.   learned helplessness.
B.   the interdependent self.
C.   self-handicapping.
D.   internal locus of control.
Answer A, Type CON

40.   Hospital patients trained to believe in their ability to control stress tend to
A.   require more pain relievers and sedatives.
B.   require fewer pain relievers and sedatives.
C.   seem more anxious to nurses attending them.
D.   seem more depressed to nurses attending them.
Answer B, Type FAC

41.   Langer and Rodin found that nursing home residents improved in alertness, activity, and happiness if they were
A.   cared for by professionals who met all their needs.
B.   cared for by affectionate, sympathetic volunteers.
C.   periodically transported to visit close friends and relatives.
D.   asked to make personal choices and given opportunities to influence nursing home policies.
Answer D, Type FAC

42. Prisoners given some control over their environments--being able to move chairs, control TV sets, and switch the lights--
    A.   become more manipulative of prison officials over time.
    B.   commit less vandalism.
    C.   experience greater stress and more health problems.
    D.   experience stronger guilt feelings over past misconduct.
    Answer B, Type FAC

43. Bandura emphasizes that self-efficacy improves as a result of
    A.   self-persuasion.
    B.   the power of positive thinking.
    C.   the complements of others.
    D.   the experience of success.
    Answer D, Type FAC

44. The tendency to perceive ourselves favorably is known as
    A.   the self-reference effect.
    B.   self-serving bias.
    C.   self-efficacy.
    D.   internal locus of control.
    Answer B, Type DEF

45. Which of the following is least representative of a self-serving bias?
    A.   "I won the election because my opponent didn't try very hard."
    B.   "I won the election because of my hard work on the campaign trail."
    C.   "I lost the election because of the political climate, which I couldn't do anything about."
    D.   "I won the election because of my knowledge and expertise."
    Answer A, Type CON

46. In their study of young married Canadians, Ross and Sicoly reported a tendency for them to
    A.   believe that their spouse contributed the most household work.
    B.   believe that they themselves contributed the most household work.
    C.   feel guilty about not carrying their fair share of work.
    D.   feel confident that their household was run fairly and efficiently.
    Answer B, Type FAC

47. After receiving an examination grade, students who do well
    A.   tend to accept personal credit.
    B.   judge the exam to be a valid measure of their competence.
    C.   tend to criticize the exam less than those who do poorly.
    D.   All of the above.
    Answer D, Type FAC

48. Jenny failed her last chemistry test. Which of the following conclusions would be most representative of a self-serving bias on Jenny's part?
    A.   "I really didn't have the motivation to study for the test."
    B.   "I lack competence in chemistry."
    C.   "I think the test questions were ambiguous and confusing."
    D.   "I didn't concentrate very hard during the test."
    Answer C, Type CON

49. For qualities that are both subjective and socially desirable, most people consider themselves to be
    A.   worse than average.

B.   about average.

C.   better than average.

D.   too different from others to permit a fair comparison.

Answer C, Type FAC

50.   A national survey asked business people to rate their own morals and values on a scale from 1-100, where 100 is perfect. Fifty percent of the people rated themselves at

A.   25.

B.   50.

C.   75.

D.   90 or above.

Answer D, Type FAC

51.   Which of the following is true?

A.   Ninety percent of business managers rate their performance as superior to their average peer.

B.   Most drivers who have been hospitalized for accidents believe themselves to be more skilled than the average driver.

C.   Most people perceive themselves as better looking than their average peer.

D.   All of the above.

Answer D, Type FAC

52.   Self-serving bias is strongest for qualities that are

A.   clearly defined.

B.   objective.

C.   socially desirable.

D.   All of the above.

Answer C, Type FAC

53.   People would be least likely to rate themselves as better than average in

A.   being punctual.

B.   being disciplined.

C.   being ethical.

D.   their ability to get along with others.

Answer A, Type FAC

54.   Nearly half of all marriages end in divorce. Yet in a study of 137 applying for a marriage license, most rated their own chance of divorce as zero. This finding illustrates

A.   false consensus.

B.   self-efficacy.

C.   unrealistic optimism.

D.   self-verification.

Answer C, Type FAC

55.   Which of the following statements is true?

A.   Students who are over-confident tend to over-prepare for exams.

B.   Students who are anxious about exams tend to blow-off studying for them.

C.   Some pessimism about an exam can motivate students to study harder and do better.

D.   None of the above.

Answer C, Type FAC

56.   In Scotland most late adolescents think they are much less likely than their peers to become infected by the AIDS virus. This best illustrates

A.   the false consensus bias.

B.   unrealistic optimism.

C.   the self-reference effect.

D.   external locus of control.

Answer B, Type FAC

57.   Jack cheats on his income taxes and consoles himself with the thought that everyone else probably cheats a little, too. This rationalization represents

A.   the fundamental attribution error.

B.   the false uniqueness effect.

C.   unrealistic optimism.

D.   the false consensus effect.

Answer D, Type CON

58.   Which of the following is particularly likely to increase our vulnerability to misfortune?

A.   a self-monitoring tendency

B.   self-analysis

C.   an interdependent self

D.   unrealistic optimism

Answer D, Type FAC

59.   The tendency to overestimate the commonality of one's opinions and undesirable behaviors is known as the

A.   self-reference effect.

B.   self-handicapping syndrome.

C.   false uniqueness effect.

D.   false consensus effect.

Answer D, Type DEF

60.   The tendency to underestimate the commonality of one's abilities and desirable behaviors is known as

A.   the self-reference effect.

B.   self-handicapping.

C.   the false uniqueness effect.

D.   the false consensus effect.

Answer C, Type DEF

61.   Which of the following is most likely to trigger a false uniqueness effect in your thinking?

A.   lying to a friend to avoid embarrassment

B.   turning down the opportunity to help out at the local homeless shelter

C.   volunteering to give blood

D.   failing your first social psychology exam

Answer C, Type CON

62.   Those who drink heavily but use seat belts will _____ the number of other heavy drinkers and _____ the number of seat belt users.

A.   overestimate; overestimate

B.   underestimate; overestimate

C.   overestimate; underestimate

D.   underestimate; underestimate

Answer C, Type CON

63.   When facing failure, high self-esteem people sustain their self-worth by

A.   perceiving other people as failing, too, and by exaggerating their superiority over others.

B.   perceiving themselves as interdependent and thus as only part of a larger group effort.

C.	engaging in altruistic acts.
D.	refusing to think about the failure and by practicing self-forgetfulness.
Answer A, Type FAC

64.	According to research by Abraham Tesser, who among the following is likely to have the strongest motive for self-esteem maintenance?
A.	an adult whose spouse depends on him or her for support
B.	an adult whose opposite-sex sibling has been fired from his or her job
C.	a child whose parents have moderate hopes for him or her
D.	an older child whose younger sibling is very talented
Answer D, Type FAC

65.	Emily and her two sisters are all musicians. According to research on the self-esteem maintenance model, Emily will be most motivated to act in ways that maintain her own self-esteem if
A.	she is the best musician of the three.
B.	her older sister is a better musician than she is.
C.	her younger sister is a better musician than she is.
D.	of the three, she is the least interested in a music career.
Answer C, Type CON

66.	In experiments, people whose self-esteem is temporarily bruised--say, by being told that they did miserably on an intelligence test--are more likely to
A.	disparage others.
B.	act altruistically.
C.	seek to develop an interdependent self.
D.	retreat into social isolation.
Answer A, Type FAC

67.	Research indicates that people with high self-esteem tend to
A.	be very modest when explaining their successes.
B.	note that there are as many weaknesses as there are strengths in their own group.
C.	see others' strengths as more important than their own.
D.	None of the above.
Answer D, Type FAC

68.	Mildly depressed people tend to
A.	be more prone to self-serving bias than are nondepressed people.
B.	see themselves as others see them.
C.	see themselves more negatively than others see them.
D.	see themselves as better than average and yet are unrealistically pessimistic.
Answer B, Type FAC

69.	Participants who worked in groups were given false feedback that they had done either well or poorly. Results indicated that, in comparison to the members of unsuccessful groups,
A.	members of successful groups claimed more responsibility for their group's performance.
B.	members of successful groups claimed less responsibility for their group's performance.
C.	males but not females of successful groups claimed more responsibility for their group's performance.
D.	females but not males of successful groups claimed more responsibility for their group's performance.
Answer A, Type FAC

70. Research on the self has made it clear that people are motivated
    A.   to assess their competence.
    B.   to verify their self-conceptions.
    C.   to enhance their self-image.
    D.   All of the above.
    Answer D, Type FAC

71. Research suggests that individual group members expect _____ rewards when their organization does well and _____ blame when it does not.
    A.   greater-than-average; greater-than-average
    B.   less-than-average; less-than-average
    C.   greater-than-average; less-than-average
    D.   less-than-average; greater-than-average
    Answer C, Type CON

72. According to the text, true humility is more like _____ than false modesty.
    A.   self-contempt
    B.   self-forgetfulness
    C.   self-handicapping
    D.   self-denial
    Answer B, Type FAC

73. According to the text, self-serving bias
    A.   can protect us from depression.
    B.   contributes to group conflict.
    C.   can motivate us to greater achievement.
    D.   All of the above.
    Answer D, Type FAC

74. Which of the following is true of the self-serving bias?
    A.   It can protect people from depression.
    B.   It can make people more vulnerable to depression.
    C.   It can lead to more accurate self-appraisals.
    D.   None of the above.
    Answer A, Type FAC

75. Barbie, Buffy, and Bambie are all in a sorority together. Candy, Kelsey, and Kara are in a different sorority together. Barbie is given a survey and winds up rating _____ as very conceited and snobby.
    A.   Candy, Kelsey, and Kara
    B.   Buffy and Bambie
    C.   everyone
    D.   no one
    Answer A, Type CON

76. According to the text, the common practice of publicly exalting one's opponents before a big game likely serves a _____ function.
    A.   self-destructive
    B.   self-protective
    C.   knowledge
    D.   self-forgetful
    Answer B, Type FAC

77. Students who were asked to write anonymously about "an important success experience"

A.   acknowledged as many personal weaknesses as strengths.
B.   seemed to write with an attitude of self-forgetfulness.
C.   recognized the contributions close friends or relatives made to their success.
D.   described themselves as achieving their successes on their own.
Answer D, Type FAC

78.   When presenting ourselves to others we sometimes put ourselves down or publicly extol an opponent's strength. According to the text, such false modesty is
A.   self-serving.
B.   masochistic.
C.   self-destructive.
D.   indicative of low self-esteem.
Answer A, Type CON

79.   People are most likely to resort to self-handicapping when
A.   the quality of their performance on a task is not particularly important.
B.   their success or failure at a task will not become public.
C.   they fear failure.
D.   they are certain of success.
Answer C, Type FAC

80.   Experimental participants guessed answers to very difficult aptitude questions and were told they had done well. While they still felt lucky, they were given a choice of drugs to take before answering the remaining questions. Most chose to take the drug they believed would
A.   improve their intellectual functioning.
B.   disrupt their thinking.
C.   reduce anxiety.
D.   keep them awake and alert.
Answer B, Type FAC

81.   Which of the following represents a way in which people self-handicap?
A.   They report feeling depressed.
B.   They procrastinate on an important project.
C.   They reduce their preparation for an important individual athletic event.
D.   All of the above.
Answer D, Type FAC

82.   David has an important tennis match in one week against the highest-rated player in the state. Instead of practicing daily, David has actually reduced his playing time since knowing he would play such a formidable opponent. Which of the following may best describe David's behavior?
A.   David has fallen victim to collective efficacy.
B.   David is making the fundamental attribution error.
C.   David is engaging in self-handicapping.
D.   David is demonstrating learned helplessness.
Answer C, Type CON

83.   Creating a handy excuse for later failure in order to protect one's self-image is known as
A.   self-handicapping.
B.   self-serving bias.
C.   internal locus of control.
D.   self-monitoring.
Answer A, Type DEF

84. The act of expressing oneself and behaving in ways designed to create a favorable impression or an impression that corresponds to one's ideals is referred to as
   A.   self-justification.
   B.   self-presentation.
   C.   self-perception.
   D.   self-management.
   Answer B, Type DEF

85. People who score high on a scale of _____ tend to act like social chameleons: they adjust their behavior in response to external situations.
   A.   social absorption
   B.   self-monitoring
   C.   affective sensitivity
   D.   self-perception
   Answer B, Type DEF

The following items also appear in the Study Guide:

86. Our perceiving ourselves as athletic, overweight, smart, or shy constitutes our
   A.   egocentric beliefs.
   B.   interdependent self.
   C.   self-schemas.
   D.   self-references.
   Answer C, Type FAC

87. When people are asked whether they would comply with demands to deliver cruel shocks or would be hesitant to help a victim if several other people were present,
   A.   they overwhelmingly deny their vulnerability to such influences.
   B.   they admit they might be influenced but in their actual behavior are not.
   C.   males deny they would be influenced, but females admit they would be.
   D.   they accurately predict their future behavior on such significant matters.
   Answer A, Type FAC

88. According to the text, research on self-knowledge suggests that
   A.   people tend to underestimate their own abilities.
   B.   people who have an interdependent self show less self-insight than those with an independent self.
   C.   people are highly accurate in predicting their own future behavior.
   D.   people's self-reports are often untrustworthy.
   Answer D, Type FAC

89. Dogs who learn a sense of helplessness by being taught they cannot escape shocks
   A.   tend to band together and as a group demonstrate collective efficacy.
   B.   tend to become highly aggressive in other situations.
   C.   more readily take the initiative to escape punishment when that becomes possible.
   D.   later fail to take the initiative in another situation when they can escape punishment.
   Answer D, Type FAC

90. Research on attribution theory challenges the notion that
   A.   most people suffer from unrealistically low self-esteem.
   B.   we tend to blame others for their own misfortune.
   C.   we strive to protect and enhance our self-esteem.
   D.   true humility consists of self-forgetfulness.
   Answer A, Type FAC

91. College students perceive themselves as far more likely than their classmates to _____ and as far less likely to _____.
   A. draw a good salary; develop a drinking problem
   B. obtain a divorce; own a home
   C. travel to Europe; be happy in their work
   D. become a mental patient; have close friendships
   Answer A, Type FAC

92. We tend to _____ the commonality of our unsuccessful behaviors and _____ the commonality of our successful behaviors.
   A. overestimate; underestimate
   B. underestimate; overestimate
   C. underestimate; underestimate
   D. overestimate; overestimate
   Answer A, Type FAC

93. Research on self-perception indicates that if we find ourselves linked to some reprehensible person, say born on the same day,
   A. we show a temporary loss of self-esteem.
   B. we form a more independent self.
   C. we form a harsher view of the person.
   D. we soften our view of the person.
   Answer D, Type FAC

94. Self-presentation, self-handicapping, and self-monitoring all reflect human efforts at
   A. self-efficacy.
   B. self-understanding.
   C. collective efficacy.
   D. impression management.
   Answer D, Type FAC

95. In completing the statement, "I am ..." Michelle responds by stating that she is the youngest in her family, belongs to a sorority, and is a member of the community orchestra. Michelle's statements most clearly reflect
   A. her possible selves.
   B. an interdependent self.
   C. a self-serving bias.
   D. a strong self-monitoring tendency.
   Answer B, Type CON

96. Because she gets poor grades no matter how hard she studies, Milly has decided not to study at all. Milly's behavior most clearly demonstrates
   A. self-serving bias.
   B. unrealistic optimism.
   C. learned helplessness.
   D. a self-monitoring tendency.
   Answer C, Type CON

97. Judging from the discussion of self-image in the text, people are least likely to see themselves as above average in
   A. leadership ability.
   B. tolerance.
   C. weight.

D.   helpfulness.

Answer C, Type CON

98.   Although Jeff frequently exceeds the speed limit by at least 10 miles per hour, he justifies his behavior by erroneously thinking that most other drivers do the same. His mistaken belief best illustrates

A.   learned helplessness.
B.   false consensus.
C.   self-monitoring.
D.   an interdependent self.

Answer B, Type CON

99.   Those who evade paying income tax but who give generously to charity will probably _____ the number of others who evade taxes and _____ the number of others who give generously to charity.

A.   overestimate; overestimate
B.   underestimate; overestimate
C.   overestimate; underestimate
D.   underestimate; underestimate

Answer C, Type CON

100.   Tomorrow morning Harry Smith has an interview that will determine whether he will be accepted into medical school. Rather than getting a good night's sleep, he is going to an all-night party with his friends. From the material presented in the text, which of the following may best describe Harry's behavior?

A.   Harry unconsciously hopes he is not accepted into medical school.
B.   Harry is making the fundamental attribution error.
C.   Harry is engaging in self-handicapping.
D.   Harry shares with his friends a sense of collective efficacy.

Answer C, Type CON

Critical Thinking Questions

101.   Give an example of false consensus and an example of false uniqueness. Clearly label which is which.

102.   Discuss the evidence for the top-down view of self-esteem. From this perspective, how can we help people with low self-esteem?

103.   Discuss the influences that help us construct our own self-concept.

104.   Is the self-serving bias adaptive or maladaptive? Defend your view.

105.   Give an example of a time when you (or someone you know) engaged in self-handicapping.

Multiple Choice Questions

1. We are especially likely to analyze and discuss why things happen when the event in question is
    A. negative or unexpected.
    B. positive or altruistic.
    C. normal or public.
    D. infrequent or private.
    Answer A, Type FAC

2. Which of the following is the most likely attribution to be made by someone in an unhappy marriage?
    A. "She was late because of heavy traffic."
    B. "She was late because she got tied up at the office."
    C. "She was late because she doesn't care about me."
    D. "She was late because it took so long to check out at the grocery store."
    Answer C, Type CON

3. Misreading and explaining a woman's warmth or friendliness as a sexual come-on is known as
    A. the gender gap.
    B. a misattribution.
    C. the fundamental attribution error.
    D. a distinctiveness attribution.
    Answer B, Type CON

4. The theory of how people explain others' behavior is known as _____ theory.
    A. dissonance
    B. attribution
    C. incentive
    D. accountability
    Answer B, Type DEF

5. Attribution theories analyze how we
    A. explain people's behavior.
    B. make decisions and solve problems.
    C. make impressions on others.
    D. form attitudes about issues.
    Answer A, Type DEF

6. Fritz Heider's "_____ psychology" analyzes the way people explain everyday events.
    A. depth
    B. structural
    C. nonobvious
    D. commonsense
    Answer D, Type FAC

7. According to Fritz Heider, we tend to attribute people's behavior to either _____ or _____ causes.
    A. internal; dispositional

B.   situational; external
C.   rational; irrational
D.   internal; external
Answer D, Type DEF

8.   Glenda has turned in an assignment late, so her instructor concludes Glenda is lazy and unmotivated. The instructor's assumption is an example of
A.   a situational attribution.
B.   a dispositional attribution.
C.   an external attribution.
D.   self-handicapping.
Answer B, Type CON

9.   Variations of attribution theory share which of the following assumptions?
A.   Attributions are either cultural or individual.
B.   Attributions are based on distinctiveness and consensus information.
C.   Attributions can generally be categorized as internal or external.
D.   Actions always correspond to dispositions.
Answer C, Type FAC

10.   Jones and Davis's theory of correspondent inferences specifies the conditions under which you are most likely to
A.   explain others' behavior in terms of your own motives.
B.   explain others' behavior in terms of conscious motives.
C.   infer people's dispositions from how they act.
D.   find actors and observers making corresponding attributions.
Answer C, Type FAC

11.   James saw a man drop a $10 bill on his way out of the store. He picked it up and gave it to the man. A correspondent inference for this act would be
A.   James is honest.
B.   James is helpful.
C.   James is nice.
D.   All of the above.
Answer D, Type CON

12.   According to theorist Harold Kelley, in making commonsense attributions to explain others' behavior, people use information about
A.   consistency, distinctiveness, and consensus.
B.   cognition, emotion, and motivation.
C.   arousal, attention, and animation.
D.   complementarity, commonality, and closure.
Answer A, Type DEF

13.   When explaining why Edgar is having trouble with his new computer, which of the following questions deals with consistency rather than with distinctiveness or consensus?
A.   Does Edgar have trouble with other computers, or only this one?
B.   Does Edgar usually have trouble with his computer?
C.   Do other people have similar problems with this computer?
D.   All of the above.
Answer B, Type FAC

14.   According to research by Norman Anderson, when integrating information about someone in forming an impression, you will probably give more weight to

A.   first impressions than later ones.
B.   traits that are important to you than traits that are not.
C.   negative information than positive.
D.   All of the above.
Answer D, Type FAC

15.   You're not really convinced that you should see the latest Robin Williams movie that Julie is raving about because Julie raves about all of his movies. You've relied on
A.   consensus information.
B.   information integration.
C.   correspondent information.
D.   distinctiveness information.
Answer D, Type CON

16.   One of social psychology's most important lesson concerns how much we are affected by our
A.   childhood experiences.
B.   personal values and standards.
C.   social environments.
D.   unconscious motives.
Answer C, Type FAC

17.   The tendency to underestimate situational influences on others' behaviors and to overestimate dispositional influences is known as the
A.   fundamental attribution error.
B.   self-serving bias.
C.   naturalistic fallacy.
D.   representativeness heuristic.
Answer A, Type DEF

18.   You notice that Devon, a classmate, has failed a quiz. You may be committing the fundamental attribution error if you conclude that
A.   Devon is a lazy student who probably did not study.
B.   the quiz was unusually difficult for all who took it.
C.   Devon probably had to work late the night before the quiz.
D.   you would probably have failed if you had taken it.
Answer A, Type CON

19.   Jones and Harris had students read debaters' speeches either supporting or attacking Cuban leader Fidel Castro. When the students were later told that the debater's position had been assigned, they

A.   assumed the debater's position merely reflected the demands of the assignment.
B.   described the speaker's position as poorly developed.
C.   concluded that to some extent the speech reflected the speaker's true beliefs.
D.   concluded that the debate coach was an effective persuader.
Answer C, Type FAC

20.   We are less likely to commit the fundamental attribution error when explaining _____ behavior.
A.   our own
B.   other people's
C.   friendly
D.   aggressive
Answer A, Type FAC

21. Students who were told that a clinical psychology graduate student had been instructed to act in a friendly manner for purposes of the experiment concluded that her behavior
    A. reflected her traits.
    B. illustrated role-playing.
    C. was situationally determined.
    D. demonstrated the illusion of control.
    Answer A, Type FAC

22. The fundamental attribution error involves the tendency to
    A. overestimate situational causes of behavior.
    B. underestimate dispositional causes of behavior.
    C. underestimate situational causes of behavior.
    D. discount dispositional causes of behavior.
    Answer C, Type DEF

23. In research by Ditto and colleagues (1997), a woman wrote positive statements about the male research participant. When the man was later told that she was ordered to write only positive statements, he
    A. realized that she didn't really like him.
    B. thought she liked him less than if she hadn't been given orders.
    C. inferred that she neither liked nor disliked him.
    D. inferred that she really liked him anyway, despite the orders she was given.
    Answer D, Type FAC

24. We tend to automatically believe that the programmed behavior of an actor reflects
    A. powerful environmental forces.
    B. a carefully prepared social script.
    C. inner dispositions.
    D. audience pressures.
    Answer C, Type FAC

25. We may overestimate the knowledge or intelligence of leaders and those with social power because
    A. we lack confidence.
    B. they typically initiate and control conversation.
    C. of the power of the confirmation bias.
    D. of the illusion of control.
    Answer B, Type CON

26. Ross, Amabile, and Steinmetz randomly assigned participants to play the part of either a quiz game contestant or the questioner, while other participants merely observed the game. Results indicated that
    A. both contestants and observers thought the questioners were more knowledgeable than the contestants.
    B. both contestants and observers thought the contestants were more knowledgeable than the questioners.
    C. observers thought the questioners were more knowledgeable, but contestants attributed the outcomes to the situation.
    D. questioners thought themselves more knowledgeable, but contestants attributed the outcomes to the situation.
    Answer A, Type FAC

27. According to research by Graham (1997), people who perceive a crime as _____ advocate _____ punishment.
    A.   uncontrollable; severe
    B.   controllable; severe
    C.   controllable; mild
    D.   justified; severe
    Answer B, Type FAC

28. The fundamental attribution error is reduced when
    A.   more than one observer accounts for the actor's behavior.
    B.   the observer does not know the personal identity of the actor.
    C.   the actor's behavior is not personally relevant to the observer.
    D.   the actor and observer switch perspectives with each other.
    Answer D, Type FAC

29. Our tendency to commit the fundamental attribution error is influenced by
    A.   the perspective we take on the situation.
    B.   self-awareness.
    C.   culture.
    D.   All of the above.
    Answer D, Type FAC

30. Recognizing our tendency to focus on the "figure" in the figure-ground relationship may help us to understand why we
    A.   engage in counterfactual thinking.
    B.   construct memories.
    C.   make the fundamental attribution error.
    D.   fall victim to the overconfidence phenomenon.
    Answer C, Type FAC

31. Videotaped confessions are more likely to lead to convictions when the tape
    A.   focuses on the confessor.
    B.   focuses on the interrogator.
    C.   focuses on both the confessor and the interrogator.
    D.   None of the above.
    Answer A, Type CON

32. According to Wicklund, Duval, and their collaborators, _____ makes people more sensitive to their own attitudes and dispositions.
    A.   self-concern
    B.   self-awareness
    C.   self-forgetfulness
    D.   self-denial
    Answer B, Type FAC

33. When self-awareness is high we are _____ likely to attribute responsibility to _____.
    A.   more; the situation
    B.   more; others
    C.   more; ourselves
    D.   less; ourselves
    Answer C, Type FAC

34. Research indicates that we tend to see our behavior as more _____ compared to other people's behavior.

A. consistent
B. extroverted
C. variable
D. self-centered
Answer C, Type FAC

35. People's impressions of someone they have often heard about from a friend are typically more _____ than their friend's firsthand impressions.
A. positive
B. variable
C. negative
D. extreme
Answer D, Type FAC

36. Our Western worldview predisposes us to assume that _____ cause events.
A. people
B. fate or chance
C. situations
D. unconscious motivation
Answer A, Type FAC

37. If John tells you his impression of Steve, your own impression of Steve will be _____ than if you'd been left to form an impression on your own.
A. more extreme
B. less extreme
C. more positive
D. more variable
Answer A, Type CON

38. Another term for the fundamental attribution error that many social psychologists prefer is
A. correspondent inference.
B. correspondence bias.
C. dispositional error.
D. potential attribution error.
Answer B, Type DEF

39. One reason psychologists study attribution errors is that
A. people are so very much aware of them.
B. they get their kicks out of playing tricks on people.
C. such errors make social psychologists feel superior.
D. such errors reveal how we think about ourselves and others.
Answer D, Type FAC

40. Which of the following statements about the biases that penetrate our thinking is true?
A. We are mostly unaware of them.
B. We are usually aware of them but deny that they play a significant role in our judgments.
C. We are aware of them and usually use them to our advantage.
D. Very few--if any--biases affect our thinking powerfully enough to harm ourselves or others.
Answer A, Type FAC

41. According to the text, the major reason for learning about social thinking and examining our errors and biases is to
A. develop more realistic self-esteem.

B.   develop our capacity for critical thinking.

C.   become more effective in influencing others.

D.   develop more positive interpersonal relationships.

Answer B, Type FAC

42.   Ross, Lepper, and Lord showed mixed research results on the deterrence effect of the death penalty to students who either favored or opposed the death penalty. Showing the two sides this identical body of mixed evidence

A.   had no effect on their preexisting opinions.

B.   narrowed the disagreement between the two sides.

C.   changed the views of the pro students but not the anti.

D.   increased the amount of disagreement between them.

Answer D, Type FAC

43.   Suppose a group of people who oppose gun control is presented with research evidence that is ambiguous about how well gun-control legislation will deter crime. Some of the evidence suggests that such laws would reduce crime, whereas other evidence suggests it would be ineffective or even backfire. After reviewing the evidence, how will most people in the group react?

A.   They will be less opposed to gun control legislation.

B.   Their attitudes will be unchanged, but they will call for more research.

C.   They will become more strongly opposed to gun control legislation.

D.   They will be more sympathetic to the opposing point of view.

Answer C, Type CON

44.   Preconceptions seem to influence our social judgments most when

A.   social information is subject to multiple interpretations.

B.   social information is clear and unambiguous.

C.   the information we have is complete.

D.   correspondence is highest.

Answer A, Type FAC

45.   Following Presidential debates, individuals typically

A.   become more moderate in their view of their preferred candidate.

B.   become even more supportive of their candidate than they were before the debate.

C.   become somewhat more favorable toward the opposing candidate.

D.   come to dislike both candidates.

Answer B, Type FAC

46.   The "Kulechov effect" (named after a Russian film director) is another illustration of

A.   the principle of belief perseverance.

B.   confirmation bias.

C.   false memories.

D.   the principle that reality is a social construction.

Answer D, Type CON

47.   Anderson, Lepper, and Ross provided people with evidence that either risk-prone or cautious people make better firefighters. Those who wrote an explanation for the findings were particularly susceptible to

A.   the fundamental attribution error.

B.   the hindsight bias.

C.   behavioral confirmation.

D.   belief perseverance.

Answer D, Type FAC

48. People tend to cling to their beliefs even in the face of contradictory evidence. This tendency is known as the
    A. belief perseverance phenomenon.
    B. belief continuity phenomenon.
    C. correspondence bias.
    D. belief disconfirmation bias.
    Answer A, Type DEF

49. One remedy for the belief perseverance phenomenon is to
    A. always attempt to justify one's position.
    B. carefully review the objective evidence.
    C. seek the opinions of others.
    D. explain why an opposite belief might be true.
    Answer D, Type FAC

50. Which of the following statements about memory is false?
    A. Memories are copies of past experiences that remain on deposit in a memory bank until withdrawn.
    B. We easily and unconsciously reconstruct our memories to suit our current knowledge.
    C. People often recall mildly pleasant events more favorably than they experienced them.
    D. We not only forget ideas and beliefs, we also forget our previous attitudes.
    Answer A, Type FAC

51. Bem and McConnell had students write essays opposing student control over university curriculum. When asked to recall how they had felt about the same issue a week earlier, most of the students
    A. remembered having held a very different attitude.
    B. could not remember how they had felt.
    C. mistakenly "remembered" having felt the same as now.
    D. admitted they had always supported student control of curriculum but pretended to oppose it in their essays.
    Answer C, Type FAC

52. When an experimenter asks people to vividly imagine a childhood incident when they knocked over a punch bowl at a wedding, _____ will later recall the event as something that actually happened.
    A. three-fourths
    B. one-half
    C. one-fourth
    D. one percent
    Answer C, Type FAC

53. On the way to his spring break at the ocean, Ben's flight was delayed 12 hours. Once on the beach he was disappointed that the condo was run-down and dirty. After the trip, Ben described his experience in nothing but positive terms. This accounting of the trip best reflects
    A. rosy retrospection.
    B. belief perseverance.
    C. confirmation bias.
    D. false memory.
    Answer A, Type CON

54. While waiting to cross the street you witness a man running a red light—causing a 3-car accident. Just after it happens, the man who ran the stoplight gets out of the car to talk to you. He tells you that the light was yellow. Later you tell police that you remembered the light being yellow, not red, when the man went through the intersection. This scenario illustrates
    A.   priming effect.
    B.   confirmation bias.
    C.   belief perseverance.
    D.   the misinformation effect.
    Answer D, Type CON

55. To retrieve a memory, you need to activate one of the strands that leads to it, a process known as
    A.   belief perseverance.
    B.   reconstruction.
    C.   priming.
    D.   induction.
    Answer C, Type DEF

56. Cognitive and affective processes that are effortless and beyond our awareness are termed
    A.   controlled.
    B.   automatic.
    C.   counter-intuitive.
    D.   schematic.
    Answer B, Type DEF

57. Steve is typically very confident about his opinions and beliefs--in fact he is usually more confident than he is accurate about certain things. Steve's thinking illustrates
    A.   illusory correlation.
    B.   the I-knew-it-all-along phenomenon.
    C.   the overconfidence phenomenon.
    D.   belief perseverance.
    Answer C, Type DEF

58. Investment experts' belief that their own expertise will enable them to select stocks that will outperform the market average best illustrates
    A.   the misinformation effect.
    B.   the overconfidence phenomenon.
    C.   the availability heuristic.
    D.   priming.
    Answer B, Type CON

59. One reason people are overconfident is that they are not inclined to seek out information
    A.   from experts.
    B.   this is objective and factual.
    C.   that involves judging estimates and comparisons.
    D.   that might disprove what they believe.
    Answer D, Type FAC

60. Dave typically reads information and watches programming that tends to support his existing beliefs. He's less inclined to seek information that might disprove his preconceptions. Dave's approach illustrates
    A.   the confirmation bias.
    B.   the misinformation effect.
    C.   the base-rate fallacy.

D.   the overconfidence phenomenon.
Answer A, Type CON

61.   The strategy of judging the likelihood of things by how well they match particular prototypes constitutes the _____ heuristic.
A.   availability
B.   representativeness
C.   vividness
D.   matching
Answer B, Type DEF

62.   Focusing on the specific individual or case being considered can push into the background useful information about the population the person came from. This is the _____ fallacy.
A.   naturalistic
B.   base-rate
C.   utilization
D.   representation
Answer B, Type DEF

63.   The tendency to conclude that a person who likes to play chess and read poetry is more likely to be a college professor of classics than a truck driver most clearly illustrates the use of
A.   the availability heuristic.
B.   the representativeness heuristic.
C.   belief perseverance.
D.   the illusion of control.
Answer B, Type CON

64.   Our tendency to judge the likelihood of an event on the basis of how readily we can remember instances of its occurrence is called the
A.   confirmation bias.
B.   representativeness heuristic.
C.   belief perseverance phenomenon.
D.   availability heuristic.
Answer D, Type DEF

65.   People's greater fear of flying than of driving may best be explained by the
A.   representativeness heuristic.
B.   confirmation bias.
C.   availability heuristic.
D.   belief perseverance phenomenon.
Answer C, Type CON

66.   "If only I hadn't called Brian when I was in a bad mood," whines Jenny, "maybe we wouldn't have had that fight and broken up!" Jenny's statement most clearly reflects
A.   the self-fulfilling prophecy.
B.   counterfactual thinking.
C.   the availability heuristic.
D.   pessimistic attributional style.
Answer B, Type CON

67.   Social psychologists refer to our tendency to imagine alternative scenarios and outcomes that might have happened, but didn't as
A.   the base-rate fallacy.
B.   automatic thinking.

C.   reflective bias.

D.   counterfactual thinking.

Answer D, Type DEF

68.   The perception of a relationship where none exists is called

A.   imaginary parallel.

B.   counterfactual thinking.

C.   illusory correlation.

D.   regression toward the average.

Answer C, Type DEF

69.   When Ward and Jenkins showed people the hypothetical results of a cloud-seeding experiment, people who believed such techniques are effective felt their faith was confirmed even though the results were a mixture of success and failure. The result illustrates

A.   the self-fulfilling prophecy.

B.   the representativeness heuristic.

C.   illusory correlation.

D.   social overconfidence.

Answer C, Type FAC

70.   Dottie has the illusory belief that there is a correlation between washing her car and the occurrence of rain in her area. According to research, Dottie is much more likely now to notice when

A.   it rains and she hasn't washed her car.

B.   it rains and she has just washed her car.

C.   it doesn't rain and she has just washed her car.

D.   All of the above.

Answer B, Type CON

71.   Dice players who throw softly to get low numbers and harder to get high numbers are demonstrating

A.   the base-rate fallacy.

B.   the illusion of control.

C.   behavioral confirmation.

D.   regression toward the average.

Answer B, Type FAC

72.   The illusion of control may arise because we fail to recognize

A.   our susceptibility to base-rate fallacy.

B.   the statistical phenomenon of regression toward the average.

C.   the operation of the representativeness heuristic.

D.   our tendency to counterfactual thinking.

Answer B, Type FAC

73.   Although Jason once scored a 270 in bowling, he has subsequently been unable to beat that record no matter how much he practices. His experience may be partially understood in terms of

A.   illusory correlation.

B.   regression toward the average.

C.   the representativeness heuristic.

D.   counterfactual thinking.

Answer B, Type CON

74.   When baseball's rookie-of-the-year has a more ordinary second year we shouldn't be surprised. This fact is easily explained by

A.   illusory correlations.
B.   the base-rate fallacy.
C.   the illusion of control.
D.   regression toward the average.
Answer D, Type CON

75.   Research indicates that, compared to unhappy people, happy people
A.   are more trusting and loving.
B.   choose long-term rewards over immediate small pleasures.
C.   tolerate more frustration.
D.   show all of the above characteristics.
Answer D, Type FAC

76.   Joseph Forgas and his colleagues found that participants' judgments of their own videotaped behaviors were more positive if, while they watched the videotape, they were
A.   in a good mood.
B.   with a stranger.
C.   distracted.
D.   either depressed or anxious.
Answer A, Type FAC

77.   Moods can affect our thinking by
A.   triggering memories associated with those moods.
B.   triggering more effortful, deep processing.
C.   triggering self-fulfilling prophecies.
D.   None of the above.
Answer A, Type FAC

78.   The tendency for one's expectations to evoke behavior that confirms the expectations is called
A.   self-fulfilling prophecy.
B.   belief confirmation.
C.   self-confirming validity.
D.   behavioral perseverance.
Answer A, Type DEF

79.   In a now-famous study, Rosenthal and Jacobson found that randomly selected elementary school students experienced a spurt in IQ score largely as a result of
A.   increased parental involvement and support.
B.   their teachers' elevated expectations.
C.   intensified academic training.
D.   educational strategies that raised their self-esteem.
Answer B, Type FAC

80.   Research has indicated that _____ can be self-fulfilling.
A.   teachers' expectations of students
B.   students' expectations of teachers
C.   experimenters' expectations of participants
D.   All of the above.
Answer D, Type FAC

81.   Snyder, Tanke, and Berscheid had male students speak by telephone with women they thought were either attractive or unattractive. When judges later analyzed the women's comments, they found that
A.   the women thought to be attractive spoke more warmly than the other women.

B.   the women thought to be unattractive tried harder to be likable and stimulated better conversation.

C.   the women thought to be attractive spoke in a more aloof and superior manner.

D.   women thought to be unattractive spoke more slowly and deliberately.

Answer A, Type DEF

82.   When our expectations lead us to act in ways that induce others to confirm those expectations, _____ is at work.

A.   illusory correlation

B.   counterfactual thinking

C.   behavioral confirmation

D.   illusion of control

Answer C, Type DEF

83.   According to research done by Miller and his colleagues, if you want young children to litter less and put trash in wastebaskets, you should probably repeatedly

A.   tell them they should be neat and tidy.

B.   congratulate them for being neat and tidy.

C.   tell them littering is a crime.

D.   tell them that people who litter are trash.

Answer B, Type FAC

84.   Research confirms that people are unlikely to confirm others' expectations when those expectations

A.   involve racial or gender stereotypes.

B.   involve the performance of altruistic behavior.

C.   conflict with a clear self-concept.

D.   are held by peers rather than by authority figures.

Answer C, Type FAC

85.   Steven Smith found that significantly more Bloomington, Indiana, residents agreed to a request to volunteer to work three hours for an American Cancer Society drive if

A.   earlier they had been asked to predict how they would react if they were to receive such a request.

B.   they had first been informed that their neighbors had refused the request to volunteer.

C.   they had first been placed in a good mood through hypnosis.

D.   they had just received a temporary boost to their self-esteem.

Answer A, Type FAC

The following items also appear in the Study Guide:

86.   According to the theory of correspondent inferences,

A.   we tend to infer that people's intentions and dispositions correspond to their actions.

B.   we tend to infer that people's intentions and dispositions correspond to our own intentions and dispositions.

C.   we tend to infer that people share the same underlying motives and values.

D.   those who have similar values tend to make the same attributions about others.

Answer A, Type DEF

87.   For a school debate, Sally has been asked to argue in favor of capital punishment. Research on the fundamental attribution error suggests that observers of Sally's speech will conclude that her arguments

A.   reflect her true attitude on the topic.

B.   reflect a tendency to present herself favorably.

C.   are weak because she was assigned to present a particular position on the topic.

D.   will lead her to experience cognitive dissonance.

Answer A, Type CON

88.   Evidence of the reasonable manner in which we form judgments of one another comes from research on

      A.   informational influence.

      B.   personal space.

      C.   the mere-exposure effect.

      D.   information integration.

Answer D, Type FAC

89.   People from collectivist cultures are more likely than Americans to

      A.   offer situational explanations for someone's actions.

      B.   offer dispositional explanations for someone's actions.

      C.   engage in self-handicapping.

      D.   offer self-serving explanations for their own behavior.

Answer A, Type FAC

90.   There is a tendency to attribute the causes of _____ behavior to the situation and to attribute the causes of _____ behavior to traits.

      A.   our own; others'

      B.   others'; our own

      C.   children's; adults'

      D.   males'; females'

Answer A, Type FAC

91.   According to the text, the fundamental attribution error may lead us to

      A.   overestimate the brilliance of our teachers.

      B.   fail to hold people responsible for their misconduct.

      C.   be lenient with convicted criminals.

      D.   All of the above.

Answer A, Type FAC

92.   The more closely we examine our theories and explain how they might be true,

      A.   the more uncertain we become of them.

      B.   the more closed we become to discrediting information.

      C.   the more open we are likely to become to discrediting information.

      D.   the more complex our theories are likely to become.

Answer B, Type FAC

93.   The incorrect belief that the letter "k" appears more often as the first letter of a word than as the third letter can be understood in terms of

      A.   the availability heuristic.

      B.   hindsight bias.

      C.   regression toward the average.

      D.   the illusion of control.

Answer A, Type CON

94.   The textbook states that a large drop in prices on the stock market sometimes illustrates

      A.   the representativeness heuristic.

      B.   the availability heuristic.

      C.   the overconfidence phenomenon.

      D.   self-fulfilling prophecy.

Answer D, Type FAC

95. Linda is 31, single, and outspoken. As a college student she was deeply concerned with discrimination and other social issues. A tendency to conclude that it is more likely that Linda is a bank teller and active in the feminist movement than simply a bank teller illustrates the powerful influence of
    A.   belief perseverance.
    B.   the availability heuristic.
    C.   regression toward the average.
    D.   the representativeness heuristic.
    Answer D, Type CON

96. Despite reading solid research evidence that cigarette smoking causes cancer, Philip continues to believe that smoking is harmless. Philip's thinking clearly reveals
    A.   belief assimilation.
    B.   belief consolidation.
    C.   belief perseverance.
    D.   operation of the availability heuristic.
    Answer C, Type CON

97. Many people firmly believe in astrology's ability to predict the future. Assuming they are presented a history of an astrologer's past predictions which in actuality show a random mix of success and failure, they are likely to
    A.   believe the astrologer is successful.
    B.   question this astrologer's predictive ability but still believe in the validity of astrology.
    C.   become very defensive.
    D.   give up their belief in the validity of astrology.
    Answer A, Type CON

98. Bob, a baseball player, makes five hits while Joe, a member of the same team, makes none in a particular game. In the next game both obtain one hit. What term used in the text explains Bob's fewer hits and Joe's increase?
    A.   overconfidence bias
    B.   base-rate fallacy
    C.   regression to the average
    D.   schemata
    Answer C, Type CON

99. What psychological term might best be used to describe the rule "I before E except after C"?
    A.   base-rate fallacy
    B.   hindsight bias
    C.   illusion of control
    D.   heuristic
    Answer D, Type CON

100. A person enters a casino and after inserting one silver dollar in a slot machine hits the jackpot. This person's tendency to continue putting money into the machine so that finally the amount lost exceeds the original winnings can perhaps best be explained in terms of
    A.   self-fulfilling prophecy.
    B.   regression toward the average.
    C.   illusion of control.
    D.   hindsight bias.
    Answer C, Type CON

Critical Thinking Questions

101. How do attributions affect how we think about and relate to one another?

102. Define the fundamental attribution error. What makes it "fundamental?"

103. Give two examples of how automatic thinking affects our feelings, thoughts, or perceptions.

104. Explain how the confirmation bias contributes to and helps explain the overconfidence phenomenon.

105. How could a teacher safeguard against self-fulfilling prophecies that might be detrimental to students?

CHAPTER FOUR
BEHAVIOR AND ATTITUDES

Multiple Choice Questions

1. An attitude is defined as _____ toward someone or something.
    A. a behavior
    B. an evaluative reaction
    C. a single belief
    D. an inclination
    Answer B, Type DEF

2. In the ABC's of attitudes, "C" stands for
    A. care.
    B. connotation.
    C. cognition.
    D. concern.
    Answer C, Type FAC

3. In the ABC's of attitudes, "A" stands for
    A. attitude.
    B. attribution.
    C. attraction.
    D. affect.
    Answer D, Type FAC

4. A person's attitude will be reflected in that person's
    A. beliefs.
    B. feelings.
    C. intentions to act.
    D. All of the above.
    Answer D, Type DEF

5. Which of the following is a component of Peter's attitude toward classical music?
    A. Peter believes that listening to classical music raises one's IQ.
    B. Peter likes the fact that a local radio plays only classical music.
    C. Peter buys classical music recordings with any extra money he earns.
    D. All of the above are part of Peter's attitude toward classical music.
    Answer D, Type CON

6. A prevailing assumption that underlies most teaching, counseling, and child rearing has been that
    A. private attitudes determine behavior.
    B. private attitudes are unrelated to behavior.
    C. feelings, behaviors, and beliefs are always consistent.
    D. feelings, behaviors, and beliefs are always inconsistent.
    Answer A, Type FAC

7. In 1964, Leon Festinger concluded that the evidence to date
    A. did not show that attitudes guide behavior.
    B. did show that attitudes guide behavior.
    C. was irrelevant to the attitude-behavior relation.

D.   None of the above.
Answer A, Type FAC

8.   In 1969 social psychologist Allan Wicker completed a review of dozens of research studies with
        the conclusion that people's stated attitudes expressed _____ of the variation in their behaviors.
        A.   very little
        B.   about half
        C.   most
        D.   virtually all
        Answer A, Type FAC

9.   In the early 1930s, Richard LaPiere traveled the United States with a Chinese couple, and they
        were received with courtesy at all but one of the hotels and restaurants they visited. Six months
        later, when LaPiere wrote those establishments and asked if they would serve members of the
        Chinese race, of those who replied,
        A.   only one said yes.
        B.   about 25 percent said yes.
        C.   about half said yes.
        D.   about 90 percent said yes.
        Answer A, Type FAC

10.   In 1969 Wicker reviewed studies of the attitude-behavior relation. Results suggested that
        A.   attitudes toward cheating were not related to actual cheating.
        B.   attitudes toward the church were only modestly related to church attendance.
        C.   racial attitudes were not related to behavior in actual situations.
        D.   All of the above.
        Answer D, Type FAC

11.   An attitude will be only weakly linked to behavior when
        A.   the attitude is not very potent.
        B.   behavior is subject to lots of other influences.
        C.   the attitude and the behavior are not measured at the same level of specificity.
        D.   All of the above.
        Answer D, Type FAC

12.   Which of the following best describes the relationship between expressed attitudes and behavior?
        A.   Expressed attitudes lead to behavioral intentions, which perfectly predict behaviors.
        B.   Past behaviors lead to behavioral intentions, which lead to expressed attitudes.
        C.   Expressed attitudes perfectly predict behaviors.
        D.   They are imperfectly related because both are subject to other influences.
        Answer D, Type FAC

13.   Which of the following statements correctly explains the bogus pipeline strategy?
        A.   Participants' expressed attitudes are interpreted to mean the exact opposite of their true
                attitudes.
        B.   Participants are deceived into believing that their true attitudes are being measured
                directly, so they do not distort their expressed attitudes.
        C.   Researchers ignore the participants' expressed attitudes and infer true attitudes from
                measures of arousal and tension.
        D.   Participants' responses are evaluated by a polygraph machine that provides a measure of
                deception and distortion.
        Answer B, Type FAC

14.   The advantage of the bogus-pipeline technique is that it

A. eliminates the need for deception in attitude research.
B. guarantees anonymity of participants' responses.
C. yields an expressed attitude that is closer to the real one.
D. guarantees that the expressed attitude will lead to action.
Answer C, Type FAC

15. Alice wonders if Justin really likes her. Since his behavior toward her may be the result of other factors besides his real attitude, the best way for her to measure his true attitude is to
A. observe his average treatment of her over time.
B. see whether he invites her to a party this weekend.
C. notice how close he sits to her in psychology class.
D. observe his reaction to the question, "Don't you like me?"
Answer A, Type CON

16. The effects of an attitude on behavior become more apparent when we look at a person's average behavior over time. This fact describes
A. the principle of aggregation.
B. regression toward the average.
C. the principle of information integration.
D. the principle of reciprocal averages.
Answer A, Type DEF

17. Snyder and Swann asked University of Minnesota men to act as jurors in a sex discrimination case. The men's previously recorded attitudes ended up predicting their verdicts only if they
A. recorded their verdicts in writing.
B. were first instructed to recall their attitudes.
C. were asked to decide quickly and impulsively.
D. first discussed their opinions with the rest of the group.
Answer B, Type FAC

18. Studies of the relationship between self-consciousness and attitudes suggest that, if you are making a decision and suddenly are induced to feel self-conscious, you will be more likely to
A. take action that is consistent with your attitudes.
B. take action that is inconsistent with your attitudes.
C. momentarily forget and fail to act on your attitudes.
D. be more vulnerable to external influences on your attitudes.
Answer A, Type FAC

19. If your goal was to increase recycling of aluminum cans through persuasion, it would be best to argue
A. for the need to protect and preserve global resources.
B. for the benefits of recycling all recyclable products.
C. for the benefits of recycling aluminum cans.
D. for the long-term dangers to the environment if we don't recycle all recyclable products.
Answer C, Type CON

20. Jack is tempted to shoplift an expensive camera even though he has a negative attitude about shoplifting. Jack is least likely to steal the camera if
A. his negative attitude about shoplifting were learned from his teachers.
B. he notices there are few customers in the store.
C. he carefully looks at himself in a mirror.
D. he has recently shoplifted items from other stores.
Answer C, Type CON

21. You are hosting a Weight Watchers party for women who have reached their goal weight. You want to provide tasty snacks, but you don't want to encourage over-eating, either. How could you arrange things to help your friends eat sensibly, in accord with their new attitudes toward eating?
    A. Put the food in the kitchen, away from the main flow of people.
    B. Spread the food out all over the house, on individual trays.
    C. Put the food on a table that is placed directly underneath your large wall mirror in the dining room.
    D. None of the above.
    Answer C, Type CON

22. A housing shortage at Cornell University forced some students to live on cots in dormitory lounges for several weeks. Although all students tended to have negative attitudes about Cornell's housing situation, only _____ acted on them.
    A. males
    B. those whose attitudes came from direct experience
    C. those who might have to experience such adverse living conditions in the future
    D. college seniors
    Answer B, Type FAC

23. Compared to attitudes formed passively, those forged in the fire of experience are more
    A. unstable.
    B. less thoughtful.
    C. more resistant to attack.
    D. more difficult to express verbally.
    Answer C, Type FAC

24. Our attitudes predict our actions when
    A. other influences on our actions are minimized.
    B. the attitude involved is specifically about the action.
    C. we are conscious of our attitudes as we act.
    D. All of the above.
    Answer D, Type FAC

25. If you want to increase the potency of your attitude toward helping the homeless, one of the most effective things you could do is
    A. read about the problem of homelessness.
    B. help out regularly at the local homeless shelter.
    C. listen to inspirational tapes on the topic of helping the needy.
    D. None of the above.
    Answer B, Type CON

26. Which of the following refers to a set of examples or research investigations that illustrate the power of self-persuasion--of attitudes following behavior?
    A. role playing
    B. the foot-in-the-door principle
    C. interracial desegregation
    D. All of the above.
    Answer D, Type FAC

27. The term _____ refers to prescribed actions expected of those who occupy a particular social position.
    A. constellation

B.   intentions
C.   role
D.   status
Answer C, Type DEF

28.   The results of Zimbardo's Stanford prison simulation indicated that
A.   prison brutality is a product of the unique traits of prisoners and guards.
B.   playing the roles of prisoners and guards can harden and embitter ordinary people.
C.   authoritarianism is a primary cause of prejudice and aggression.
D.   crowding is a primary cause of prison violence.
Answer B, Type FAC

29.   You've just been promoted to the role of supervisor at work. You feel awkward and uncomfortable in your new position. Research on role-playing suggests
A.   this discomfort will increase over time.
B.   others will not treat you fairly in your new position.
C.   over time you will get comfortable with your new role.
D.   your attitude and feelings toward your new role will not change over time.
Answer C, Type CON

30.   Saying is most likely to become believing when
A.   we have said something positive but not negative.
B.   we already tend to believe it anyway.
C.   we are not forced into saying it.
D.   we are given no choice but to say it.
Answer C, Type FAC

31.   Experiments suggest that if you want people to do a big favor for you, one technique is to get them to do a small favor first; this is known as the _____ technique.
A.   insufficient justification
B.   overjustification
C.   foot-in-the-door
D.   door-in-the-face
Answer C, Type DEF

32.   According to the foot-in-the-door principle, if you get someone to agree to a small request, he or she will
A.   later comply with a larger request.
B.   expect you to return the favor later.
C.   experience reactance and refuse requests for all later favors.
D.   see himself or herself as altruistic and do similar favors for other people.
Answer A, Type DEF

33.   In a study by Freedman and Fraser, Californians were found to be more willing to agree to post an ugly "Drive Carefully" sign prominently in their front yards if they
A.   were offered a small compensation for their effort.
B.   had previously scored high on a survey of attitudes favoring more stringent traffic laws.
C.   had earlier complied with a smaller request to display a safe-driving window sign.
D.   had first refused to comply with a smaller request to sign a safe-driving petition.
Answer C, Type FAC

34.   You agree to buy a new computer at a terrific price. Then the sales associate charges you for software you thought was included in the original package. You've been
A.   victimized by the overjustification effect.

B. low-balled.

C. victimized by post-decision dissonance.

D. All of the above.

Answer B, Type CON

35. For the foot-in-the-door principle to work, the initial compliance--signing a petition, wearing a lapel pin, stating one's intention--must be

A. granted without much thought.

B. voluntary.

C. socially approved.

D. granted to a powerful authority figure.

Answer B, Type FAC

36. The low-ball technique is a strategy for

A. improving one's self-concept.

B. measuring a person's attitude.

C. reducing physical aggression.

D. getting people to agree to something.

Answer D, Type DEF

37. A sales representative comes to your home and asks you to try a water filter system for a week, absolutely free, so you agree. He returns the next week and offers you an expensive contract to continue to rent the system and you agree. You are most clearly a victim of

A. self-monitoring.

B. the overjustification effect.

C. the foot-in-the-door phenomenon.

D. impression management.

Answer C, Type CON

38. The text cites the escalation of United States involvement in the Vietnam war as an example of

A. the power of initial commitments to lead to further action consistent with those commitments.

B. the effects of the low-ball technique.

C. how saying becomes believing.

D. the overjustification effect.

Answer A, Type FAC

39. Disparaging an innocent victim leads an aggressor to justify further hurtful behavior. Research studies show that this pattern occurs especially when the aggressor

A. identifies with the victim as similar to himself or herself.

B. engages in verbal but not physical aggression.

C. is coerced into the attack by threats from superiors.

D. is coaxed but not threatened or coerced into aggression.

Answer D, Type FAC

40. Aggressors are likely to hate and blame their victims, illustrating

A. the power of the low-ball technique.

B. the principle of self-presentation.

C. the insufficient justification effect.

D. the power of actions to influence attitudes.

Answer D, Type CON

41. Which of the following statements about the effects of moral and immoral action is correct?

A. Just as immoral actions corrode the conscience of those who perform them, moral actions affect the actor in positive ways.
B. People induced to act in evil ways quickly renounce this pattern, while those coaxed to do good continue the pattern.
C. Moral acts are internalized only if they are prompted by significant rewards or threats.
D. None of the above.
Answer A, Type FAC

42. Freedman asked young children not to play with an enticing robot toy by threatening some with severe punishment and others with only a mild penalty. Much later the same children had an opportunity to play with the robot again, this time with no threat of punishment. Results showed that the children
A. given the mild deterrent were first to play with the robot.
B. given the mild deterrent mostly resisted playing with it.
C. who played with the robot later feared being punished.
D. previously given the severe threat showed a great deal of anxiety when they neared the robot.
Answer B, Type FAC

43. Children seem more likely to internalize their decisions to obey rules when the deterrent they are threatened with is _____ and they are given _____.
A. strong; no choice about how to behave
B. mild; no choice about how to behave
C. mild; a choice about how to behave
D. strong; a reward for obeying the rules
Answer C, Type FAC

44. Findings indicate that since the U.S. Supreme Court's 1954 decision to desegregate schools, the percentage of white Americans favoring integrated schools has
A. declined slightly in those states most affected by the ruling.
B. more than doubled and now includes nearly everyone.
C. increased only in those states not affected by the decision.
D. remained essentially unchanged.
Answer B, Type FAC

45. Findings on racial attitudes and behavior suggest that
A. you can't legislate morality.
B. changes in racial attitudes have followed changes in racial behavior.
C. interracial behavior improves only after attitudes change.
D. desegregation has tended to make people more prejudiced.
Answer B, Type FAC

46. According to the text, since the 1954 Supreme Court decision to desegregate schools
A. Whites' expressed attitudes toward Blacks have grown more negative.
B. Blacks' expressed attitudes toward Whites have grown more positive.
C. the percentage of Whites favoring integrated schools has declined by more than 50%.
D. the percentage of Whites favoring integrated schools has more than doubled.
Answer D, Type FAC

47. An analysis of social movements suggests that
A. totalitarian attitudes determine genocidal behavior.
B. attitudes often follow behavior.
C. attitudes are rarely influenced by behavior at the level of social movements.

D.   brainwashing has no psychological basis.
Answer B, Type FAC

48.   Historians suggest that, in Nazi Germany, citizens who were reluctant to support the Nazi regime experienced a profound inconsistency between their private beliefs and
   A.   running a private business in Germany.
   B.   enrolling their children in German schools.
   C.   reciting the public greeting "Heil Hitler" as a conformist greeting.
   D.   saluting the German flag but not the swastika.
   Answer C, Type FAC

49.   Which of the following is not an effective component of a brainwashing program?
   A.   escalating very gradually the demands made of the prisoner
   B.   offering large bribes for compliance with requests
   C.   eliciting regular participation from the prisoner rather than allowing him to be a passive recipient of propaganda
   D.   having prisoners write self-criticism or utter public confessions
   Answer B, Type FAC

50.   Which theory assumes that we observe our actions for clues about our own attitudes and beliefs?
   A.   self-presentation
   B.   cognitive dissonance
   C.   self-justification
   D.   self-perception
   Answer D, Type DEF

51.   Impression management is to _____ as cognitive dissonance is to _____.
   A.   overjustification; insufficient justification
   B.   Bem; Festinger
   C.   self-monitoring; self-presentation
   D.   self-presentation; self-justification
   Answer D, Type CON

52.   No one wants to look foolishly inconsistent according to _____ theory.
   A.   self-perception
   B.   self-justification
   C.   self-presentation
   D.   social orientation
   Answer C, Type DEF

53.   Making a good impression is a way of life for people
   A.   low in self-monitoring.
   B.   high in self-monitoring
   C.   low in self-perception.
   D.   high in self-perception
   Answer B, Type FAC

54.   David has a strong set of internal principles for his beliefs and behaviors and always says what he thinks and believes what he says. He would probably score _____ on a measure of _____.
   A.   high; self-monitoring
   B.   low; self-monitoring
   C.   high; cognitive dissonance
   D.   low; self-perception
   Answer B, Type CON

55. Cognitive dissonance theory was formulated by
    A. James Laird.
    B. William James.
    C. Leon Festinger.
    D. Daryl Bem.
    Answer C, Type FAC

56. Cognitive dissonance theory proposes that we experience _____ when our beliefs are _____.
    A. fear; uncertain
    B. pleasure; inconsistent
    C. tension; inconsistent
    D. arousal; consistent
    Answer C, Type FAC

57. Dissonance is
    A. an uncomfortable state of tension.
    B. a stimulating state of arousal.
    C. an enjoyable state of uncertainty.
    D. a frightening state of consistency.
    Answer A, Type DEF

58. We experience dissonance when we have
    A. made a decision between two equally attractive alternatives.
    B. acted in ways that are not consistent with previously stated attitudes.
    C. insufficient justification for performing a costly act.
    D. All of the above.
    Answer D, Type FAC

59. Festinger and Carlsmith had experimental participants perform a dull task but paid them to lie by telling a prospective participant that the task had been enjoyable. Results showed that the participants who were paid _____ came to believe the task had been _____.
    A. $1; tedious and boring
    B. $1; interesting and enjoyable
    C. $20; interesting and enjoyable
    D. $1; frightening
    Answer B, Type FAC

60. Though she is opposed to capital punishment, Lisa is asked to give a speech in favor of it to round out a class debate. Dissonance theory predicts that her true attitude will undergo the most change if she
    A. makes a speech implying capital punishment is really wrong.
    B. agrees to give the speech but only if she tells both sides.
    C. agrees to give the speech without special incentives.
    D. agrees to give the speech for a large reward.
    Answer C, Type CON

61. The magnitude of the felt dissonance is greater when
    A. there is insufficient justification for the behavior.
    B. there is overjustification for the behavior.
    C. there is no choice over the behavior.
    D. there are others engaged in the same behavior.
    Answer A, Type FAC

62. Research on dissonance theory suggests that the attitudes-follow-behavior effect is strongest when
    A. people have some choice in their behavior.
    B. the behavior has undesirable consequences.
    C. the person feels they should have foreseen the consequences of their behavior.
    D. All of the above.
    Answer D, Type FAC

63. In applying the principle of cognitive dissonance to have others develop their own internal standards for new behavior, managers, teachers, and parents should use _____ to elicit the desired behavior.
    A. reminders of their legitimate authority
    B. only social punishments and rewards
    C. promises rather than threats
    D. the smallest possible incentive
    Answer D, Type FAC

64. Research indicates that after making important decisions that involve choosing between equally attractive alternatives, we
    A. experience very little cognitive dissonance once the choice is made.
    B. reduce dissonance by trying to think about something else.
    C. reduce dissonance by downgrading the rejected alternative.
    D. reduce dissonance by verbalizing the weaknesses of the chosen alternative.
    Answer C, Type FAC

65. Researcher Jack Brehm had women rate the desirability of various appliances before and after they had chosen one to keep for themselves. Brehm found that after the women had chosen a particular appliance, they
    A. decreased their rating of its desirability.
    B. expressed increased interest in learning about the others.
    C. increased their rating of its desirability.
    D. increased their rating of how desirable the others were.
    Answer C, Type FAC

66. Beth is torn between buying a Toyota Camry and a Honda Accord—two equally attractive options. After finally deciding on the Toyota, Beth will likely
    A. regret her decision for as long as she owns the car.
    B. think about all the positive features of the Honda.
    C. dwell on the negative features of the Toyota.
    D. think about and even upgrade all the positive features of the Toyota.
    Answer D, Type CON

67. Deciding-is-believing causes voters to indicate more esteem and confidence in a candidate
    A. long before they vote.
    B. just before they vote.
    C. just after they vote.
    D. just after the results are known.
    Answer C, Type FAC

68. Which of the following statements is true?
    A. People feel more confident just after betting on a horse than just before betting.
    B. Contestants at a carnival game feel more confident of winning before agreeing to play than just after agreeing to play.

C.   Voters are more confident in a candidate just before voting than just after voting.
D.   All of the above.
Answer A, Type FAC

69.   Based on the findings of James Laird's research on self-perception, if you want to feel happier you should
A.   compare yourself to those who are worse off.
B.   act happy by smiling.
C.   assume an unhappy expression like frowning.
D.   reward yourself after you have met your goals.
Answer B, Type CON

70.   William James, self-perception theory, and research findings all suggest that
A.   your gait can influence how you feel.
B.   your posture can influence how you feel.
C.   your facial expressions can influence how you feel.
D.   All of the above.
Answer D, Type FAC

71.   Wells and Petty asked students to listen to a tape-recorded radio editorial while testing the fit of earphone headsets. The students later said they agreed more with the editorial they had heard on the tape if they had been
A.   distracted and unable to listen carefully.
B.   wearing the lightest, most comfortable headsets.
C.   given the choice of which editorial they would hear.
D.   instructed to test the headsets by nodding.
Answer D, Type FAC

72.   The muscle-flex effect (more positive ratings of stimuli when arms are flexed upward) is most effective
A.   for initially negative stimuli.
B.   for initially positive stimuli.
C.   for initially neutral stimuli.
D.   for familiar and well-liked stimuli.
Answer C, Type FAC

73.   The overjustification effect is best explained in terms of _____ theory.
A.   self-perception
B.   cognitive dissonance
C.   self-monitoring
D.   self-presentation
Answer A, Type FAC

74.   Jeremy loses his former interest in doing arithmetic after his teacher promises him $1 for each problem he solves correctly. Which theory best explains Jeremy's loss of interest in arithmetic?
A.   self-perception theory
B.   cognitive dissonance theory
C.   self-presentation theory
D.   self-monitoring theory
Answer A, Type CON

75.   According to the overjustification effect, promising children a reward for doing what they intrinsically enjoy will
A.   lead to more enjoyment in the activity.

B.   lead to less enjoyment in the activity.

C.   increase the time and effort they put into the activity.

D.   encourage them to do the activity on their own, without the promise of future rewards.

Answer B, Type FAC

76.   Myra's neighbor, a little boy, practices his saxophone loudly and annoyingly. According to the overjustification effect, if Myra wants to get him to quit playing, she should

A.   threaten to make him miserable if he keeps playing.

B.   pay him to quit playing.

C.   pay him a small amount to quit playing and then offer him more and more.

D.   pay him to play and then offer him less and less.

Answer D, Type CON

77.   As self-perception theory implies, the overjustification effect can be avoided, because _____ reward does not diminish intrinsic interest in an action, since people can still attribute the action to their own motivation.

A.   an uninformative

B.   an unanticipated

C.   a social

D.   an excessive

Answer B, Type FAC

78.   The major difference between dissonance theory and self-perception theory is that the former relies on the motivating effects of _____, while the latter does not.

A.   behavior

B.   self-awareness

C.   tension

D.   self-inference

Answer C, Type FAC

79.   In dissonance experiments, the attitudes-follow-behavior effect _____ when participants _____.

A.   becomes stronger; drink alcohol

B.   becomes stronger; have no choice in their behavior

C.   disappears; exercise

D.   disappears; drink alcohol

Answer D, Type FAC

80.   A comparison of theories explaining attitude-behavior relationships concludes that dissonance conditions do indeed arouse tension, especially when those conditions threaten

A.   self-worth.

B.   physical discomfort.

C.   as-yet-unformed attitudes.

D.   None of the above.

Answer A, Type FAC

81.   A comparison of dissonance theory and self-perception theory suggests that _____ theory really explains _____.

A.   dissonance; attitude formation

B.   dissonance; behavior change

C.   self-perception; attitude change

D.   self-perception; attitude formation

Answer D, Type FAC

82. Harry has always strongly believed that it is wrong to shoplift. But after he himself shoplifts some inexpensive jewelry, his attitude toward shoplifting becomes less harsh. Which theory best accounts for this attitude shift?
   A. role-playing theory
   B. self-monitoring theory
   C. self-perception theory
   D. cognitive dissonance theory
   Answer D, Type CON

83. A powerful practical lesson of the chapter on attitudes and behavior is that if we want to change ourselves in some important way, it is best to
   A. wait for the insight and inspiration needed to see it through.
   B. plan carefully before undertaking any action.
   C. arm ourselves with incentives and motives beforehand.
   D. go ahead and take action even if we don't feel like it.
   Answer D, Type FAC

84. Bower and Masling gave students a list of bizarre correlations to remember. They found that students recalled most if they had
   A. invented their own explanations for them.
   B. been given good explanations of them by experts.
   C. been given extra time to study them.
   D. reviewed concrete examples for each one.
   Answer A, Type FAC

85. Confirming the value of self-produced lessons, philosopher-psychologist William James asserted that "the great maxim which the teacher ought never to forget" is that no student should ever be asked to receive information without
   A. being given time to process it.
   B. knowing how it is supposed to be applied.
   C. being instructed in its proper use.
   D. having a chance to react to it.
   Answer D, Type FAC

These items also appear in the Study Guide:

86. Which of the following is a technique for measuring attitudes?
   A. self-monitoring pipeline
   B. foot-in-the-door phenomenon
   C. low-ball technique
   D. bogus pipeline
   Answer D, Type FAC

87. Based on recent social-psychological research, which of the following statements is true?
   A. Our attitudes and our behavior are unrelated.
   B. Our attitudes determine our behavior but our behavior does not determine our attitudes.
   C. Our behavior determines our attitudes but our attitudes do not determine our behavior.
   D. Under certain circumstances attitudes do predict behavior.
   Answer D, Type FAC

88. When a movie version was made of William Golding's novel Lord of the Flies,
   A. the youngsters who acted it out became the creatures prescribed by their roles.
   B. hypnosis was used to get the youngsters to live up to their roles.
   C. action therapy was necessary to get the youngsters to unlearn their roles.

D.   the foot-in-the-door phenomenon led the youngsters who acted it out to become uncivilized and brutal.

Answer A, Type FAC

89.   Which of the following is cited in the text as an example of how changing behavior can alter attitudes?
A.   civil rights legislation
B.   prohibition
C.   traffic laws
D.   capital punishment legislation

Answer A, Type FAC

90.   The theory that states we adopt certain attitudes in order to justify our past actions is _____ theory.
A.   self-perception
B.   self-presentation
C.   cognitive dissonance
D.   psychological reactance

Answer C, Type DEF

91.   The gradual escalation of demands and active participation were described as key elements in
A.   the overjustification effect.
B.   brainwashing.
C.   the underjustification effect.
D.   the low-balling effect.

Answer B, Type FAC

92.   Both cognitive dissonance theory and self-perception theory provide an explanation for the
A.   hindsight bias.
B.   insufficient justification effect.
C.   overjustification effect.
D.   Both B and C.

Answer B, Type FAC

93.   Which of the following is a component of Mary's attitude toward smoking?
A.   Mary believes smoking is harmful to one's health.
B.   Mary dislikes the fact that people are permitted to smoke in vehicles of public transportation.
C.   Mary is actively working for legislation that would outlaw the sale of cigarettes.
D.   All of the above are part of Mary's attitude toward smoking.

Answer D, Type CON

94.   A car salesman offers to sell a customer a new car for $17,000 which is a very attractive price. After the customer signs the papers to purchase at that price, the salesman seeks final approval from the manager. He returns to tell the customer that the manager will sell the car for $17,700. The customer still agrees to buy. The customer was a victim of
A.   the overjustification effect.
B.   low-balling.
C.   brainwashing.
D.   the door-in-the-face phenomenon.

Answer B, Type CON

95.   Nicole loses her former interest in playing the piano after her father promises to pay her $2 for each hour of practice. This illustrates the _____ effect.

A.   insufficient justification
B.   low-ball
C.   overjustification
D.   door-in-the-face
Answer C, Type CON

96.   Although John is strongly opposed to stricter parking regulations on campus, he is asked to write a paper supporting them. Dissonance theory predicts that his attitude will undergo the most change if he
A.   refuses to write the paper.
B.   agrees to write the paper for $200.
C.   agrees to write the paper for no pay.
D.   refuses to write the paper even after being offered $20.
Answer C, Type CON

97.   Milford has always strongly believed that it is wrong to cheat. But after he himself cheats on a chemistry quiz, his attitude toward cheating becomes significantly less harsh. What best accounts for this attitude shift?
A.   cognitive dissonance theory
B.   self-perception theory
C.   reinforcement theory
D.   role-playing theory
Answer A, Type CON

98.   In unfamiliar social situations Philip always sizes up his audience before stating an opinion. He only makes statements he knows others will support. Philip would probably obtain a high score on a scale of
A.   self-monitoring.
B.   low-balling.
C.   internal control.
D.   social comparison.
Answer A, Type CON

99.   In which of the following situations would cognitive dissonance theorists predict that the person is experiencing dissonance?
A.   Dan is trying to decide whether to buy a new or used bicycle.
B.   Just as Mike finishes mowing the lawn, it begins to rain.
C.   Sara has just been accepted into law school.
D.   Nancy has just chosen to attend City College rather than State University after receiving equally attractive scholarship offers from both.
Answer D, Type CON

100.   "Let me see, do I like Chinese food? I guess I do because I eat at a Chinese restaurant twice a month." The process reflected in this internal dialogue is best understood in terms of
A.   cognitive dissonance theory.
B.   self-perception theory.
C.   reinforcement theory.
D.   equity theory.
Answer B, Type CON

Critical Thinking Questions

101. Describe one of your important attitudes. Include cognitive, affective, and behavioral components.

102. "We are likely to act ourselves into a way of thinking." Discuss the evidence for this statement.

103. The general concept of consistency between attitudes and behavior is important to both self-presentation theory and cognitive dissonance theory. Compare and contrast how these two theories use this concept.

104. Compare and contrast self-perception theory and dissonance theory.

105. Discuss the evidence that arousal is an important element of dissonance.

CHAPTER FIVE
GENES, CULTURE, AND GENDER

Multiple Choice Questions

1. Given the prevalence of ethnic conflict and racial hostilities worldwide, it is not surprising that historian Arthur Schlesinger calls _____ "the explosive problem of our times."
    A.   social anarchy
    B.   social diversity
    C.   totalitarianism
    D.   mindless conformity
    Answer B, Type FAC

2. Aliens who abducted a very small sample of humans, each from different cultures, would likely conclude that
    A.   their participants are members of different species.
    B.   although all are human, the participants are more different than alike.
    C.   when brought together on the alien planet, the humans were unable to find anything in common.
    D.   humans everywhere are intensely social creatures.
    Answer D, Type CON

3. Darwin proposed the process of natural selection, whereby
    A.   he could explain animal and human mate selections.
    B.   nature selects traits that best equip organisms to survive in their environment.
    C.   human sexual behavior could be understood in evolutionary terms.
    D.   None of the above.
    Answer B, Type FAC

4. Evolutionary psychology
    A.   involves studying how natural selection predisposes traits and social behaviors.
    B.   is the study of diversity within evolutionarily-linked species.
    C.   involves studying animal social behavior.
    D.   is the study of prehistoric behavior and mental process.
    Answer A, Type DEF

5. Evolutionary psychology
    A.   highlights human diversity.
    B.   highlights human mating preferences.
    C.   highlights universal human nature.
    D.   highlights gender differences in the need for human affiliation.
    Answer C, Type FAC

6. Psychologists refer to the enduring behaviors, ideas, attitudes, and traditions shared by a large group of people and transmitted from one generation to the next as
    A.   evolutionary heritage.
    B.   social heritage.
    C.   the collective unconscious.
    D.   culture.
    Answer D, Type DEF

7.   A cultural perspective
     A.   highlights human adaptability.
     B.   highlights universals in human nature.
     C.   highlights the role of our evolved genes in determining cultural patterns.
     D.   None of the above.
     Answer D, Type FAC

8.   Which of the following is shaped by where and when we live?
     A.   how we define beauty
     B.   how we define social justice
     C.   whether we tend to be expressive or reserved
     D.   All of the above.
     Answer D, Type FAC

9.   Human kinship is to the _____ perspective as social diversity is to the _____ perspective.
     A.   evolutionary; cultural
     B.   cognitive; psychoanalytic
     C.   humanistic; cultural
     D.   biological; humanistic
     Answer A, Type CON

10. The cultural perspective is to _____ as the evolutionary perspective is to _____.
     A.   Brown; Darwin
     B.   social norms; human adaptability
     C.   social roles; hormonal factors
     D.   human adaptability; natural selection
     Answer D, Type CON

11. Evolutionary psychology is the study of the evolution of _____ using the principles of _____.
     A.   cultures; natural selection
     B.   behavior; conditioning
     C.   cultures; conditioning
     D.   behavior; natural selection
     Answer D, Type DEF

12. The fact that all human societies engage in communal sharing, rank people by authority and status, and have ideas about economic justice would be emphasized by the _____ perspective.
     A.   psychoanalytic
     B.   communitarian
     C.   evolutionary
     D.   cultural
     Answer C, Type FAC

13. The fact that people worldwide vary greatly in their dress habits and the specific foods they eat would be emphasized by the _____ perspective.
     A.   cultural
     B.   individualistic
     C.   evolutionary
     D.   psychoanalytic

Answer A, Type FAC

14. Norms
A. describe what most others do.
B. are rules for accepted and expected behavior.
C. prescribe proper behavior.
D. All of the above.
Answer D, Type DEF

15. Seven-year-old Mary says "Thank you" after opening each birthday present she receives because her family considers it to be proper behavior. This best illustrates the influence of a
A. norm.
B. schema.
C. role.
D. stereotype.
Answer A, Type CON

16. Social norms
A. make social interactions run smoothly.
B. lead us to feel uncomfortable when they are violated.
C. may control us so successfully that we hardly sense their presence.
D. All of the above.
Answer D, Type FAC

17. The incest taboo
A. is very difficult for evolutionary psychologists to explain.
B. is no longer considered a universal norm.
C. is violated more often than psychologists once believed.
D. All of the above.
Answer C, Type FAC

18. The buffer zone we like to maintain around our bodies is called
A. private territory.
B. protective covering.
C. personal space.
D. intimacy quotient.
Answer C, Type DEF

19. Although there are many unoccupied tables in the restaurant, Rudolph decides to sit at the same table in the chair right next to James. James feels uncomfortable because Rudolph has violated
A. his social role.
B. his personal space.
C. Brown's universal norm.
D. the personal rights taboo.
Answer B, Type CON

20. Which of the following illustrates a violation of Roger Brown's universal norm?
A. Jennifer is raped by her step-father.
B. Howard sits too close to John during a business luncheon.
C. Seth, an undergraduate, invites his social psychology professor out for a drink.
D. Kim, the office supervisor, invites Ken, a new employee, to lunch.
Answer C, Type CON

21. There is a universal norm governing the tendency for people to
A. excuse themselves when they accidentally make physical contact with strangers.

B.   avoid eye contact with people they do not know.
C.   feel indebted to friends or relatives.
D.   talk to higher-status people and strangers in the same respectful way.
Answer D, Type FAC

22.   In languages that distinguish between the two forms of "you," the familiar form is used with
       _____ and the respectful form is used with _____.
       A.   children; adults
       B.   intimates; strangers
       C.   inferiors; superiors
       D.   All of the above.
       Answer D, Type FAC

23.   A _____ is a set of norms that defines how people in a given social position ought to behave.
       A.   role
       B.   social status
       C.   tradition
       D.   performance standard
       Answer A, Type DEF

24.   It takes a whole cluster of _____ to define a role.
       A.   traditions
       B.   relationships
       C.   positions
       D.   norms
       Answer D, Type DEF

25.   The more you occupy and internalize a role,
       A.   the more socially awkward you may feel.
       B.   the less self-conscious you feel.
       C.   the more discrepant your attitudes and actions become.
       D.   All of the above.
       Answer B, Type FAC

26.   By the flip of a coin toss, Shelly found herself assigned to the role of warehouse manager. Tim
       remained in his position in the stock-room. After a week it is likely that
       A.   Shelly will come to see herself as more capable and deserving of her position than others
             in the stock-room.
       B.   Tim and others in the stock-room will come to see Shelly as more capable and deserving
             of her position than they did at first.
       C.   both a and b.
       D.   None of the above.
       Answer C, Type CON

27.   The changes undergone by heiress-turned-revolutionary Patricia Hearst in the early 1970s
       illustrate the power exerted by situations in defining roles. Commenting on this phenomenon,
       social psychologist Philip Brickman notes, "Nowhere is social psychology farther apart from
       public consciousness than in its understanding of _____."
       A.   how things become real for people.
       B.   the destructiveness of which humans are capable.
       C.   the differences between being rich and poor.
       D.   the pervasiveness of social class in one's consciousness.
       Answer A, Type FAC

28. In many everyday and laboratory situations, people assigned a superior status come to see themselves as
    A. overwhelmed by responsibilities that detract from the quality of life.
    B. underqualified and in jeopardy of losing their position.
    C. having a special obligation to follow the social responsibility norm.
    D. superior performers who merit favorable treatment.
    Answer D, Type FAC

29. Pairs of New York City women first solved arithmetic problems as individuals and then worked together on additional problems, with one of the women designated "boss" and the other "assistant." When the women returned to working individually, the former "bosses" now solved _____ problems and the former "assistants" solved _____ problems than they had in the first round.
    A. more; fewer
    B. fewer; more
    C. more; more
    D. fewer; fewer
    Answer A, Type FAC

30. Having people play a demeaning role seems to undermine their feelings of
    A. individualism.
    B. collectivism.
    C. self-efficacy.
    D. empathy.
    Answer C, Type FAC

31. According to the text, role reversal can
    A. increase conflict between partners.
    B. lead to a loss of self-efficacy.
    C. be used to improve communication and understanding.
    D. make role conflict more severe.
    Answer C, Type FAC

32. The characteristics people associate with male and female define
    A. gender.
    B. sexuality.
    C. sex roles.
    D. sex differences.
    Answer A, Type DEF

33. Compared to women, men
    A. are more likely to commit suicide.
    B. are more vulnerable to anxiety disorders.
    C. are less likely to become alcoholic.
    D. All of the above.
    Answer A, Type FAC

34. Compared to men, women
    A. are more likely to be able to wiggle their ears.
    B. have a somewhat better sense of smell.
    C. are more creative.
    D. None of the above.
    Answer B, Type FAC

35. Males and females are alike in
    A. vocabulary.
    B. intelligence.
    C. self-esteem.
    D. All of the above.
    Answer D, Type FAC

36. During the 1970s, many scholars worried that studies of gender differences might
    A. lead to the conclusion that males and females are fundamentally the same, and thus to social upheaval.
    B. reinforce stereotypes, and that gender differences might be interpreted as women's deficits.
    C. lead to the conclusion that males are inferior to women, and thus to a reverse form of sexism.
    D. replace more basic and important research on processes of social influence and interpersonal relationships.
    Answer B, Type FAC

37. In rating their feelings regarding "men" and "women," most
    A. people rate women more favorably than men.
    B. people rate men more favorably than women.
    C. people rate men and women the same.
    D. men rate men more favorably, and most women rate women more favorably.
    Answer A, Type FAC

38. In general, women more than men give priority to
    A. independence.
    B. creativity.
    C. skill mastery.
    D. close relationships.
    Answer D, Type FAC

39. As children, girls are more likely than boys to
    A. play in groups.
    B. display conflict.
    C. display sharing.
    D. All of the above.
    Answer C, Type FAC

40. In groups, men talk more _____, while women talk more _____.
    A. about others; about themselves
    B. about people; about issues
    C. to give information; to show support
    D. to show support; to criticize
    Answer C, Type FAC

41. Men are more likely than women to gravitate toward jobs that
    A. reduce inequalities.
    B. enhance inequalities.
    C. require empathy skills.
    D. enhance independence.
    Answer B, Type FAC

42. When surveyed, women are far more likely than men to describe themselves as having

A. empathy for others.
B. difficulty with important relationships.
C. envy of others.
D. problems expressing their emotions.
Answer A, Type FAC

43. Women are more likely than men to
A. make a charitable bequest from estate money.
B. buy greeting cards.
C. describe themselves as empathetic.
D. All of the above.
Answer D, Type FAC

44. After seeing victims of an earthquake on television, women are more likely than men to
A. inform others of the event.
B. demonstrate the just world phenomenon.
C. express empathy.
D. distract themselves with some leisure activity.
Answer C, Type CON

45. When they want empathy and understanding, men turn to _____ and women turn to

_____ .
A. men; women
B. women; men
C. men; men
D. women; women
Answer D, Type FAC

46. Which of the following couples is likely to experience the greatest marital satisfaction?
A. gentle Bill and empathic Sue
B. ambitious Nick and assertive Lucy
C. warm Mike and independent Jan
D. competitive Rob and nurturant Jane
Answer A, Type CON

47. In every known society, men, relative to women
A. have poorer vocabularies.
B. are more communitarian.
C. are socially dominant.
D. have higher self-esteem.
Answer C, Type FAC

48. In group situations, men are more likely than women to
A. interrupt others.
B. smile less.
C. stare more.
D. All of the above.
Answer D, Type FAC

49. Research on gender differences indicates that
A. throughout the world hunting and fishing are primarily men's activities.
B. in some parts of the world women are as likely to murder women as men are to murder men.
C. in Canada, the male-to-female arrest rate for murder is 3 to 1.

D.   All of the above.
Answer A, Type FAC

50.   Research findings show that compared to men, women
A.   are more likely to smile.
B.   are better at reading others' emotions.
C.   are more skilled at expressing emotions nonverbally.
D.   All of the above.
Answer D, Type FAC

51.   Women get evaluated less favorably than men when
A.   their leadership is autocratic.
B.   their leadership is democratic.
C.   they speak with deference and politeness.
D.   none of the above.
Answer A, Type FAC

52.   In both aggressive behavior and communication styles
A.   gender differences are invariable.
B.   gender differences fluctuate with the context.
C.   gender differences are uninfluenced by culture.
D.   None of the above.
Answer D, Type FAC

53.   Research on sexual behavior indicates that
A.   in their physiological and subjective responses to sexual stimuli, women and men are
       "more similar that different."
B.   males are more likely than females to initiate sexual activity.
C.   about half as many men as women cite affection for the partner as a reason for first
       intercourse.
D.   All of the above.
Answer D, Type FAC

54.   Across cultures, men
A.   prefer younger mates.
B.   prefer women with physical features that suggest fertility.
C.   desire kindness, love, and mutual attraction.
D.   All of the above.
Answer D, Type FAC

55.   When a 1990 Gallup survey asked respondents whether upbringing or biology accounted for
       gender differences,
A.   most said "upbringing."
B.   most said "biology."
C.   nearly equal numbers said "upbringing" and "biology."
D.   most men said "biology," and most women said "upbringing."
Answer C, Type FAC

56.   Evolutionary psychologists suggest that males are sexually assertive while females are more
       selective of sexual partners because
A.   worldwide, males outnumber females.
B.   each strategy is likely to promote gene survival.
C.   males and females are socialized differently.
D.   of differences in brain chemistry.

Answer B, Type FAC

57. Higher than normal levels of testosterone have been found in
    A.   violent male criminals.
    B.   boisterous fraternity members.
    C.   National Football League players.
    D.   All of the above.
    Answer D, Type FAC

58. As people mature to middle age and beyond,
    A.   gender differences in interpersonal behavior decrease.
    B.   gender differences in interpersonal behavior increase.
    C.   androgyny in men decreases.
    D.   androgyny in women decreases.
    Answer A, Type FAC

59. Given their present analysis of gender differences, evolutionary psychologists would have greatest difficulty explaining why
    A.   a young man would engage in casual sex with many female partners.
    B.   a young woman would engage in casual sex with many male partners.
    C.   a woman would prefer to marry a man who is slightly older than herself.
    D.   a woman would rather marry a man who is wealthy than one who is physically attractive.
    Answer B, Type CON

60. A person who is both _____ would be considered androgynous.
    A.   assertive and nurturant
    B.   intelligent and athletic
    C.   moral and competent
    D.   good and evil
    Answer A, Type FAC

61. Cameron has qualities like assertiveness, a traditionally masculine trait, as well as nurturance, a quality associated with traditional femininity. Cameron could be described as
    A.   gender-ambivalent.
    B.   role-conflicted.
    C.   androgynous.
    D.   gender-diffused.
    Answer C, Type CON

62. Evolutionary explanations of gender differences have been criticized because they
    A.   underestimate the role of genetic factors.
    B.   do not explain cultural changes in behavior that occur over relatively short periods of time.
    C.   deny the role of hormonal factors.
    D.   rely too heavily on the experimental method in formulating and testing hypotheses.
    Answer B, Type FAC

63. Evolutionary psychology has been criticized for
    A.   hindsight bias.
    B.   unethical treatment of human participants.
    C.   use of unrepresentative samples.
    D.   functional fixedness.
    Answer A, Type FAC

64. Evolutionary psychologists respond to their critics by saying

A. the criticisms are "flat-out wrong."
B. cultural explanations are guilty of hindsight explanations.
C. their field is an empirical science that tests its predictions with a variety of data.
D. All of the above.

Answer D, Type FAC

65. A set of behavior expectations for males or females defines a gender
A. type.
B. role.
C. identity.
D. position.

Answer B, Type DEF

66. The term gender role refers to
A. enduring behaviors, attitudes, and traditions transmitted from one generation to the next.
B. a set of behavior expectations for males or females.
C. a rule for accepted and expected behavior.
D. the personality characteristics by which people define male and female.

Answer B, Type DEF

67. From studies of gender differences worldwide, it would seem that gender socialization gives girls _____ and boys _____.
A. "arms"; "legs"
B. "roots"; "wings"
C. "feet"; "hands"
D. "ears"; "eyes"

Answer B, Type FAC

68. Compared to boys, girls in countries everywhere spend more time _____ and less time _____.
A. helping with housework; in unsupervised play
B. in unsupervised play; in school
C. helping with child care; helping with housework
D. playing; working

Answer A, Type FAC

69. When Zanna and Pack led women to believe that they would meet an attractive, unattached, nonsexist man who liked strong, ambitious women, the women
A. behaved more intelligently and solved more problems.
B. presented themselves in "traditionally feminine" terms.
C. experienced a great deal of conflict over how they should present themselves.
D. denigrated him as being probably not very attractive at all.

Answer A, Type FAC

70. When Williams, Best, and their collaborators asked university students in 14 cultures questions such as "Should women do the housework?" and "Should women be more concerned with promoting their husband's career than their own?" they found that in nearly every culture women students had _____ egalitarian views than their male peers.
A. significantly more
B. slightly more
C. slightly less
D. significantly less

Answer B, Type FAC

71. Gender roles are more distinct in _____ societies than in _____ societies.
    A. agricultural; nomadic, food-gathering
    B. nomadic, food-gathering; industrialized
    C. industrialized; agricultural
    D. pastoral; agrarian
    Answer A, Type FAC

72. Which of the following is true of American gender roles?
    A. Since 1970, increasing numbers of women have been training to become lawyers, doctors, and dentists.
    B. In 1993, only a small minority of Americans still stated that the "ideal family situation" is one in which "father has a job and mother stays home and cares for the children."
    C. From 1965 to 1985, the proportion of housework done by men remained constant.
    D. All of the above.
    Answer A, Type FAC

73. Data regarding the percentage of women in managerial positions suggests that in industrialized societies
    A. gender roles vary enormously across cultures.
    B. gender roles are very consistent across cultures.
    C. women are as likely as men to hold managerial positions.
    D. None of the above.
    Answer A, Type FAC

74. The Nurture Assumption refers to the belief that
    A. women are more caring and care-giving than men.
    B. women are expected to be more caring and care-giving than men.
    C. the way parents bring up their children governs who their children become.
    D. the way parents bring up their children has very little to do with who their children become.
    Answer A, Type FAC

75. One dramatic finding from developmental psychology is that two children in the same family are, on average,
    A. as different from one another as two children selected at random.
    B. more likely to share the same general personality characteristics than two children selected at random.
    C. completely uninfluenced by their genetic heritage.
    D. None of the above.
    Answer A, Type FAC

76. Twin and adoption studies indicate that genetic influences explain approximately _____ of individual variations in personality traits.
    A. 0 to 10 percent
    B. 10 percent
    C. 25 percent
    D. 50 percent
    Answer D, Type FAC

77. Judith Rich Harris argues that 40 to 50 percent of the personality differences between siblings can be explained by
    A. the sex of the child.
    B. parental influence.

C.   peer influence.

D.   sibling rivalry.

Answer C, Type FAC

78.   In both human and primate cultures, change comes primarily from

A.   the process of natural selection.

B.   the young.

C.   the influence of parents and grandparents.

D.   the environment.

Answer B, Type FAC

79.   The idea that natural selection and cultural selection cooperate in producing genetically advantageous traits is what evolutionary psychologists call

A.   shared environment.

B.   coevolution.

C.   functionalism.

D.   codeterminism.

Answer B, Type DEF

80.   According to the text, what term best describes the relationship between biology and culture?

A.   competition

B.   interaction

C.   interpolation

D.   reciprocation

Answer B, Type FAC

81.   If the presence of others improves performance on easy tasks but hinders performance on difficult tasks, the presence of others and task difficulty are said to

A.   compete.

B.   accentuate.

C.   interact.

D.   interpolate.

Answer C, Type CON

82.   A very strong cultural norm dictates that males should be taller than their female mates. This height norm is cited in your text as evidence that

A.   relationship behavior is influenced more by biology than culture.

B.   gender roles are essentially cultural and thus completely arbitrary.

C.   what is biologically "fit" may be culturally disastrous.

D.   biology and culture interact to develop gender-role norms.

Answer D, Type FAC

83.   In her book Sex Differences in Social Behavior, Alice Eagly theorizes that in adult life, the immediate causes of gender differences in social behavior are

A.   the roles that reflect a sexual division of labor.

B.   biologically-based differences in power and aggressiveness.

C.   learned habits reinforced by social rewards like affection.

D.   rules and laws that legislate and maintain the status quo.

Answer A, Type FAC

84.   What can we conclude about the relationship between persons and situations?

A.   Individuals vary in how they interpret and react to a given situation.

B.   People choose many of the situations that influence them.

C.   People often create their social situations.

D.   All of the above.
Answer D, Type FAC

85.   In the final analysis, the text suggests that what most religions encourage we should also do:
        View ourselves as _____ and others as _____.
        A.   influenced by our environments; free agents
        B.   free agents; influenced by their environments
        C.   free agents; free agents
        D.   influenced by our environments; influenced by their environments
        Answer B, Type FAC

These items also appear in the Study Guide:

86.   Norms, according to the text,
        A.   are composed of a set of roles.
        B.   prescribe proper behavior.
        C.   are social behaviors of typical or average people.
        D.   are laws that govern the distribution of social rewards.
        Answer B, Type DEF

87.   Which of the following is true?
        A.   There are really no truly universal norms.
        B.   Religion does not exist in some societies.
        C.   Norms can liberate us from preoccupation with what we are saying and doing.
        D.   A "pedestrian" would be an example of a role.
        Answer C, Type FAC

88.   Which of the following friendship norms seems to be universal?
        A.   Respect the friend's privacy.
        B.   Make eye contact while talking.
        C.   Don't divulge things said in confidence.
        D.   All of the above.
        Answer D, Type FAC

89.   The study of how natural selection predisposes adaptive traits and behavior is called
        A.   behavioral genetics.
        B.   biological behaviorism.
        C.   evolutionary psychology.
        D.   genetic psychology.
        Answer C, Type DEF

90.   Research indicates that a gender difference exists in
        A.   vocabulary.
        B.   intelligence.
        C.   age at which infants walk.
        D.   smiling.
        Answer D, Type FAC

91.   A noticeable difference has not been found between males and females in
        A.   happiness.
        B.   judging emotion on people's faces.
        C.   suicide rate.
        D.   frequency of smiling.
        Answer A, Type FAC

92. Research on possible hormonal influences on aggression has indicated that
    A.   testosterone levels influence animal aggression but not human aggression.
    B.   violent male criminals have higher than normal testosterone levels.
    C.   gender differences in aggression are clearly unrelated to hormonal differences.
    D.   administering testosterone reduces aggression in most animals.
    Answer B, Type FAC

93. Who of the following maintain the least personal space?
    A.   British
    B.   Americans
    C.   Arabs
    D.   Scandinavians
    Answer C, Type FAC

94. A study of Australian married couples found that marital satisfaction was highest when
    A.   both partners possessed feminine traits.
    B.   both partners possessed androgynous traits.
    C.   both partners possessed masculine traits.
    D.   the male possessed feminine traits and the female possessed masculine traits.
    Answer A, Type FAC

95. Which of the following is true of the relationship between persons and situations?
    A.   a given situation affects different people differently
    B.   people choose many of their situations
    C.   people help create the situations that affect them
    D.   All of the above are true
    Answer D, Type FAC

96. Which of the following illustrates Roger Brown's "universal norm"?
    A.   Brothers do not have sexual relations with their sisters in Daneria.
    B.   The King of Sindab invites subjects to his castle for dinner before they invite him to their huts for dinner.
    C.   Friends in Transylvania do not divulge things said in confidence.
    D.   Males rather than females initiate sexual relations in Wallonia.
    Answer B, Type CON

97. William is gentle and affectionate with his children but independent and assertive in running his business. What term best describes his personality?
    A.   androgynous
    B.   gender diffused
    C.   gender schematic
    D.   inter-role patterned
    Answer A, Type CON

98. "Drivers are expected to keep to the right on a two-lane road" would be an example of what the text calls a
    A.   norm.
    B.   role.
    C.   position.
    D.   status.
    Answer A, Type CON

99. Which of the following would be least likely to be considered a role?
    A.   college president

B.   bicyclist
C.   father
D.   wife
Answer B, Type CON

100.   The evolutionary perspective is to the cultural perspective as _____ is to _____.
A.   gender role; social role
B.   coevolution; empathy
C.   role; norm
D.   human kinship; human diversity
Answer D, Type FAC

Critical Thinking Questions

101.   Explain the hindsight criticism of evolutionary psychology. From your perspective, how important is this criticism?

102.   Imagine yourself going to the head of a very long line for a popular movie and cutting in. What are the likely consequences of such norm violation? How does this scenario illustrate the function(s) of social norms?

103.   How would evolutionary psychology explain Brown's universal norm that forms of address communicate social status and that advances in intimacy are initiated by the higher status person?

104.   Harris (1996) argues that if you left a group of children with their same schools, neighborhoods, and peers but switched parents, those children "would develop into the same sort of adults." What then is the role of parenting? How do parents influence the development of their children?

105.   What are the pros and cons of seeing ourselves as free agents while viewing others as influenced by their environments?

Multiple Choice Questions

1. American and European psychologists view going along with group pressure in such a way that they customarily refer to it with all except which of the following terms?
    A. conformity
    B. cooperation
    C. compliance
    D. submission
    Answer B, Type FAC

2. In Japan, going along with others is a sign of
    A. maturity.
    B. mindlessness.
    C. incompetence.
    D. irresponsibility.
    Answer A, Type FAC

3. _____ is a change in behavior or belief as a result of real or imagined group pressure.
    A. Conformity
    B. Consensus
    C. Obedience
    D. Submission
    Answer A, Type DEF

4. Conformity that involves publicly acting in accord with social pressure while privately disagreeing is called
    A. acceptance.
    B. compliance.
    C. mindlessness.
    D. reactance.
    Answer B, Type DEF

5. Conformity that involves both acting and believing in accord with social pressure is called
    A. acceptance.
    B. cooperation.
    C. compliance.
    D. social sensitivity.
    Answer A, Type DEF

6. Sincere inward conformity is to _____ as insincere outward conformity is to _____.
    A. acceptance; reactance
    B. reactance; submission
    C. obedience; compliance
    D. acceptance; compliance
    Answer D, Type CON

7.   Kenny is scolded by his mother and told to stand in the corner quietly for three minutes. While standing in the corner he mutters, "I may be standing, but inwardly I'm sitting." Kenny has been _____, but displays no sign of _____.
A.   compliant; conformity
B.   obedient; conformity
C.   obedient; acceptance
D.   compliant; obedience
Answer C, Type CON

8.   Jennifer thinks it's stupid to dress up to go to church, given that she never dresses up any other time. Yet she dresses up anyway in order to fit in. Her behavior reflects the process of
A.   compliance.
B.   acceptance.
C.   reactance.
D.   informational social influence.
Answer A, Type CON

9.   As a freshman, Tim became a vegetarian in order to fit in with his new friends. Now, as a senior, Tim would never consider eating meat again. What process does Tim's experience illustrate?
A.   compliance
B.   acceptance
C.   reactance
D.   social facilitation
Answer B, Type CON

10.   Tisha started going to church only because her boyfriend wanted to go. She continues to go now, even though she broke up with him, because she really gets a lot out of the service. What principle does Tisha's experience illustrate?
A.   the false consensus effect
B.   the foot-in-the-door principle
C.   acceptance can increase cohesion
D.   acceptance sometimes follows compliance
Answer D, Type CON

11.   In his classic study of _____, Sherif had participants in groups call out estimates of the distance a small point of light appeared to move in a dark room.
A.   obedience
B.   group cohesiveness
C.   norm formation
D.   psychological reactance
Answer C, Type FAC

12.   At one time, aircraft had constant rather than blinking lights on the wingtips. When pilots in formation tried to follow the constant lights of the aircraft in front of them, they veered off course. This is perhaps best explained by
A.   illusory correlation.
B.   normative influence.
C.   psychological reactance.
D.   the autokinetic effect.
Answer D, Type CON

13.   The autokinetic phenomenon refers to
A.   a false group consensus.

B.   an illusion of perceived movement.

C.   a form of self-efficacy.

D.   an influential bias in social judgment.

Answer B, Type DEF

14.   Sherif's study of the autokinetic phenomenon best illustrates

A.   normative influence.

B.   informational influence.

C.   obedience.

D.   compliance.

Answer B, Type FAC

15.   A year after his original study, Sherif's participants were retested alone and gave answers that supported the original group's norm. This suggests that the process involved was really

A.   reactance.

B.   compliance.

C.   obedience.

D.   acceptance.

Answer D, Type FAC

16.   An accomplice of the experimenter is called a

A.   co-investigator.

B.   conspirator.

C.   counterfeit.

D.   confederate.

Answer D, Type DEF

17.   Jacobs and Campbell (1961) used the Sherif paradigm to study the transmission of norms. They found that inflated estimates lasted for

A.   three generations.

B.   five generations.

C.   ten generations.

D.   more than ten generations.

Answer B, Type FAC

18.   In spring of 1954, Seattle residents were alarmed by widespread reports of damage by a mysterious windshield-pitting agent. The true cause of public concern was most likely

A.   fallout from recent Pacific testing of the H-bomb.

B.   mass suggestibility.

C.   psychological reactance.

D.   the autokinetic phenomenon.

Answer B, Type FAC

19.   Sociologist David Phillips and colleagues report that _____ increase after well-publicized and celebrity suicides.

A.   suicides

B.   private airplane crashes

C.   fatal auto accidents

D.   All of the above.

Answer D, Type FAC

20.   Solomon Asch's studies of conformity differ in important ways from those of Muzafer Sherif because

A.   Asch's participants faced a more ambiguous task.

B.   Sherif's participants were dealing with facts rather than opinions.

C.   Asch's participants could clearly see the correct judgment.

D.   Sherif's participants were in the physical presence of the pressuring group while Asch's participants were not.

Answer C, Type FAC

21.   While control participants were correct about line-length judgments more than 99 percent of the time in Asch's conformity study, his naive participants conformed to the incorrect judgments of others _____ of the time.

A.   12 percent

B.   37 percent

C.   65 percent

E.   87 percent

Answer B, Type FAC

22.   Asch's conformity experiments were high in

A.   mundane realism.

B.   experimental realism.

C.   acceptance.

D.   stimulus ambiguity.

Answer B, Type FAC

23.   Richard Crutchfield's variation of Asch's experiment contained more _____ than Asch's because the procedure _____.

A.   experimental control; was automated

B.   mundane realism; used all real participants

C.   experimental realism; was automated

D.   experimental control; used all real participants

Answer A, Type FAC

24.   The Sherif, Asch, and Crutchfield results are all startling because none of the studies employed any

A.   judgments about ambiguous stimuli.

B.   groups larger than four persons.

C.   experimental realism.

D.   open, obvious pressure to conform.

Answer D, Type FAC

25.   Social psychology's most famous and controversial experiments were conducted by

A.   Sherif.

B.   Milgram.

C.   Asch.

D.   Watson.

Answer B, Type FAC

26.   In response to the ethical controversy surrounding his experiments, Milgram wrote that stress and risk to self-esteem are higher for _____ than for participants in his experiments.

A.   participants in Zimbardo's prison experiment

B.   students taking course examinations

C.   parents raising children

D.   None of the above

Answer B, Type FAC

27. The experimenter in Milgram's study used all but which of the following verbal prods to encourage participants to continue?
    A. "It is absolutely essential that you continue."
    B. "You will be penalized if you refuse to go on."
    C. "You have no other choice, you must go on."
    D. "The experiment requires that you continue."
    Answer B, Type FAC

28. When Milgram asked 100 psychiatrists, college students, and middle-class adults to predict the results of his experiment, the respondents said that they thought _____ would _____.
    A. they themselves; never begin to administer shock
    B. they themselves; disobey by about 135 volts
    C. other people; disobey by about 210 volts
    D. other people; would go all the way to 450 volts
    Answer B, Type FAC

29. When Milgram conducted his first series of experiments with a sample of 20- to 50-year-old men, he found that over 60 percent of them
    A. refused to deliver shocks beyond 150 volts.
    B. refused to deliver shocks past the 300-volt level.
    C. went clear to 450 volts.
    D. asked to be released from the experiment by 135 volts.
    Answer C, Type FAC

30. In a follow-up series of experiments after his initial study, Milgram made the learner's protests more compelling by having him complain of a heart condition, then scream and plead for release, and finally refuse to answer. With this added condition,
    A. a majority of participants still fully obeyed the experimenter's demands.
    B. teachers were more reluctant to deliver initial shocks.
    C. learners became more real and personal to the teacher.
    D. fewer participants went to 450 volts.
    Answer A, Type FAC

31. When the participants in Milgram's studies were surveyed afterward about their participation in the obedience experiment, most said
    A. they did not regret having participated.
    B. they deeply regretted having participated.
    C. they were glad to have helped but felt the study should never be repeated.
    D. they experienced guilt over their actions as participants.
    Answer A, Type FAC

32. Which of the following was found to be a factor that influenced obedience in Milgram's research?
    A. the victim's emotional distance
    B. the closeness of the authority
    C. the presence of other defiant teachers
    D. All of the above.
    Answer D, Type FAC

33. When Milgram varied his experiment so that teachers had to physically force the learner's hand onto a shock plate in order to administer punishment, compliance to the experimenter's orders
    A. dropped to almost zero.
    B. dropped to 10 percent.

C.   dropped to 30 percent.
D.   actually increased to almost 80 percent.
Answer C, Type FAC

34.   In Milgram's studies, obedience was highest when
      A.   teachers were required to put the learner's hand onto a shock plate.
      B.   the learner was in the same room as the teacher.
      C.   the learner did not complain of a heart condition.
      D.   the learner was remote and silent.
      Answer D, Type FAC

35.   From the results of Milgram's studies that manipulated the distance between teacher and learner, one could conclude that
      A.   it would be more disturbing to ignore many people starving in a foreign land than a single neighbor who needs food.
      B.   it would be more disturbing to kill another with one's bare hands than with a gun.
      C.   ironically it may be more difficult to dehumanize a stranger than a close friend.
      D.   group cohesiveness breeds aggression.
      Answer B, Type CON

36.   In Milgram's research, when the experimenter gave the commands by telephone instead of in person, full obedience
      A.   dropped to zero.
      B.   dropped to 21 percent.
      C.   dropped to 50 percent.
      D.   increased to 73 percent.
      Answer B, Type FAC

37.   Obedience to a legitimate authority is highest when
      A.   the authority speaks loudly.
      B.   the authority is physically close.
      C.   the self-esteem of the target is low.
      D.   the authority gives the order by telephone.
      Answer B, Type FAC

38.   In order for a person to be more willing to obey authoritative orders that conflict with his or her own personal standards,
      A.   the authority must be perceived as legitimate.
      B.   the probable victims must be as close as possible.
      C.   the authority figure must be as distant as possible.
      D.   All of the above.
      Answer A, Type FAC

39.   In one variation on his original experiment, Milgram arranged for a confederate "clerk" (posing as a fellow participant) to assume command in the experimenter's absence. As a result of this manipulation,
      A.   most teachers agreed to comply with the orders of their fellow group member.
      B.   the teachers competed with him and with each other for the role of leader.
      C.   participants became more positive about their roles in this cohesive group, and some even became enthusiastic.
      D.   80 percent of the teachers refused to comply fully.
      Answer D, Type FAC

40. In a study by Hofling and colleagues, 22 hospital nurses were telephoned by an unknown physician and ordered to administer an obvious drug overdose. Results showed that
    A. most would not act on the order unless the caller named a familiar physician as reference.
    B. most nurses refused to comply unless given the order in writing.
    C. less experienced nurses complied but more experienced ones challenged the order.
    D. all but one proceeded to comply without delay.
    Answer D, Type FAC

41. When Milgram's experimental series was reenacted in Bridgeport, Connecticut, far from the prestige and authority of Yale University, the proportion of participants who fully complied with orders to shock the learner _____ compared to the Yale rate.
    A. remained unchanged
    B. decreased to 48 percent
    C. decreased to 25 percent
    D. decreased to 10 percent
    Answer B, Type FAC

42. When Milgram assigned two confederates to act as fellow teachers with a third teacher, the real participant, and then had the two confederates defy the experimenter, the presence of defiant peers
    A. pressured the participant to comply more fully with the experimenter's orders.
    B. led 90 percent of the participants to also disregard the experimenter.
    C. led 60 percent of the participants to also disregard the experimenter.
    D. made it easier for participants to feel anonymous while shocking the learner.
    Answer B, Type FAC

43. Milgram's variation in which two "fellow participants" (actually confederates) defied the experimenter's commands demonstrates that
    A. conformity can be constructive.
    B. obedience to a legitimate authority is absolute.
    C. peers have little influence over an individual's likelihood of obeying a legitimate authority.
    D. obedience can be liberating.
    Answer A, Type FAC

44. In Milgram's research, participants were most likely to obey the experimenter's commands when the experimenter was _____ and the victim was _____.
    A. distant; distant
    B. close; close
    C. distant; close
    D. close; distant
    Answer D, Type FAC

45. Both Asch's conformity studies and Milgram's obedience studies illustrate
    A. the power of the situation.
    B. the fact that we are cognitive misers.
    C. the prevalence of conforming personalities in American culture.
    D. All of the above.
    Answer A, Type FAC

46. The fact that the voltage in Milgram's research increased in 15 volt increments allowed obedient participants to

A.	take out their increasing aggression on the learner.
B.	reduce their dissonance somewhat as the experiment progressed.
C.	deliver whatever severity of shock they felt was appropriate.
D.	None of the above.
Answer B, Type FAC

47.	Milgram and Sabini (1983) had student confederates violate a norm by asking New York City subway riders to give up their seat. Which of the following is true about this research?
A.	Only five percent of the subway riders gave up their seat.
B.	Ninety-five percent of subway riders gave up their seat, but only if a reason was given.
C.	The student confederates enjoyed the experiment and had no difficulty violating the norm.
D.	The student confederates were extremely uncomfortable violating the norm.
Answer D, Type FAC

48.	The text suggests that in our everyday lives, the experience of _____ illustrates an unintended drift toward self-harm, similar to the same incremental action experienced by Milgram's participants and the German civil servants who worked for the Nazis.
A.	mistrust
B.	procrastination
C.	overeating
D.	social rejection
Answer B, Type FAC

49.	To believe that Milgram's obedient participants were particularly hostile and aggressive kinds of people is
A.	a correct inference.
B.	to commit the fundamental attribution error.
C.	to ignore the power of behavior to shape attitudes.
D.	to ignore the strength of positive internal dispositions.
Answer B, Type FAC

50.	According to Milgram, the most fundamental lesson to be learned from his study of obedience is that
A.	people are naturally inclined to be hostile and aggressive.
B.	the desire to be right is one of the strongest human motives.
C.	even ordinary people, who are not particularly hostile, can become agents of destruction.
D.	people value their freedom and uniqueness and react negatively when it is taken from them.
Answer C, Type FAC

51.	Which of the following is not one of the factors that has been found to significantly influence one's conformity to the group?
A.	requiring the individual's response to be made in public
B.	increasing the size of the group from 6 to 10 members
C.	increasing the status of the group
D.	having the group's agreement be unanimous rather than reflect some disagreement
Answer B, Type FAC

52.	Bibb Latané's _____ theory proposes that social influence increases with the immediacy and size of the group.
A.	social impact
B.	individuation

C. reactance
D. elaboration likelihood

Answer A, Type DEF

53. Research on group size and conformity has shown that
   A. as group size increases, conformity decreases.
   B. two groups of three persons elicit more conformity than one group of six persons.
   C. group size influences conformity in teenagers but not in adults.
   D. the conformity of females is more significantly influenced by group size than is the conformity of males.

Answer B, Type FAC

54. According to conformity research, a group's social power is deflated when it loses its
   A. agenda.
   B. anonymity.
   C. unanimity.
   D. heterogeneity.

Answer C, Type FAC

55. A practical lesson of much conformity research is that it is easier to stand up for something if you
   A. believe the matter is trivial.
   B. do so all at once instead of paving the way with smaller actions and hints.
   C. go it alone and face the criticism independently.
   D. get someone else to stand up with you.

Answer D, Type FAC

56. Charlie wants to play a trick on his best friend, Bill. He wants to get Bill to agree that a green jacket is actually blue. Conformity research suggests that he will most likely succeed if
   A. one other friend agrees to go along with Charlie's trick.
   B. four other friends agree to go along, but a fifth friend calls the jacket green.
   C. five friends agree to go along with Charlie's trick.
   D. None of the above – no one would call green blue.

Answer C, Type CON

57. In Milgram's original studies of obedience, he found that participants who were _____ were most likely to be obedient and deferential.
   A. the victims of past abuse
   B. of low status
   C. female
   D. professionals used to giving orders

Answer B, Type FAC

58. In experiments, people have been found to conform more when they must _____ than when they are allowed to _____.
   A. respond publicly; write down their responses in private
   B. commit themselves in writing; announce their responses in public
   C. think before acting; react spontaneously
   D. explain their responses; keep silent

Answer A, Type FAC

59. Which of the following has been found to increase the likelihood of conformity?
   A. making private responses following group pressure
   B. a high status group

C.   making a public commitment prior to group pressure

D.   a divided group

Answer B, Type FAC

60.   In calling sports decisions, umpires and referees rarely change their decisions as a result of a player's objection. This may be an example of how

A.   status produces psychological reactance.

B.   a we-they feeling has evolved between professional sports players and officials.

C.   the umpire or referee seeks to maintain emotional distance from players.

D.   public commitment reduces susceptibility to social influence.

Answer D, Type CON

61.   Once the President has announced his position on a major foreign policy matter, he is unlikely to change his mind. This most likely reflects the fact

A.   of we-they polarity between the political parties.

B.   that public commitment reduces susceptibility to social influence.

C.   that the high status of the office elicits a need for uniqueness.

D.   that higher-status people are more susceptible to psychological reactance.

Answer B, Type CON

62.   Going along with the crowd in order to avoid rejection is called

A.   emotional influence.

B.   normative influence.

C.   cohesion-based influence.

D.   informational influence.

Answer B, Type DEF

63.   Going along with the crowd because they appear to know more about the situation than you do is called

A.   pluralistic influence.

B.   normative influence.

C.   cohesion-based influence.

D.   informational influence.

Answer D, Type DEF

64.   _____ influence is based on a person's desire to be _____.

A.   Normative; correct

B.   Informational; correct

C.   Informational; accepted

D.   Normative; unique

Answer B, Type DEF

65.   Normative influence commonly leads to _____, whereas informational influence commonly leads to _____.

A.   conformity; reactance

B.   acceptance; consensus

C.   compliance; obedience

D.   compliance; acceptance

Answer D, Type FAC

66.   Why do people conform?

A.   They want to be liked and approved.

B.   They want to be right.

C.   They are morally weak.

D.   A and B

Answer D, Type FAC

67.   Jodi wears slacks or jeans almost all the time, rejecting skirts and dresses as too formal and sexist. However, when she is invited to attend an honors reception, she borrows a skirt to wear so she will fit in with the other guests. This is an example of

A.   normative social influence.

B.   self-efficacy.

C.   psychological reactance.

D.   informational social influence.

Answer A, Type CON

68.   You see a person lying in the street in apparent discomfort. Unsure of whether he needs help, you observe that while other people notice him, no one else stops to offer help. Because no one else stops, you conclude that he must not need help but is probably only drunk. Your decision shows the effects of

A.   normative social influence.

B.   informational social influence.

C.   compliance.

D.   the boomerang effect.

Answer B, Type CON

69.   Researchers have explored several areas in search of the conformer. Which of the following is one of those areas?

A.   gender

B.   personality

C.   culture

D.   All of the above

Answer D, Type FAC

70.   To explain the small gender difference in conformity by saying that women are more concerned with interpersonal relations is to attribute the difference to

A.   culture.

B.   personality.

C.   the situation.

D.   social roles.

Answer B, Type FAC

71.   Eagly and Wood believe that gender differences in conformity may actually be a product of

A.   sexism on the part of researchers who expect it to occur.

B.   hormonal influences and unlearned predispositions.

C.   men's and women's typical social roles.

D.   feelings of intimidation by males' greater physical power.

Answer C, Type FAC

72.   Personality characteristics best predict an individual's

A.   likelihood of performing a specific action in a given situation.

B.   likelihood of performing a specific action repeatedly over time.

C.   average behavior across many situations.

D.   None of the above.

Answer C, Type FAC

73.   Personality predicts behavior better than situational forces do when

A.   a single behavior is being predicted rather than one's average behavior.

B. the trait is specific to a particular situation.
C. the participants are women compared to men.
D. All of the above.
Answer B, Type FAC

74. When the influence of the situation is _____, the consequent behavior is likely to be a result of _____.

A. weak; individual personalities
B. weak; external circumstances
C. strong; internal forces
D. strong; dispositions
Answer A, Type FAC

75. According to theorist Kurt Lewin, "every psychological event" depends on
A. cultural filtering.
B. learned behavior patterns.
C. both the person and the environment.
D. instinctive emotional predispositions.
Answer C, Type FAC

76. Which of the following statements about cross-cultural research on conformity is true?
A. Findings using the Asch procedure have found similar conformity rates in most countries, except among the Bantu of Zimbabwe, a tribe with strong sanctions against nonconformity.
B. When Milgram compared the conformity of French and Norwegian students, the French consistently conformed more.
C. Recent conformity studies in Britain, Canada, and the United States have indicated more conformity than was observed two or three decades ago.
D. All of the above.
Answer A, Type FAC

77. Which of the following statements is true of conformity and obedience?
A. They are primarily collectivistic phenomena.
B. They are primarily individualistic phenomena.
C. They are universal phenomena that vary by culture.
D. They are universal phenomena that are uninfluenced by culture.
Answer C, Type FAC

78. Compared to people in individualistic countries, those in collectivistic countries are
A. more likely to express psychological reactance.
B. more responsive to others' influence.
C. more susceptible to the fundamental attribution error.
D. None of the above.
Answer B, Type FAC

79. When social pressure threatens a person's sense of _____, he or she is likely to rebel.
A. belonging
B. freedom
C. achievement
D. meaning or purpose in life
Answer B, Type FAC

80. High school students Chas and Marnie have been dating each other casually. When Marnie's parents tell her to stop seeing Chas and ask her to go out with "nicer boys," Marnie announces

that she and Chas are actually "in love" and have decided to go steady. Marnie's behavior most likely illustrates the effects of
A.   the false uniqueness effect.
B.   the fundamental attribution error.
C.   the self-serving bias.
D.   psychological reactance.
Answer D, Type CON

81.   The motive to protect or restore one's sense of freedom is known as
A.   rebellion.
B.   disobedience.
C.   resistance.
D.   reactance.
Answer D, Type DEF

82.   Psychological reactance theory may help explain why
A.   drinking on campus is heavier for underage drinkers than for legal-age drinkers.
B.   a toddler, ignoring a toy, protests and demands that toy back when a playmate begins to play with it.
C.   the demand for and value placed on an object is greater when the object is perceived to be rare or hard to get.
D.   All of the above.
Answer D, Type CON

83.   In a study by Snyder, students who were told that their personal attitudes were nearly identical to those of 10,000 other students _____ when they participated in a conformity experiment.
A.   were judged most attractive by their fellow participants
B.   were more willing to obey the experimenter's request to make a public commitment to a popular cause
C.   took on additional attitudes as well as the mannerisms of the majority
D.   asserted their individuality by being nonconformist
Answer D, Type FAC

84.   When William McGuire and his Yale University colleagues invited children to "tell us about yourself," they found that the children were most likely to mention their
A.   sex.
B.   nationality.
C.   distinctive attributes.
D.   most common personal characteristics.
Answer C, Type FAC

85.   Milly has blonde hair, a sister and a brother, and parents who are both teachers. Milly was born in the Netherlands and her family moved to New York when she was six. She attends a state university in the Midwestern United States and majors in journalism. If you asked Milly to "tell us about yourself," she is most likely to mention that
A.   she has blonde hair.
B.   she has a brother and a sister.
C.   she was born in the Netherlands.
D.   her parents both attended college.
Answer C, Type CON

These items also appear in the Study Guide:

86.   Studies involving _____ most clearly demonstrate social influence taking the
       form of acceptance.
       A.   judgments of the length of lines
       B.   judgments of the autokinetic phenomenon
       C.   shocking innocent victims
       D.   None of the above demonstrate acceptance
       Answer B, Type FAC

87.   Which of the following social-psychological principles is <u>not</u> illustrated by the conformity
       literature?
       A.   behavior shapes attitudes
       B.   the fundamental attribution error
       C.   the inoculation effect
       D.   the power of the situation
       Answer C, Type FAC

88.   How social pressure may lead us to perform immoral acts is best illustrated by studies of
       A.   psychological reactance.
       B.   spontaneous self-concept.
       C.   obedience to authority.
       D.   informational influence.
       Answer C, Type FAC

89.   The effect of group size on conformity has been explained by _____ theory.
       A.   cognitive dissonance
       B.   social norm
       C.   psychological reactance
       D.   social impact
       Answer D, Type FAC

90.   Normative influence is to informational influence as _____ is to _____.
       A.   autokinetic effect; cohesiveness
       B.   compliance; acceptance
       C.   conformity; reactance
       D.   acceptance; reactance
       Answer B, Type CON

91.   Which of the following is true regarding individual differences in conformity?
       A.   Females conform slightly more than males.
       B.   French participants conform slightly more than Norwegian participants.
       C.   People's self-esteem test scores are excellent predictors of conformity.
       D.   American participants conform slightly more than German participants.
       Answer A, Type FAC

92.   Compared to Euro-American cultures, Asian cultures are more likely to teach their children
       A.   independence.
       B.   collectivism.
       C.   to follow their own conscience.
       D.   to respect another's privacy.
       Answer B, Type FAC

93. After hearing a respected medical authority lecture about the value of eating fresh fruits and vegetables, Joshua includes more of them in his diet. This change in Joshua's eating patterns is an example of
A. normative social influence.
B. psychological reactance.
C. informational social influence.
D. social facilitation.
Answer C, Type CON

94. Peter hates to wear ties anywhere. Nevertheless he wears one to his sister's wedding to avoid the disapproval of his family. This is an example of
A. identification.
B. informational social influence.
C. normative social influence.
D. psychological reactance.
Answer C, Type CON

95. Ancient astronomers who observed the stars occasionally saw a star that seemed to move very abruptly. This is probably an example of
A. the autokinetic effect.
B. the inoculation effect.
C. astronomical impact theory.
D. normative social influence.
Answer A, Type CON

96. In light of the Milgram studies, to believe that soldiers who shoot innocent civilians as a consequence of following orders are unusually cruel is to
A. make the fundamental attribution error.
B. engage in self-serving bias.
C. overlook the effect of cultural differences on conformity.
D. underestimate the influence of personality differences on conformity.
Answer A, Type CON

97. Philip hates to attend concerts but goes because his wife wants him to. After three years Philip comes to genuinely enjoy concerts. This is an example of
A. how acceptance can lead to compliance.
B. how compliance can lead to acceptance.
C. the boomerang effect.
D. how psychological reactance can lead to acceptance.
Answer B, Type CON

98. A psychiatrist who interviewed 40 of Milgram's participants a year after their participation concluded that
A. none had been harmed.
B. many were suspicious of all authorities.
C. a minority had lowered self-esteem.
D. most regretted having served in Milgram's study.
Answer A, Type FAC

99. Milly generally likes to go home to visit her family during vacation. However, after her father tells her she must be home during spring vacation, Milly decides to remain at college. We can probably best understand Milly's behavior in terms of
A. reaction formation.

B.   regression.

C.   psychological reactance.

D.   self-serving bias.

Answer C, Type CON

100.   John has red hair, has two brothers, one sister, and was born in Chicago. Both his parents were born in this country and are lawyers. If you asked John to "tell us about yourself," he is most likely to mention that

A.   he has two brothers.

B.   he has red hair.

C.   his father has a college education.

D.   he was born in this country.

Answer B, Type CON

Critical Thinking Questions

101.   Describe the normative and informational influence pressures operating in Milgram's obedience experiments.

102.   How are both the power of the situation and the power of the person evident in the results of Asch's conformity research?

103.   Unanimity, status, and cohesion are all factors that influence when people conform. Explain the impact of each of these factors on conformity in terms of normative and/or informational influence pressures.

104.   John wants to go out with Sue, but Sue is playing "hard-to-get." John is all the more intrigued and motivated to get a date with Sue. Explain this scenario in terms of reactance theory.

105.   "Conformity is neither all bad or all good." Do you agree? Why or why not?

Multiple Choice Questions

1. According to the text, those who wish to influence our behavior will seek to change our
   A. experiences.
   B. environments.
   C. attitudes.
   D. social relationships.
   Answer C, Type FAC

2. According to the text, persuasion in everyday life is
   A. diabolical.
   B. inevitable.
   C. avoidable.
   D. None of the above.
   Answer B, Type FAC

3. According to the text, persuasion efforts to change attitudes toward _____ have been successful while efforts to change attitudes toward _____ have been unsuccessful.
   A. marijuana use; tobacco use
   B. seat belt use; tobacco use
   C. tobacco use; marijuana use
   D. marijuana use; seat belt use
   Answer D, Type FAC

4. The response of most Americans to massive media campaigns urging automobile seat belt use suggests that our behavior is strongly influenced by
   A. the illusion of invulnerability.
   B. the availability heuristic.
   C. the vivid or emotion-arousing appeal.
   D. television as an irresistible medium of propaganda.
   Answer A, Type FAC

5. According to the text, the factor that determines whether we call attempts at persuasion "education" or "propaganda" is whether
   A. we believe them or not.
   B. we know the communicator or not.
   C. the message is rational or emotional in tone.
   D. the message is one-sided or two-sided.
   Answer A, Type FAC

6. To answer questions about effective persuasion, social psychologists usually study persuasion the way some geologists study erosion:
   A. by surveying the populations most directly affected.
   B. by conducting massive, wide-scale observational studies.
   C. by observing the effects of various factors in brief controlled experiments.
   D. by designing simulations of real-world effects and analyzing the components of the most accurate models.
   Answer C, Type FAC

7. According to the text, actual social psychological studies of the various factors that influence persuasion produce effects that are _____ and that are most potent on _____.
    A.   large; our central values
    B.   small; our central values
    C.   large; weak attitudes that don't touch our values
    D.   small; weak attitudes that don't touch our values
    Answer D, Type FAC

8. People who are motivated and able to think through an issue are best persuaded by
    A.   central route processing.
    B.   peripheral route processing.
    C.   heuristic route processing.
    D.   the elaboration likelihood model.
    Answer A, Type FAC

9. Persuasion that occurs when people are influenced by incidental cues, such as a speaker's attractiveness, is referred to as _____ route persuasion.
    A.   central
    B.   peripheral
    C.   subconscious
    D.   emotional
    Answer B, Type DEF

10. Which of the following is a characteristic of central route persuasion?
    A.   It uses systematic arguments.
    B.   It relies heavily on the communicator's attractiveness.
    C.   It employs rule-of-thumb heuristics to persuade.
    D.   Its effectiveness depends on a two-step flow of communication.
    Answer A, Type DEF

11. An automobile manufacturer who produces advertisements associating his cars with a young, attractive family enjoying picnics is most clearly using
    A.   central route persuasion.
    B.   peripheral route persuasion.
    C.   two-step flow of communication.
    D.   social implosion.
    Answer B, Type CON

12. A computer manufacturer who produces advertisements comparing his product with other competing models on features and prices is most clearly using
    A.   central route persuasion.
    B.   peripheral route persuasion.
    C.   attitude inoculation.
    D.   sleeper effect.
    Answer A, Type CON

13. For people who think carefully about issues, persuasion
    A.   depends on the strength or cogency of the arguments.
    B.   depends on their own cognitive responses to the persuasive appeal.
    C.   does not depend much on the expertise of the source of the persuasive appeal.
    D.   All of the above.
    Answer D, Type FAC

14. Attitude change that has followed the central route is more likely to
    A. persist.
    B. resist attack.
    C. influence behavior.
    D. All of the above.
    Answer D, Type FAC

15. John doesn't care at all about the legalization of marijuana, but in class he listened to a speech in favor of it. All else equal, John is most likely to be persuaded if
    A. the message contains short, cogent arguments.
    B. the message contains information about the benefits of marijuana use that he can think about and evaluate.
    C. the message is delivered by a fast talker.
    D. None of the above.
    Answer C, Type CON

16. Two primary components of credibility are
    A. confidence and attractiveness.
    B. confidence and trustworthiness.
    C. expertise and trustworthiness.
    D. expertise and similarity.
    Answer C, Type DEF

17. Over time the impact of a message from a noncredible source may _____ , a phenomenon known as the
    A. decrease; sleeper effect.
    B. increase; sleeper effect.
    C. decrease; status effect.
    D. increase; status effect.
    Answer B, Type DEF

18. You will be perceived as more credible if you
    A. speak with a higher pitch.
    B. speak with great emotion.
    C. speak slowly, carefully articulating each phrase.
    D. speak confidently, without hesitating.
    Answer D, Type FAC

19. Perceptions of trustworthiness can be increased by
    A. giving direct eye contact to one's audience.
    B. telling the audience your intent to persuade.
    C. arguing in a straightforward way for one's own self-interest.
    D. arguing for the position the audience expects of you.
    Answer A, Type FAC

20. A local charity is recruiting college sorority members to help them canvass to raise money. Of the following individuals, who are equally well-known and popular on campus, who should be the most persuasive in raising funds?
    A. Marcie, well known for her stinginess when it comes to money
    B. Jennifer, well known for her outgoing and fun-loving personality
    C. Mary, well known for her generosity and compassion
    D. Beth, well known for her leadership abilities
    Answer A, Type CON

21. A congressman argues that the government should be more aggressive in its campaign to get citizens to stop smoking. He will appear more credible and persuasive if he
    A. represents a district dependent on tobacco farming.
    B. is a former employee of the American Cancer Society.
    C. has once been a lobbyist for the television industry.
    D. comes from a religiously conservative region where many people believe it is wrong to smoke.
    Answer A, Type CON

22. A citizens' group that favors strict restriction of gun sales is preparing a communication to present to various community groups. If they want their message to seem most credible and sincere, which member of their group should present it?
    A. Smitty, who owns a local sports store and sells guns
    B. Betty, an x-ray technician who works at the local hospital
    C. Jacob, whose son was killed by an accidental gunshot
    D. Maurice, a psychologist and expert on human aggression
    Answer A, Type CON

23. In a study by Miller and colleagues, Los Angeles residents who listened to tape-recorded messages on topics like "the dangers of drinking coffee" rated fast speakers as being _____ than slow speakers.
    A. less objective
    B. less intelligent
    C. more believable
    D. more manipulative
    Answer C, Type FAC

24. One reason why fast speech may be more persuasive is that it
    A. typically has a higher pitch.
    B. tends to prevent counterarguing.
    C. is associated with greater intensity.
    D. is more comprehensible.
    Answer B, Type FAC

25. Physical appeal and similarity are two important factors that determine a communicator's
    A. credibility.
    B. status.
    C. attractiveness.
    D. trustworthiness.
    Answer C, Type DEF

26. When it comes to matters of objective reality or fact, we are most influenced by
    A. attractive others.
    B. similar others.
    C. trustworthy others.
    D. dissimilar others.
    Answer D, Type FAC

27. People who are similar to ourselves will be more influential than those who are dissimilar to us in persuading us about all of the following questions except:
    A. Which soft drink tastes best?
    B. Is being honest more important than being loving?
    C. Who would make the best President?

D.   What North American city gets the most annual rainfall?
Answer D, Type CON

28.   Jim is not completely confident in the strength of the persuasiveness of his arguments. To
       increase his degree of influence, Jim ought to
       A.   provide refreshments for his audience.
       B.   play pleasant background music as the audience gathers.
       C.   tell a few really good jokes at the beginning of his speech.
       D.   do all of the above.
       Answer D, Type CON

29.   _____ audiences are more persuaded by _____.
       A.   Well-educated; rational appeals
       B.   Uninvolved; how much they like the communicator
       C.   Highly involved; reasoned arguments
       D.   All of the above.
       Answer D, Type FAC

30.   According to the text, Americans' voting preferences are most predictable from their
       A.   emotional reactions to the candidates.
       B.   beliefs about the candidates' likely behavior.
       C.   beliefs about the candidates' traits.
       D.   involvement in the election.
       Answer A, Type FAC

31.   Janis and his colleagues found that if Yale students were allowed to consume peanuts and Pepsi
       while reading persuasive messages, they
       A.   felt manipulated and resisted influence.
       B.   were more convinced by the messages.
       C.   were distracted and showed poorer comprehension of the messages.
       D.   viewed the communicator as more attractive but less credible.
       Answer B, Type FAC

32.   Compared to happy people, unhappy people ruminate more before reacting to a persuasive
       message and thus are
       A.   more vulnerable to emotional appeals.
       B.   less easily swayed by weak arguments.
       C.   less involved in judging persuasive messages.
       D.   more vulnerable to one-sided messages.
       Answer B, Type FAC

33.   Fear-arousing messages have proven potent in convincing people to
       A.   cut down on smoking.
       B.   brush their teeth more often.
       C.   drive carefully.
       D.   All of the above.
       Answer D, Type FAC

34.   Fear-arousing messages are effective if they
       A.   also tell people how to avoid the danger.
       B.   raise a moderate but not high level of fear.
       C.   are presented by similar rather than dissimilar communicators.
       D.   follow the peripheral rather than the central route of persuasion.
       Answer A, Type FAC

35. According to the text, health warnings on cigarette ads are ineffective because they
    A.   lack source credibility.
    B.   lack vividness.
    C.   generate too much fear.
    D.   lack logical appeal.
    Answer B, Type FAC

36. When the fear aroused by a persuasive message is relevant to a pleasurable activity (e.g., sex or smoking), the result is often
    A.   intensified fear.
    B.   reduced fear.
    C.   immediate behavioral change.
    D.   denial.
    Answer D, Type FAC

37. Nazi propaganda was effective because it
    A.   was vivid.
    B.   used emotional, often fear-arousing appeals.
    C.   gave specific instructions on how to deal with the "Jewish threat."
    D.   All of the above.
    Answer D, Type FAC

38. People who disagree with conclusions drawn by a newscaster rate the newscaster as being more
    A.   biased.
    B.   inaccurate.
    C.   untrustworthy.
    D.   All of the above.
    Answer D, Type FAC

39. Aronson, Turner, and Carlsmith found that only a _____ source elicited considerable opinion change when advocating a position greatly discrepant from the recipient's.
    A.   credible
    B.   physically appealing
    C.   fear-arousing
    D.   personally familiar
    Answer A, Type FAC

40. Communicators with little credibility are most effective in changing the opinions of other people when they advocate positions that
    A.   arouse the emotions of the audience.
    B.   arouse intense dissonance in the audience.
    C.   differ only moderately from the positions of the audience.
    D.   differ markedly from the positions of the audience.
    Answer C, Type FAC

41. If you are a credible authority and your audience isn't much concerned with your issue, you ought to
    A.   advocate an extremely discrepant view.
    B.   advocate a moderately discrepant view.
    C.   advocate a slightly discrepant view.
    D.   present a short message.
    Answer A, Type FAC

42. A highly discrepant message is least likely to be persuasive if the audience

A.   is deeply involved in the issue.

B.   is youthful.

C.   views the communicator as credible.

D.   is in a happy mood.

Answer A, Type FAC

43.   A message presenting only one side of an issue will be more effective than a two-sided communication if

A.   the issue is of great personal significance to the audience and tends to elicit strong emotion.

B.   the communicator has only moderate credibility or attractiveness.

C.   the audience tends to agree with the advocated position and will not hear the opposing side.

D.   the audience is well-informed and is already aware of the opposing arguments.

Answer C, Type FAC

44.   After Germany's defeat in World War II, radio broadcasts were designed to warn Army infantry that the war in the Pacific would probably last another two years. Soldiers who already initially agreed with that message were more persuaded by a(n) _____ version.

A.   logical

B.   emotional

C.   two-sided

D.   one-sided

Answer D, Type FAC

45.   A group of concerned students who drive to school each day came to a meeting about the possibility of more parking restrictions on campus. As a representative of the college administration in favor of the restrictions, you ought to

A.   present only strong arguments in favor of the new restrictions.

B.   present the most extreme version of the plan to restrict parking.

C.   present both sides of the issue.

D.   present an emotional appeal.

Answer C, Type CON

46.   What refers to the fact that, other things being equal, information presented first usually has the most influence?

A.   the primacy effect

B.   the recency effect

C.   the shaping effect

D.   priming

Answer A, Type DEF

47.   In experiments where people succeed on a guessing task half the time and fail half the time, people perceive those whose successes come early as

A.   likely to have cheated.

B.   more able than those whose early experience is failure.

C.   less attractive than those whose successes come later.

D.   having lost interest in the task.

Answer B, Type FAC

48.   In an election campaign debate, Kelly makes her statement to the audience first and is immediately followed by her opponent, Stuart. The election is not held till two weeks later. If

both messages were persuasive and the debate was the deciding factor, the election results should show the influence of

A. the recency effect.
B. the primacy effect.
C. a two-step flow of communication.
D. the credibility-discrepancy effect.

Answer B, Type CON

49. Using the transcript of an actual criminal case, Gary Wells and his colleagues found that a defense attorney's opening statement was more effective if presented before, rather than after, the prosecution's presentation of evidence. This finding illustrates

A. the recency effect.
B. the primacy effect.
C. the sleeper effect.
D. social implosion.

Answer B, Type FAC

50. When information that is presented last has the most influence, a _____ is said to have occurred.

A. halo effect
B. primacy effect
C. recency effect
D. serial position effect

Answer C, Type DEF

51. Which of the following statements about the recency effect is true?

A. Recency effects are more common than primacy effects.
B. It is more likely to occur when a delay occurs before the audience is asked to commit to a choice.
C. It probably occurs because early arguments have faded from memory.
D. All of the above.

Answer C, Type FAC

52. The way a message is delivered constitutes the _____ of communication.

A. channel
B. route
C. flow
D. process

Answer A, Type DEF

53. In testing the impact of the spoken word, Crawford (1974) found that _____ spontaneously recalled hearing a sermon opposing racial bigotry.

A. no one
B. 10 percent
C. 30 percent
D. 90 percent

Answer B, Type FAC

54. In comparing the actions of 180 different students before and after a "Keep Our Campus Beautiful" poster campaign, Paloutzian found that _____ more passers-by picked up test litter after the campaign than had done so before the campaign.

A. no
B. two

C.   25 percent
D.   80 percent
Answer B, Type FAC

55. According to the text, which of the following is one of the hurdles a persuasive message must clear in order to change attitudes and behavioral intentions?
A.   Is the message comprehended?
B.   Is the message believed?
C.   Is the message remembered?
D.   All of the above.
Answer D, Type FAC

56. For minor issues, the impact of a persuasive appeal is likely to increase with
A.   novelty.
B.   complexity.
C.   emotional intensity.
D.   repetition.
Answer D, Type FAC

57. A simple rule that summarizes the effects of the media's influence on attitude change is that persuasion decreases
A.   as the significance and familiarity of the issue increases.
B.   as the complexity of the issue increases.
C.   as the significance and familiarity of the issue decreases.
D.   if the issue is trivial.
Answer A, Type FAC

58. Persuasion studies demonstrate that the major influence on important beliefs and attitudes appears to be
A.   television.
B.   print media like newspapers and magazines.
C.   our contact with people.
D.   major social institutions and the values they foster.
Answer C, Type FAC

59. The two-step flow of communication suggests that
A.   media influences have little effect on people's attitudes.
B.   media influences only have an effect on opinion leaders, but the influence stops there.
C.   media influences may have a big indirect effect on the culture.
D.   None of the above.
Answer C, Type FAC

60. In reflecting on their college experience, most former students say they learned more from _____ than from any other source.
A.   class assignments and in-class experiences
B.   contacts with friends and fellow students
C.   specific books and readings
D.   professors and other role models
Answer B, Type FAC

61. The process by which media influence often occurs through opinion leaders, who in turn influence others, is referred to as
A.   the sleeper effect.
B.   an indirect channel of communication.

C.   the opinion leader effect.
D.   a two-step flow of communication.
Answer D, Type DEF

62.   Which of the following illustrates media influence through a two-step flow of communication?
A.   A teenager buys a video game she saw advertised both on television and in a favorite magazine.
B.   A domestic car manufacturer sponsors a television program about the defectiveness of many foreign imports.
C.   A candidate for political office answers questions from members of a studio audience on live television.
D.   A man buys a new laundry detergent after hearing it recommended by a friend who read that it was both effective and environmentally safe in a consumer magazine article.
Answer D, Type CON

63.   All else equal, the order of persuasiveness (from most to least) seems to be
A.   written, live, videotaped, audiotaped.
B.   written, audiotaped, videotaped, live.
C.   live, videotaped, audiotaped, written.
D.   live, written, audiotaped, videotaped.
Answer C, Type FAC

64.   Peter is opposed to capital punishment and has, on the basis of extensive research, developed some complex but compelling arguments to support his position. In attempting to persuade others of the validity of his arguments, he should present them
A.   on a videotape.
B.   on an audiotape.
C.   in writing.
D.   on live television.
Answer C, Type CON

65.   Research suggests that people with _____ are the easiest to influence.
A.   low self-esteem
B.   moderate self-esteem
C.   high self-esteem
D.   None of the above; there is no relationship between self-esteem and susceptibility to influence.
Answer B, Type FAC

66.   The idea that attitudes change as people grow older is known as the _____ explanation of age differences in attitudes.
A.   life cycle
B.   generational
C.   belief differentiation
D.   psychosocial crisis
Answer A, Type DEF

67.   In the study of age differences in attitudes, there is very little evidence for
A.   maturation effects.
B.   life cycle effects.
C.   generational effects.
D.   conservatism effects.
Answer B, Type FAC

68. Which of the following is true regarding age differences in attitudes?
    A.   People's racial attitudes tend to be most liberal in their 30s and 40s.
    B.   People in their 50s and 60s tend to have more conservative sexual attitudes than they had in their 30s and 40s.
    C.   Attitudes formed in the teens and 20s tend to be stable thereafter.
    D.   All of the above are true.
    Answer C, Type FAC

69. Schuman and Scott found that when they asked people to name the most important national or world events of the last half century, most recalled
    A.   tragedies like war and assassinations.
    B.   achievements like peace accords and moon landings.
    C.   recent rather than long-ago news events.
    D.   events from their teens and early adulthood.
    Answer D, Type FAC

70. Freedman and Sears found that California high schoolers did not change their attitudes in response to a talk entitled "Why Teenagers Should Not Be Allowed to Drive" if they
    A.   had a moderate, rather than a high or low, level of self-esteem.
    B.   were of lower intelligence.
    C.   were male.
    D.   had been forewarned that the talk was coming.
    Answer D, Type FAC

71. Keela wants to persuade her parents to help pay for a study trip abroad this summer. She will have a more difficult time succeeding if
    A.   her parents are forewarned of her intent to convince them.
    B.   she has the trip coordinator call to reassure them.
    C.   her parents are not particularly intelligent or analytical.
    D.   her parents have a moderate level of self-esteem.
    Answer A, Type CON

72. Jennifer, a single mom, needs to ask her parents for money. To minimize their objections to her request, she should
    A.   warn them ahead of time of her need.
    B.   have her busy, distracting little toddler along when she makes her request.
    C.   write out her request for them to consider.
    D.   make her request over the phone.
    Answer B, Type CON

73. Political ads that use words to promote the candidate while visual images keep the viewer occupied to prevent analysis of the words are most clearly employing
    A.   the technique of classical conditioning.
    B.   the two-step flow of communication.
    C.   the sleeper effect.
    D.   distraction to inhibit counterarguing.
    Answer D, Type FAC

74. Analytical people are to _____ as image-conscious people are to _____.
    A.   central route persuasion; peripheral route persuasion
    B.   the primacy effect; the recency effect
    C.   life-cycle explanation; generational explanation
    D.   personal influence; media influence

Answer A, Type CON

75. Which of the following techniques has been used to stimulate people's thinking in response to a persuasive message?
    A. having different speakers present separate arguments rather than the same speaker present all the arguments
    B. using rhetorical questions such as, "Are you better off for having voted for so-and-so four years ago?"
    C. making people in the audience feel responsible for passing along the persuasive message
    D. All of the above.
    Answer D, Type FAC

76. Asking rhetorical questions, repeating the message, and using multiple speakers to deliver a message all stimulate the audience's thinking and make _____ messages _____ persuasive.
    A. strong; more
    B. weak; less
    C. Both A and B.
    D. None of the above.
    Answer C, Type FAC

77. In the central versus peripheral route theory of persuasion, what matters most is
    A. what we think in response to a message.
    B. how much knowledge we have about an issue.
    C. how we feel about the communicator.
    D. how many times the message is repeated.
    Answer A, Type FAC

78. Cults like the Unification Church and Jim Jones's People's Temple typically recruit and retain members by exploiting
    A. the sleeper effect.
    B. the foot-in-the-door phenomenon.
    C. the recency effect.
    D. attitude inoculation.
    Answer B, Type FAC

79. People most vulnerable to cults are usually
    A. under age 25.
    B. facing a personal crisis.
    C. middle-class.
    D. All of the above.
    Answer D, Type FAC

80. The success of religious cults is explained by their effective use of
    A. escalating behavioral commitments.
    B. persuasion principles.
    C. isolating group members.
    D. All of the above.
    Answer D, Type FAC

81. Charles Kiesler recommends that one way to stimulate people's thinking so they become more committed to their positions is to
    A. mildly attack their position.
    B. strongly attack their position.
    C. mildly support their position.

D.   strongly support their position.
Answer A, Type FAC

82.   Exposing people to weak attacks on their attitudes that stimulate thinking in support of the initial attitude is known as
A.   central route persuasion.
B.   attitude inoculation.
C.   psychological reactance.
D.   the boomerang effect.
Answer B, Type DEF

83.   The text indicates that inoculation procedures have been successful in
A.   increasing drivers' use of seat belts.
B.   reducing children's aggression.
C.   reducing teenage smoking rates.
D.   increasing adults' charitable contributions.
Answer C, Type FAC

84.   Research on attitude inoculation suggests that religious educators are wise to avoid
A.   the two-step flow of communication.
B.   forewarning followers that outsiders will question their beliefs.
C.   using charismatic leaders to attract new converts.
D.   creating a "germ-free ideological environment."
Answer D, Type FAC

85.   Inoculation research suggests that
A.   ineffective persuasion can harden people against later persuasive appeals.
B.   children are helpless victims of television advertising.
C.   the best way to inoculate attitudes is to mount an all-out strong attack on the attitude.
D.   None of the above.
Answer A, Type FAC

These items also appear in the Study Guide:

86.   The central route is to _____ as the peripheral route is to _____.
A.   analytical; motivated
B.   similarity; attractiveness
C.   heuristics; incidental cues
D.   high effort; low effort
Answer D, Type CON

87.   Social psychologists study persuasion primarily through
A.   experiments.
B.   surveys.
C.   case studies.
D.   participant observation.
Answer A, Type FAC

88.   Which of the following is one of the four major factors studied by psychologists in research on effective persuasion?
A.   the function of communication
B.   the setting of communication
C.   the channel of communication
D.   the length of communication

Answer C, Type FAC

89. Wood and Eagly reported that when a speaker presents _____, we are more likely to attribute the message to compelling evidence and thus to be persuaded by it.
    A.   a popular rather than an unpopular position
    B.   an unexpected rather than an expected position
    C.   an emotional rather than a rational appeal
    D.   a political rather than a religious position
    Answer B, Type FAC

90. People who argue against their own self-interest
    A.   are effective in persuading a female audience but not in persuading a male audience.
    B.   are effective with an intelligent audience but not with an unintelligent audience.
    C.   are viewed as inconsistent and thus lose their effectiveness.
    D.   are viewed as more credible and are thus more influential.
    Answer D, Type FAC

91. "Similar" communicators are more effective in persuading on _____ than on _____.
    A.   radio; television
    B.   judgments of fact; matters of value
    C.   political issues; religious beliefs
    D.   matters of value; judgments of fact
    Answer D, Type FAC

92. What is the effect of a fear-arousing communication?
    A.   Fear renders a communication ineffective.
    B.   Generally the more frightened people are, the more they respond.
    C.   Evoking a low level of fear is effective, but producing a high level of fear is not.
    D.   Fear appeals are effective with women but boomerang with men.
    Answer B, Type FAC

93. When researchers went to the homes of people from 12 churches shortly after they heard sermons opposing racial bigotry, they found that ____ percent spontaneously recalled the sermons.
    A.   10
    B.   30
    C.   50
    D.   70
    Answer A, Type FAC

94. Life-cycle and generational explanations both attempt to explain
    A.   why the content of messages changes over time.
    B.   why people have different attitudes depending on their age.
    C.   why a particular communicator has a different effect on people of different ages.
    D.   how an emotional appeal builds to a climax in terms of its impact.
    Answer B, Type FAC

95. An attractive or similar communicator would be most effective in changing beliefs about the
    A.   health benefits of eating fruits and vegetables.
    B.   dangers of marijuana use.
    C.   dangers of driving without wearing seat belts.
    D.   advantages of living in a small town versus the country or a large city.
    Answer D, Type CON

96. A gun manufacturer delivers a speech against stricter gun legislation. Because he clearly has a vested interest, his arguments have little initial impact on the audience. However, several weeks later, a survey of the audience indicates that his impact was much greater than first thought. This would be an example of
   A. the recency effect.
   B. the sleeper effect.
   C. social implosion.
   D. attitude inoculation.
   Answer B, Type CON

97. You have been asked to design an advertising campaign urging people to stop drinking alcohol. To be most effective, your message should arouse
   A. no fear.
   B. a moderate level of fear.
   C. a low level of fear.
   D. a high level of fear.
   Answer D, Type CON

98. You have been asked to prepare a speech opposing capital punishment. To be most effective in convincing those who strongly favor the death penalty, you should present
   A. a one-sided communication.
   B. a two-sided communication.
   C. an emotional appeal.
   D. an audiotaped appeal.
   Answer B, Type CON

99. You are one of two candidates being interviewed for a position as superintendent of the city school system. You are notified that one candidate will be interviewed tomorrow evening and the other a week later. The school board will make a decision immediately after the second candidate has been interviewed. If you want the job
   A. you should try to be interviewed first.
   B. you should try to be interviewed last.
   C. you should try to be interviewed first but only if the school board is composed of college graduates and the other candidate is controversial.
   D. you should try to be interviewed first but only if you are more attractive than the other candidate.
   Answer B, Type CON

100. According to research presented in the text, the mass media may be most effective in influencing
   A. whether one becomes a Democrat or Republican.
   B. whether a person believes in God or not.
   C. the brand of shampoo a person buys.
   D. one's attitude toward capital punishment.
   Answer C, Type CON

Critical Thinking Questions

101. Describe a familiar television commercial and analyze the elements of persuasion that it uses. Does it promote and/or assume central or peripheral route processing?

102. Describe the ways in which a typical sales person (e.g., someone selling cars or insurance) will seek to enhance his or her perceived credibility in your eyes. Keep in mind the two components of credibility when developing your answer.

103. When would it be best to present your persuasive appeal to an audience in a good mood versus a bad mood? Why?

104. You've been hired to develop an information campaign to prevent Jr. High School students from taking up smoking. Your boss wants you to use a scare-tactic approach. What must you do to construct a fear-appeal that is maximally effective?

105. Persuasion effects are typically complex. Most variables will increase persuasion in some situations but decrease persuasion in others. Choose two message-relevant factors and describe their complex effects.

Multiple Choice Questions

1. According to group dynamics expert Marvin Shaw, one thing that all groups have in common is that their members
    A.   share a common goal.
    B.   have well-defined roles.
    C.   enjoy free and open communication.
    D.   interact.
    Answer D, Type DEF

2. Which of the following is a defining characteristic of a group?
    A.   Two or more people belong to it.
    B.   Its members influence one another.
    C.   Its members perceive one another as "us."
    D.   All of the above.
    Answer D, Type DEF

3. Which of the following is probably not a group as that term is defined in your text?
    A.   a doctor with her patient
    B.   three people who share the same taxi and decide who gets dropped off first
    C.   four people working together on a class project
    D.   five people riding the city bus
    Answer D, Type CON

4. Which of the following can occur in a minimal group situation?
    A.   social facilitation
    B.   minority influence
    C.   group polarization
    D.   groupthink
    Answer A, Type FAC

5. On exam day, a student you don't know sits near you. This person is best described as
    A.   a confederate.
    B.   a coactor.
    C.   an ingroup member.
    D.   a comrade.
    Answer B, Type CON

6. A coactor is someone who
    A.   does the same task as you at the same time.
    B.   helps and cooperates with you.
    C.   competes with you on a single task.
    D.   imitates you.
    Answer A, Type DEF

7. Who among the following would be considered coactors?
    A.   20 people doing sit-ups in an exercise class
    B.   two people playing chess against each other

C.   12 competitors running in a cross-country race
D.   three friends chatting pleasantly before class starts
Answer A, Type CON

8. In one of social psychology's earliest experiments, Norman Triplett found that children told to wind string on a fishing reel as quickly as possible did their task much faster when
A.   competing with other children.
B.   each worked alone.
C.   they worked in the presence of coactors.
D.   they had first practiced with their teammates.
Answer C, Type FAC

9. When the mere presence of others strengthens the dominant response, _____ has occurred.
A.   coaction
B.   competition
C.   social facilitation
D.   group polarization
Answer C, Type DEF

10. The mere presence of others has been found to boost people's performance when they are
A.   crossing out designated letters on printed pages.
B.   memorizing nonsense syllables.
C.   performing complex multiplication problems.
D.   completing a complex maze.
Answer A, Type FAC

11. The social-facilitation effect has been found to apply to
A.   people performing simple motor tasks.
B.   chickens eating grain.
C.   ants excavating sand.
D.   All of the above.
Answer D, Type FAC

12. Zajonc resolved the conflicting findings on how the presence of others influences performance with the help of the well-established principle in experimental psychology that arousal
A.   enhances whatever response tendency is dominant.
B.   interferes with the performance of simple tasks.
C.   inhibits coordination of efforts.
D.   weakens competing motives.
Answer A, Type FAC

13. The presence of others is likely to lead to better performance in _____ and to worse performance in _____.
A.   solving a crossword puzzle; sweeping a sidewalk
B.   raking leaves; solving complex mathematical problems
C.   playing golf; raking leaves
D.   solving complex mathematical problems; solving a crossword puzzle
Answer B, Type CON

14. Lee scored in the 99th percentile on the verbal portion of the SAT. She loves to put her verbal skills to use in solving anagrams. Lee would most likely perform at her best
A.   alone.
B.   in the mere presence of others also solving anagrams.
C.   after receiving positive feedback.

D.   after receiving negative feedback.
Answer B, Type CON

15.   Michaels and his colleagues watched students play pool in the student union at Virginia Tech. When four observers came up to watch the pool players, _____ players did _____ than they had when playing without the audience.
A.   good; slightly worse
B.   good; even better
C.   poor; slightly better
D.   poor; significantly better
Answer B, Type FAC

16.   Nearly 300 studies confirm that social arousal _____ performance on easy tasks and _____ performance on difficult tasks.
A.   hurts; boosts
B.   facilitates; boosts
C.   boosts; hurts
D.   hurts; facilitates
Answer C, Type FAC

17.   The primary effect of a crowd is that it
A.   enhances performance.
B.   enhances arousal.
C.   hurts performance.
D.   enhances social responsibility.
Answer B, Type FAC

18.   Freedman and his colleagues had an accomplice listen to a humorous tape or watch a movie with other participants. When all sat close together, the accomplice
A.   was liked less by males and liked more by females.
B.   could more readily induce the group to express hostility toward the experimenter.
C.   could more readily induce the group to laugh and clap.
D.   could more readily distract the group from attending to the tape or movie.
Answer C, Type FAC

19.   Evans tested 10-person groups of University of Massachusetts students in either a small, crowded room or a larger, more spacious room. Those in the crowded room were found to
A.   make more errors on both simple and complex tasks.
B.   make more errors on complex tasks but not on simple tasks.
C.   complete both simple and complex tasks more quickly.
D.   complete simple tasks more quickly and complex tasks more slowly.
Answer B, Type FAC

20.   Evidence that contradicts Zajonc's mere presence theory of social facilitation is that when observers are blindfolded, their presence
A.   does not boost performance on a simple task.
B.   hinders performance on a complex task.
C.   boosts performance on a simple task.
D.   is a distraction that leads to poorer performance on both simple and complex tasks.
Answer A, Type FAC

21.   Social psychologists refer to our concern for how others are evaluating us as
A.   social fear.
B.   evaluation apprehension.

C.   evaluation phobia.

D.   coactor anxiety.

Answer B, Type DEF

22. In one experiment, joggers on a jogging path at the University of California at Santa Barbara sped up as they came upon a woman seated on the grass--but only if she was

A.   facing them.

B.   facing away from them.

C.   someone they knew.

D.   a stranger.

Answer A, Type FAC

23. What is it about others that causes arousal?

A.   they facilitate concentration

B.   they are attractive

C.   they create evaluation apprehension

D.   All of the above

Answer C, Type FAC

24. Sanders and his colleagues have suggested that we are aroused in the presence of others, not only because of evaluation apprehension, but because we

A.   engage in social comparison.

B.   become deindividuated.

C.   get distracted.

D.   need to belong.

Answer C, Type FAC

25. According to the "distraction hypothesis," the mere presence of others can cause arousal because one experiences a conflict between

A.   paying attention to the task and paying attention to the other people.

B.   wanting to perform well and wanting to complete the task.

C.   one's social role and one's personal self-image.

D.   following instructions and making one's own decisions.

Answer A, Type FAC

26. According to the text, the idea that the mere presence of others produces some arousal even without evaluation apprehension or distraction is supported by the finding that

A.   some people publicly violate social norms.

B.   people's color preferences are stronger when they make judgments with others present.

C.   social facilitation effects occur among children.

D.   social facilitation effects occur among strangers.

Answer B, Type FAC

27. Research on social facilitation suggests that the design of new office buildings in which private offices are replaced with large, open areas may

A.   invade privacy and disrupt worker morale.

B.   improve communication and build employee morale.

C.   disrupt creative thinking on complex tasks.

D.   disrupt performance of routine clerical tasks.

Answer C, Type CON

28. Social loafing refers to the tendency for people to

A.   perform an unfamiliar task more poorly when others are present.

B.   violate social norms when no one is watching.

C.   be insensitive to the needs of others.

D.   exert less effort when they pool their efforts toward a common goal.

Answer D, Type DEF

29.   Social loafing occurs in situations in which people

      A.   pool their efforts toward a common goal.

      B.   are not accountable as individuals.

      C.   feel little evaluation apprehension.

      D.   All of the above.

Answer D, Type DEF

30.   In a study by Latané and his colleagues, participants were asked to shout and clap as loud as possible. Participants produced the most noise when they

      A.   thought they were shouting alone.

      B.   thought there was one other person shouting with them.

      C.   thought there were five other people shouting with them.

      D.   were not feeling any evaluation apprehension.

Answer A, Type FAC

31.   In a study by Ingham, blindfolded participants were placed in the first position in a tug-of-war apparatus. Participants pulled hardest when they

      A.   were part of a five-person team.

      B.   were part of a three-person team.

      C.   were part of a two-person team.

      D.   knew they were pulling alone.

Answer D, Type FAC

32.   Social loafing would be most likely to occur in

      A.   college students working on a group project for which they will all receive the same grade.

      B.   factory workers who are each paid according to how many lamps they assemble.

      C.   a group of golfers competing for first place in a tournament.

      D.   political candidates who hope to win a seat on the city council.

Answer A, Type CON

33.   For simple tasks, _____ occurs when observation increases evaluation apprehension, whereas _____ occurs when the pooling of effort lowers evaluation apprehension.

      A.   social facilitation; social loafing

      B.   social loafing; group polarization

      C.   deindividuation; social loafing

      D.   social loafing; deindividuation

Answer A, Type FAC

34.   Making group members' performance individually identifiable seems to be one effective strategy for reducing

      A.   social facilitation.

      B.   social loafing.

      C.   minority influence.

      D.   group polarization.

Answer B, Type FAC

35.   People in groups will loaf less when

      A.   the task is challenging.

      B.   the task is important and involving.

C.   the group is cohesive.

D.   All of the above.

Answer D, Type FAC

36.   People in groups loaf less when

    A.   all group members have comparable levels of self-esteem.

    B.   the group is made up of a small number of friends.

    C.   they work on a simple task with strangers.

    D.   the task is aversive.

    Answer B, Type FAC

37.   Research suggests that social loafing does not occur in

    A.   Israel's kibbutz farms.

    B.   China's collective factories.

    C.   Cuba's collective farms.

    D.   Japan.

    Answer A, Type FAC

38.   Which of the following is likely to occur under conditions of deindividuation?

    A.   police brutality

    B.   screaming at a referee during a NCAA tournament game

    C.   stealing

    D.   All of the above

    Answer D, Type FAC

39.   Which of the following circumstances contributes to people becoming deindividuated?

    A.   They are immersed in a large group.

    B.   They are physically anonymous.

    C.   They are involved in arousing, distracting activities.

    D.   All of the above.

    Answer D, Type DEF

40.   A loss of both self-awareness and evaluation apprehension can lead to

    A.   social facilitation.

    B.   powerful minority influence effects.

    C.   coactor effects.

    D.   Deindividuation.

    Answer D, Type DEF

41.   People are more likely to bait a person to jump off a bridge when it is dark and

    A.   the crowd is small.

    B.   the crowd is large.

    C.   the crowd is made up of people with authoritarian personalities.

    D.   the crowd is frustrated.

    Answer B, Type FAC

42.   Zimbardo explained the greater vandalism of an abandoned car left in New York than one left in Palo Alto in terms of the greater _____ of the large city.

    A.   poverty

    B.   frustration

    C.   anonymity

    D.   competitiveness

    Answer C, Type FAC

43. Zimbardo reported that women who were masked and hooded in KKK-style hoods and robes tended to _____ than women who were visible and wore name tags.
   A. administer longer shocks to a victim
   B. engage in greater social loafing
   C. make riskier decisions
   D. make more contact and reveal more personal information
   Answer A, Type FAC

44. On Halloween night, Diener and colleagues conducted a study of trick-or-treat theft at homes scattered throughout the Seattle area. Given a chance to steal candy, the children who were _____ were most likely to commit transgressions.
   A. anonymous and alone
   B. anonymous and in a group
   C. frustrated and alone
   D. frustrated and in a group
   Answer B, Type FAC

45. Based on research cited in the text, who is most likely to honk aggressively at someone stopped at a green light?
   A. The male driver of a sport utility vehicle.
   B. The male driver of a convertible.
   C. The female drive of a convertible.
   D. Any driver of a car with the top up.
   Answer D, Type CON

46. In a study at the University of Georgia, women who donned white nurses' uniforms and were made anonymous became _____ than when their names and personal identities were emphasized.
   A. less sympathetic to patients' needs
   B. more sympathetic to patients' needs
   C. less aggressive in administering shock
   D. more aggressive in administering shock
   Answer C, Type FAC

47. Compared to self-aware people, deindividuated people are
   A. less responsive to the situation.
   B. less likely to act without thinking about their own values.
   C. less self-regulated.
   D. more restrained.
   Answer C, Type FAC

48. "It was such an exciting game," your friend insists. "We were all shouting and clapping together, everyone was in sync. When our team won, I realized I was jumping up and down, screaming, right along with everyone else. I don't know what got into me!" Your friend's reactions best illustrate the process of
   A. social facilitation.
   B. risky shift.
   C. deindividuation.
   D. groupthink.
   Answer C, Type CON

49. In which of the following groups is deindividuation least likely to occur?
   A. in a jury where a guilty verdict requires unanimous agreement

B.	at a Ku Klux Klan rally where new members are being inducted
C.	in a high school pep rally attended by almost all students
D.	in the audience at an Independence Day parade celebrating the benefits of individual freedom
	Answer A, Type CON

50.	Which of the following pairs are most clearly opposites?
	A.	group polarization and group consensus
	B.	groupthink and the accentuation phenomenon
	C.	minority influence and leadership
	D.	deindividuation and self-awareness
	Answer D, Type CON

51.	People who are made self-aware, by acting in front of a mirror or TV camera, for example, have been found to
	A.	exhibit increased self-confidence.
	B.	behave more consistently with their attitudes.
	C.	be less thoughtful in analyzing complex social issues.
	D.	be more vulnerable to persuasive appeals that run counter to social norms.
	Answer B, Type FAC

52.	Research on group polarization began with the erroneous conclusion that group discussion leads to
	A.	a risky shift.
	B.	groupthink.
	C.	pluralistic ignorance.
	D.	group moderation.
	Answer A, Type FAC

53.	Group polarization occurs when group discussion _____ group members' initial inclinations.
	A.	challenges
	B.	reverses
	C.	neutralizes
	D.	strengthens
	Answer D, Type DEF

54.	The fact that people associate mostly with others whose attitudes are similar to their own suggests the prevalence of naturally occurring
	A.	social facilitation.
	B.	groupthink.
	C.	minority influence.
	D.	group polarization.
	Answer D, Type FAC

55.	Investigations of the risky shift eventually led to the conclusion that this group phenomenon was really a tendency for group discussion to
	A.	reverse the group's original leanings.
	B.	accentuate group members' initial leanings.
	C.	arouse and distract members so their self-awareness is reduced.
	D.	favor illusory thinking in supporting the group's leader.
	Answer B, Type FAC

56. Myers and Bishop organized groups of prejudiced and nonprejudiced high school students and asked them to respond to issues involving racial attitudes, both before and after group discussion. Results showed that after within-group discussion, _____ became _____.
    A. all students; more prejudiced
    B. all students; less prejudiced
    C. between-group differences; smaller
    D. between-group differences; greater
    Answer D, Type FAC

57. Which of the following describes the accentuation phenomenon?
    A. Initial differences among college student groups become less marked over time in college as a result of exposure to new information.
    B. Initial differences among college student groups become sharper and greater with more time in college.
    C. Discussions with like-minded others stimulate creative thought and reduce the extremism of opinions.
    D. The benefits of group membership become more apparent the longer one is part of the group.
    Answer B, Type DEF

58. The text suggests that the extremism of terrorist organizations is very likely the result of the naturally occurring process of
    A. group polarization.
    B. pluralistic ignorance.
    C. social loafing.
    D. social facilitation.
    Answer A, Type FAC

59. Individuals who believe that physician-assisted suicide should be legalized meet to discuss the issue. Research on group interaction suggests that after discussion the individuals will be
    A. more likely to question the wisdom of legalizing physician-assisted suicide.
    B. even more convinced that physician-assisted suicide should be legalized.
    C. sharply divided over whether physician-assisted suicide should be legalized.
    D. opposed to the legalization of physician-assisted suicide.
    Answer B, Type CON

60. What underlying processes help to explain the occurrence of group polarization?
    A. informational influence and normative influence
    B. minority influence and social facilitation
    C. psychological reactance and deindividuation
    D. social comparison and self-censorship
    Answer A, Type FAC

61. The fact that active participation in discussion produces more polarization is best explained by
    A. informational influence processes.
    B. normative influence processes.
    C. cognitive miser theory.
    D. a decrease in pluralistic ignorance.
    Answer A, Type FAC

62. According to Festinger, it is human nature to want to evaluate our opinions by
    A. comparing ourselves with others.
    B. designing everyday tests of their validity.

C.   engaging in frequent introspection.

D.   actively studying the results of scientific research.

Answer A, Type FAC

63.   _____ is a false impression of how other people are thinking, feeling, or responding.

A.   Social rationalization

B.   Social censorship

C.   Pluralistic ignorance

D.   Group delusion

Answer C, Type DEF

64.   Research by Baron and colleagues (1996) demonstrated that merely hearing one's opinion about the comforts of a dental chair corroborated by another led to

A.   more extreme ratings of the chair.

B.   a moderation of opinion about the chair.

C.   informational influence among dental students.

D.   more positive ratings of both the dental chair and the dentist.

Answer A, Type FAC

65.   Research on the underlying processes producing group polarization indicates that persuasive arguments predominate on issues having a(n) _____ basis and social comparison predominates on issues having a _____ basis.

A.   emotional; factual

B.   personal; social

C.   factual; value-laden

D.   economic; psychological

Answer C, Type FAC

66.   Failing to ask questions in class because you assume everyone else understands best exemplifies

A.   groupthink.

B.   pluralistic ignorance.

C.   social loafing.

D.   self-handicapping.

Answer B, Type CON

67.   Norman Triplett is to _____ as Irving Janis is to _____.

A.   social facilitation; social loafing

B.   deindividuation; group polarization

C.   groupthink; social loafing

D.   social facilitation; groupthink

Answer D, Type CON

68.   Groupthink can be defined as

A.   a tendency to suppress dissent in the interests of group harmony.

B.   a tendency to sacrifice group cohesiveness in favor of task orientation and problem focus.

C.   enhancement of problem-solving capacity as a result of several persons joining together to work on the same problem.

D.   reduced self-awareness as a result of group immersion and social anonymity.

Answer A, Type DEF

69.   Janet is a very directive leader of a highly cohesive student group on campus. When discussing important policy decisions the group will be at greatest risk for groupthink if it is also

A.   isolated from dissenting viewpoints.

B. composed of majority and minority students.

C. composed of only minority students.

D. prone to pluralistic ignorance.

Answer A, Type CON

70. According to the text, groupthink symptoms can be viewed as

A. most likely to emerge in collectivistic cultures.

B. a collective form of moral failure.

C. a collective form of dissonance reduction.

D. a collective form of informational influence.

Answer C, Type FAC

71. Which of the following comments is most likely to be made in a group characterized by groupthink?

A. "We have been in agreement on matters in the past and I hope that will continue."

B. "Joe, why don't you play devil's advocate and challenge the course of action most of us seem to prefer?"

C. "I think we need some outsiders to come in and critique our decision before we proceed."

D. "We have made some stupid mistakes in the past. Let's work carefully and not make the same errors again."

Answer A, Type CON

72. "Mindguards" protect group leaders from

A. unfair criticism.

B. disagreeable facts.

C. susceptibility to illusions.

D. stereotyped views of the opponents.

Answer B, Type FAC

73. Pressures toward uniformity are most clearly reflected in which of the following symptoms of groupthink?

A. an illusion of invulnerability

B. a stereotyped view of the opponent

C. self-censorship

D. rationalization

Answer C, Type FAC

74. Which of the following is not a prescriptive strategy to prevent groupthink from developing?

A. One or more members should be assigned the position of devil's advocate.

B. Group members should be kept together as one unit and not divided into separate discussion subgroups.

C. Outsiders should attend the meetings and challenge the group's views.

D. After reaching a preliminary decision, the group should call a second-chance meeting and ask each member to express remaining doubts.

Answer B, Type FAC

75. Closed-mindedness is most clearly fostered by which of the following symptoms of groupthink?

A. rationalization

B. unquestioned belief in the group's morality

C. an illusion of unanimity

D. conformity pressure

Answer A, Type FAC

76. Research on brainstorming reveals that people working _____ will generate _____ good ideas.
   A. alone; fewer
   B. alone; more
   C. in large groups; more
   D. in small group; more
   Answer B, Type FAC

77. Which of the following is not a determinant of minority influence?
   A. defections from the majority
   B. self-confidence
   C. consistency
   D. open-mindedness
   Answer D, Type FAC

78. Research indicates that minorities are most influential when they
   A. make use of two-sided rather than one-sided appeals.
   B. unswervingly stick to their position.
   C. argue positions that are greatly discrepant from the majority position.
   D. show respect for the majority position.
   Answer B, Type FAC

79. Minority influence is most likely to have an impact through
   A. central route persuasion.
   B. peripheral route persuasion.
   C. normative influence processes.
   D. the foot-in-the-door principle.
   Answer A, Type FAC

80. Moscovici believes that a minority's following the majority usually reflects _____ and a majority's following a minority usually reflects _____.
   A. public compliance; genuine acceptance
   B. genuine acceptance; public compliance
   C. public compliance; public compliance
   D. genuine acceptance; genuine acceptance
   Answer A, Type FAC

81. Confident minorities are most likely to influence the majority on matters of _____ than on matters of _____.
   A. law; fashion
   B. political importance; social importance
   C. opinion; fact
   D. gender bias; racial bias
   Answer C, Type FAC

82. The process by which certain group members motivate and guide the group defines
   A. social facilitation.
   B. goal arousal.
   C. leadership.
   D. expert power.
   Answer C, Type DEF

83. Tim is excellent at organizing his employees, setting goals and focusing on achieving those goals for the company. Tim excels in

A.   social leadership.
B.   laissez faire leadership.
C.   task leadership.
D.   masculine leadership.
Answer C, Type CON

84.   Research on leadership indicates that
A.   all great leaders share certain traits.
B.   effective supervisors tend to score high on both task and social leadership.
C.   the most effective leaders typically deviate significantly from a group's standards or norms.
D.   All of the above.
Answer B, Type FAC

85.   Effective, charismatic leaders typically have
A.   a compelling vision of some desired state of affairs.
B.   an ability to communicate goals in clear and simple language.
C.   enough optimism and faith in the group to inspire members to follow them.
D.   All of the above.
Answer D, Type DEF

The following items also appear in the Study Guide:

86.   Which form of social influence discussed in Chapter 8 does not necessarily involve an interacting group?
A.   group polarization
B.   groupthink
C.   minority influence
D.   social facilitation
Answer D, Type FAC

87.   Which of the following is true?
A.   People's color preferences are stronger when they make judgments with others present.
B.   Ants excavate less sand in the presence of other ants.
C.   In the presence of others, students take more time to learn a simple maze and less time to learn one that is complex.
D.   Joggers run more slowly when jogging with someone else.
Answer A, Type FAC

88.   Social facilitation and social loafing have been explained in terms of difference in
A.   evaluation concern.
B.   informational influence.
C.   cognitive dissonance.
D.   group polarization.
Answer A, Type FAC

89.   Which of the following is false?
A.   Groups of friends loaf less than groups of strangers.
B.   Israel's communal kibbutz farms have outproduced Israel's noncollective farms.
C.   Research completed in Japan, Thailand, and India indicates that social loafing does not occur in less individualistic, more group-centered cultures.
D.   Students pumped exercise bikes more energetically when they knew they were being individually monitored than when they thought their output was being pooled with that of other riders.

90. Experiments show that people in groups loaf less when
    A. the task is challenging.
    B. they are in an unfamiliar setting.
    C. they have a strong sense of external control.
    D. the task is routine.
    Answer A, Type FAC

91. The term "risky shift" was used to refer to the finding of
    A. groups being riskier than individuals.
    B. individuals being riskier than groups.
    C. males being riskier than females.
    D. people becoming less risky as they grow older.
    Answer A, Type FAC

92. Tom, a successful foreman in a large furniture factory, emphasizes the attainment of production goals and sets high standards for the workers under him. Tom's style is an example of _____ leadership.
    A. normative
    B. task
    C. autocratic
    D. Type A
    Answer B, Type CON

93. The presence of others would be most likely to improve performance on
    A. raking up leaves.
    B. solving crossword puzzles.
    C. learning foreign language words.
    D. solving complex mathematical puzzles.
    Answer A, Type CON

94. Who among the following would be considered coactors?
    A. four people doing push-ups in an exercise class
    B. two people playing bridge
    C. eight competitors running a 5-kilometer race
    D. All of the above.
    Answer A, Type CON

95. After an exciting soccer game in which the home team loses, a crowd of fans throws garbage and begins to tear up the field. This behavior is best understood in terms of
    A. group polarization.
    B. deindividuation.
    C. groupthink.
    D. social facilitation.
    Answer B, Type CON

96. Which of the following is least likely to be considered a group as defined in the text?
    A. a husband and wife talking over dinner
    B. a committee of eight discussing the problem of neighborhood crime
    C. four seven-year-olds playing hide-and-go-seek
    D. seven people waiting at a bus stop
    Answer D, Type CON

97. The presence of others would be least likely to improve performance in

A.   playing chess.
B.   weight lifting.
C.   running.
D.   the broad jump.
Answer A, Type CON

98.   Social loafing would be least likely to occur
A.   in a boys' club trying to raise money by holding a Saturday car wash.
B.   in a relay race in which each team member's performance is timed.
C.   in a community garden where each family is expected to contribute whatever free time they have.
D.   in a work crew building a new highway.
Answer B, Type CON

99.   Individuals who tend to favor stiff penalties for drunk drivers come together to discuss various ways of dealing with the problem of intoxicated drivers. The group polarization hypothesis predicts that after group discussion,
A.   the individuals will favor even more severe penalties for drunk drivers.
B.   the individuals will tend to become more tolerant of drunk drivers.
C.   the individuals will be divided into two opposing groups as to the best way to deal with drunk drivers.
D.   the individuals will favor a rehabilitation program rather than a jail sentence for drunk drivers.
Answer A, Type CON

100.   Which of the following is a comment you are least likely to hear being made within a group characterized by groupthink?
A.   "Our critics are not very smart."
B.   "Our past decisions have always been right."
C.   "Let's make the decision and get out of here. I've got more important things to do."
D.   "It seems to me we are all in agreement on this, so let's proceed."
Answer C, Type CON

Critical Thinking Questions

101.   Explain the role of evaluation apprehension in both social facilitation and social loafing.

102.   "Self-awareness is the opposite of deindividuation." Explain.

103.   Explain group polarization in terms of normative and informational influence.

104.   Describe how the symptoms of groupthink illustrate self-justification, self-serving bias, and conformity.

105.   Explain why minority influence often leads to genuine acceptance rather than simply public compliance.

CHAPTER NINE
PREJUDICE: DISLIKING OTHERS

Multiple Choice Questions

1. Prejudice is defined as
   A. an inaccurate idea about a group based on insufficient information.
   B. a negative attitude toward a group and its individual members.
   C. an intentional or unintentional policy of discriminating against outgroups.
   D. a cognitive categorization based on overgeneralizations.
   Answer B, Type DEF

2. Prejudice biases us against an individual based solely on
   A. the person's appearance and behavior.
   B. our past experience with similar persons.
   C. the person's identification with a particular group.
   D. our present emotional state.
   Answer C, Type FAC

3. Which of the following clearly meets the definition of a stereotype?
   A. Mary believes she is underpaid as an administrative secretary.
   B. Gretchen believes the British are cool and unexcitable.
   C. Kershon believes sport utility vehicles are safe.
   D. All of the above.
   Answer B, Type CON

4. According to Lee Jussim and colleagues, stereotypes may be
   A. positive.
   B. accurate.
   C. inaccurate.
   D. All of the above.
   Answer D, Type FAC

5. Prejudice is to discrimination as attitude is to
   A. policy.
   B. belief.
   C. behavior.
   D. generalization.
   Answer C, Type CON

6. Racism refers to
   A. institutional practices that subordinate people of a given race.
   B. individuals' prejudicial attitudes toward people of a given race.
   C. individuals' discriminatory behavior toward people of a given race.
   D. All of the above.
   Answer D, Type DEF

7. Jimmy often expresses his dislike of Hispanics, believing them to be shiftless and untrustworthy. As long as he can get away with it, he never hires them to work for his company.
   A. Jimmy is displaying stereotype threat.
   B. Jimmy is probably a victim of realistic group conflict theory.

C.   Jimmy is best characterized as prejudiced.

D.   Jimmy is best characterized as racist.

Answer D, Type CON

8.   A state police force has set a height requirement of 5 feet 10 inches for all officers. This requirement is irrelevant to job effectiveness but generally excludes Hispanics, Asians, and women from the force. Such a requirement most clearly reflects

A.   racism and sexism.

B.   scapegoating and ingroup bias.

C.   stereotyping and prejudice.

D.   Gause's law and realistic conflict theory.

Answer A, Type CON

9.   To judge from what Americans tell survey takers, racial prejudice toward African-Americans

A.   is today worse than ever.

B.   has decreased since the early 1940s.

C.   has actually increased since the early 1980s.

D.   decreased from 1940 to 1960, then increased until 1980, and has since stabilized.

Answer B, Type FAC

10.   In the 1940s, researchers Kenneth Clark and Mamie Clark gave African-American children a choice between Black dolls and White dolls. Results showed that most

A.   chose the Black dolls.

B.   chose the White dolls.

C.   refused to choose between them.

D.   used the dolls in aggressive symbolic play.

Answer B, Type FAC

11.   Compared to the 1940s, racial prejudice

A.   is no longer fashionable to express.

B.   has completely disappeared.

C.   surfaces under conditions where it is both safe and unsafe to express it.

D.   None of the above.

Answer A, Type FAC

12.   The phenomenon of "greatest prejudice in the most _____ social realms" seems universal.

A.   public

B.   intimate

C.   profitable

D.   traditional

Answer B, Type FAC

13.   White people who were asked to use electric shocks to "teach" a task, delivered no more shock to a Black person than to a White person except when

A.   they were angered.

B.   the recipient could not retaliate.

C.   the recipient did not know who did it.

D.   any of the above conditions were true.

Answer D, Type FAC

14.   Research on discriminatory behavior in the U.S. indicates that it

A.   is practiced primarily by White males against Black males.

B.   occurs when it can hide behind the screen of some other motive.

C.   occurs wherever it is not legally prohibited.

D.   is primarily motivated by economic gain.
Answer B, Type FAC

15.   According to the text, modern racism is
       A.   seldom consciously intended.
       B.   subtle.
       C.   likely to occur behind the screen of some other motive.
       D.   All of the above.
       Answer D, Type FAC

16.   Patricia Devine suggests that even for the low-prejudice person, overcoming prejudice is like
       learning to
       A.   break a bad habit.
       B.   play a musical instrument.
       C.   write a novel.
       D.   walk a tightrope.
       Answer A, Type FAC

17.   Research has confirmed the phenomenon of automatic stereotyping and prejudice, in which
       A.   people stereotype ingroup members automatically.
       B.   people feel squeamish when they think about Blacks and homosexuals.
       C.   cognitively activated stereotypes influence people to behave in a biased, prejudiced
               manner.
       D.   None of the above.
       Answer C, Type FAC

18.   When low-prejudiced people are aware of the gap between how they should respond and how
       they do respond to outgroup members, they primarily
       A.   feel guilty.
       B.   feel angry.
       C.   feel hopeless.
       D.   All of the above.
       Answer A, Type FAC

19.   Ideas about how men and women ought to behave are called _____, whereas ideas about how
       women and men do behave are called _____.
       A.   gender-role norms; gender stereotypes
       B.   gender stereotypes; gender-role norms
       C.   gender preferences; gender roles
       D.   sexist attitudes; sexists stereotypes
       Answer A, Type DEF

20.   The belief that Italians are passionate is an example of _____; the refusal to hire Hispanics is an
       example of _____.
       A.   a stereotype; discrimination
       B.   a stereotype; prejudice
       C.   racism; prejudice
       D.   discrimination; racism
       Answer A, Type CON

21.   Which of the following is false?
       A.   Strong gender stereotypes continue to exist.
       B.   Few women accept gender stereotypes.
       C.   Gender stereotypes are generally stronger than racial stereotypes.

D.   Stereotypes are not prejudices.
Answer B, Type FAC

22. Jackman and Senter (1981) found that both men and women thought that
    A.   women make better leaders.
    B.   women are more "emotional."
    C.   men and women are equally assertive.
    D.   men and women are equally compassionate.
    Answer B, Type FAC

23. Porter, Geis, and Jennings showed participants a picture of a group of graduate students working
    together on a project and asked participants to guess which member contributed the most to the
    group. When the pictured group was mixed sex, the participants chose
    A.   a woman only if she was seated at the head of the table.
    B.   a woman only if she appeared to be the oldest member of the group.
    C.   a woman only if women in the group outnumbered the men.
    D.   None of the above.
    Answer D, Type FAC

24. By 1988, _____ Americans said they would vote for a qualified woman whom their party
    nominated for President.
    A.   9 in 10
    B.   7 in 10
    C.   5 in 10
    D.   3 in 10
    Answer A, Type FAC

25. A review of research on gender attitudes suggests
    A.   that most people have gut-level negative emotions about women even though they
         describe them favorably.
    B.   a "women-are-wonderful" effect.
    C.   that most people express more admiration than affection for women.
    D.   that men and women are viewed as equally understanding and helpful.
    Answer B, Type FAC

26. Which of the following is an example of benevolent sexism?
    A.   "Women have a superior sense of compassion."
    B.   "Wives are controlling of their husbands."
    C.   "Women are less skilled in mathematics than men."
    D.   All of the above.
    Answer A, Type CON

27. Which of the following statements is true?
    A.   Experiments have not demonstrated any overall tendency to devalue women's work.
    B.   Both males and females tend to deprecate women's work.
    C.   Males tend to deprecate women's work while females do not.
    D.   Females but not males tend to deprecate women's work.
    Answer A, Type FAC

28. Deonn believes that prejudice toward Black women is very common, but she doesn't believe that
    she has suffered from discrimination. Her perceptions best reflect
    A.   personal/group discrimination discrepancy.
    B.   biased gender-role norms.
    C.   illusory correlations.

D.   a privileged socioeconomic background.
Answer A, Type CON

29.   When Ian Ayres and his colleagues visited Chicago area car dealers and used a uniform strategy to negotiate the lowest price on a new car, dealers charged _____ the highest average price.
    A.   White males
    B.   White females
    C.   Black males
    D.   Black females
    Answer D, Type FAC

30.   Most women believe that sex discrimination
    A.   has affected them personally.
    B.   affects most working women.
    C.   both A and B.
    D.   neither A nor B.
    Answer B, Type FAC

31.   Sex-selective abortions and infanticide in China and India have led to _____ "missing women."
    A.   seven million
    B.   seventy-six thousand
    C.   seventy-six million
    D.   twenty million
    Answer C, Type FAC

32.   In which of the following groups do individual members believe that their group is discriminated against and at the same time deny suffering any personal disadvantage?
    A.   unemployed people
    B.   African Americans
    C.   out-of-the-closet lesbians
    D.   All of the above.
    Answer D, Type FAC

33.   Which of the following does the text cite as a social source of prejudice?
    A.   scapegoating
    B.   authoritarianism
    C.   just-world phenomenon
    D.   unequal status
    Answer D, Type FAC

34.   The text indicates that, until recently, prejudice was greatest in regions where slavery was practiced. This fact is clearly consistent with the principle that _____ breeds prejudice.
    A.   frustration
    B.   unequal status
    C.   conformity
    D.   authoritarianism
    Answer B, Type FAC

35.   Knowing that members of Group X in Transylvania have primary responsibility for making the law is likely to lead people to conclude that members of Group X
    A.   reflect the full variation of abilities, traits, and interests that are present in the larger population.

B.   have traits that fit their legislative role.

C.   tend to have authoritarian personalities and are thus somewhat prejudiced.

D.   None of the above.

Answer B, Type CON

36.   A consistent finding concerning Christianity in North America is that, in comparison to non-members, church members show _____ than nonmembers.

A.   more racial prejudice

B.   less racial prejudice

C.   more sexism but less racism

D.   more conformity but less authoritarianism

Answer A, Type FAC

37.   Which of the following could explain the correlation found between religion and racial prejudice?

A.   People with less education may be both more fundamentalist and more prejudiced.

B.   Prejudice may "cause" religion by leading people to create religious ideas that support their prejudices.

C.   Religion may cause prejudice by leading people to believe that everyone has free will, so minorities are to blame for their own victimization.

D.   All of the above.

Answer D, Type FAC

38.   Which of the following is true?

A.   Faithful church attenders are more prejudiced than occasional attenders.

B.   Those who score highest on Gallup's "spiritual commitment" index are less accepting of a person of another race moving in next door.

C.   Those for whom religion is an end in itself express less prejudice than those for whom religion is more a means to an end.

D.   All of the above.

Answer C, Type FAC

39.   A consistent finding is that however religious commitment is assessed,

A.   the less devout are less prejudiced.

B.   commitment bears no relation to prejudice.

C.   the very devout are less prejudiced.

D.   the very devout are the most prejudiced.

Answer C, Type FAC

40.   Gordon Allport has concluded, "The role of _____ is paradoxical. It makes prejudice and it unmakes prejudice."

A.   power

B.   religion

C.   self-esteem

D.   education

Answer B, Type FAC

41.   Word, Zanna, and Cooper had White Princeton University men interview both White and Black job applicants. When the applicant was Black, the interviewers _____ than when the applicant was White.

A.   ended the interview sooner

B.   sat farther away from the applicant

C.   made more speech errors

D.   All of the above.
Answer D, Type FAC

42.   Stereotype threat refers to
A.   the greater likelihood that minority groups will be negatively stereotyped.
B.   the tendency for stereotypes to change over time.
C.   the tendency for stereotyping to lead to prejudice and discrimination.
D.   a disruptive concern that one's behavior will verify a negative stereotype.
Answer D, Type DEF

43.   Unfortunately, Mr. Smith, a high school speech teacher, communicates to his class that he thinks boys tend to be less anxious and thus make better speeches than girls do. As a result, some of the girls in his class become apprehensive in preparing and giving speeches in Mr. Smith's class. The girls are experiencing
A.   stereotype threat.
B.   the just-world phenomenon.
C.   the scapegoating effect.
D.   personal/group discrimination discrepancy.
Answer A, Type CON

44.   Betsy and Tina, both third-graders in the same classroom, are assigned by their teacher to different groups that will compete in a spelling bee. Betsy and Tina each believe that their own group is composed of the better spellers. The girls' beliefs best illustrate
A.   the just-world phenomenon.
B.   ingroup bias.
C.   the fundamental attribution error.
D.   authoritarianism.
Answer B, Type CON

45.   Ingroup bias can be promoted
A.   by the mere experience of people's being formed into groups.
B.   only by the consistent lesson that other groups are inferior.
C.   only by the repeated experience that one's ingroup is superior.
D.   only by direct competition between ingroup and outgroups.
Answer A, Type FAC

46.   According to social identity theory, people readily
A.   categorize themselves and others.
B.   identify with certain groups.
C.   compare their group with other groups.
D.   All of the above.
Answer D, Type FAC

47.   A group that is perceived as distinctive from one's own group is generally called
A.   an outgroup.
B.   a low-status group.
C.   a minimal group.
D.   ingroup favoritism.
Answer A, Type DEF

48.   Ingroup bias will result when the groups formed
A.   share at least one demographic characteristic (e.g., racial identity).
B.   share a birthday.
C.   share the last digit in their social security number.

D.   All of the above.
Answer D, Type FAC

49.   Research suggests that we are most prone to ingroup bias when
      A.   the ingroup is lower in status than the outgroup.
      B.   one's self-esteem has just been threatened.
      C.   we identify very strongly with the ingroup.
      D.   All of the above.
      Answer D, Type FAC

50.   If prejudice is a social norm, many people will follow the path of least resistance and conform to
      the fashion. Thus once established, prejudice is maintained largely by
      A.   pressure.
      B.   inertia.
      C.   conscious effort.
      D.   social engineering.
      Answer B, Type FAC

51.   Studies of Whites by Thomas Pettigrew in South Africa in the 1950s, when apartheid ruled,
      revealed that those who _____ were also most prejudiced.
      A.   had the most education
      B.   conformed most to other social norms
      C.   were the most disadvantaged
      D.   had the greatest amount of social power
      Answer B, Type FAC

52.   Conformity is to _____ sources of prejudice as authoritarianism is to _____
      sources of prejudice.
      A.   social; emotional
      B.   emotional; cognitive
      C.   cognitive; social
      D.   social cognitive
      Answer A, Type CON

53.   Children of _____ have less stereotyped views of men and women.
      A.   authoritarian parents
      B.   employed women
      C.   devoutly religious parents
      D.   bisexual men
      Answer B, Type FAC

54.   Cultural attitudes are embodied and reinforced in
      A.   schools.
      B.   films and television.
      C.   politics.
      D.   All of the above.
      Answer D, Type FAC

55.   In examining photographs of people in magazines and newspapers, Dane Archer and his
      colleagues found that, relative to the average female photo, the average male photo is more likely
      to
      A.   emphasize the face.
      B.   emphasize the body.
      C.   include the situational context.

D.   display a standing posture.
Answer A, Type FAC

56.   In research in Germany, Norbert Schwarz and Eva Kurz confirmed that people whose faces are prominent in photos seem
       A.   more physically attractive.
       B.   less powerful.
       C.   younger.
       D.   more intelligent and ambitious.
       Answer D, Type FAC

57.   More lynchings of Blacks took place in the old South during years when cotton prices were low, suggesting that prejudice is partly explained by
       A.   ingroup bias.
       B.   the just-world hypothesis.
       C.   displaced aggression.
       D.   institutional supports.
       Answer C, Type FAC

58.   In a famous experiment by Miller and Bugelski, college-age men staying at a summer camp were asked to state their attitudes toward Japanese and Mexicans. Some did so before, and then after, being forced to stay in camp to take tests rather than going to a long-awaited free evening at a theater. Results most clearly supported
       A.   realistic group conflict theory.
       B.   the scapegoat theory of prejudice.
       C.   the principle that unequal status breeds prejudice.
       D.   the just-world hypothesis.
       Answer B, Type FAC

59.   Realistic group conflict theory suggests that prejudice arises
       A.   whenever people try to live together.
       B.   when a new group moves into an area.
       C.   between groups who fail to communicate clearly with each other.
       D.   when groups compete for scarce resources.
       Answer D, Type DEF

60.   The ecological principle that maximum competition will exist between species that have identical needs is known as
       A.   realistic group conflict theory.
       B.   Gause's law.
       C.   the frustration-aggression relation.
       D.   species-ism
       Answer B, Type DEF

61.   In one study at Northwestern University, members of _____ sororities were more disparaging of other sororities than were members of _____ sororities.
       A.   academic honors; athletic
       B.   athletic; academic honors
       C.   higher-status; lower-status
       D.   lower-status; higher-status
       Answer D, Type FAC

62.   Frustration, the need for status and belonging, and authoritarianism are all
       A.   social sources of prejudice.

B.   cognitive sources of prejudice.
C.   emotional sources of prejudice.
D.   personality sources of prejudice.
Answer C, Type FAC

63.   You are given a novel problem that you believe reflects creativity and intelligence. You fail. When asked to rate students at a rival school, you are more likely than a control group who did not fail to
A.   rate them lower and your own school higher.
B.   rate them higher than students at your own school.
C.   express prejudice against students at your own school.
D.   express prejudice against the experimenter.
Answer A, Type CON

64.   When Grube, Kleinhesselink, and Kearney had men view young women's videotaped job interviews, men with low self-acceptance disliked
A.   women with low self-esteem.
B.   dependent, traditional women.
C.   physically attractive women.
D.   strong, nontraditional women.
Answer D, Type FAC

65.   Individuals with authoritarian tendencies have
A.   an intolerance for weakness.
B.   a punitive attitude.
C.   a submissive respect for ingroup authority.
D.   All of the above.
Answer D, Type DEF

66.   A belief in the superiority of one's own ethnic and cultural group and a corresponding disdain for all other groups is called
A.   conservatism.
B.   ethnocentrism.
C.   scapegoating.
D.   ingroup authoritarianism.
Answer B, Type DEF

67.   An important conclusion of research on the authoritarian personality is that prejudices against different minorities
A.   are not founded in hostility.
B.   tend to coexist in the same individuals.
C.   have an institutional origin and are maintained by institutional supports.
D.   are a by-product of normal thinking processes.
Answer B, Type FAC

68.   One researcher of right-wing authoritarians concludes that such people
A.   are mentally ill.
B.   suffer from severe childhood sexual abuse.
C.   are "equal opportunity bigots."
D.   All of the above.
Answer C, Type FAC

69.   Which of the following statements is true?
A.   Stereotyped beliefs and prejudiced attitudes exist because of social conditioning.

B. Stereotyped beliefs and prejudiced attitudes exist because they enable people to displace hostilities.

C. Stereotyped beliefs and prejudiced attitudes exist as by-products of normal thinking processes.

D. All of the above.

Answer D, Type FAC

70. Which of the following statements is true?

A. Categorization can provide useful information about people with minimum effort.

B. It is difficult to resist categorizing people into groups.

C. Categorization provides a cognitive foundation for prejudice.

D. All of the above.

Answer D, Type FAC

71. The phrase "they are all alike, but we are diverse" reflects

A. outgroup bias.

B. the outgroup homogeneity effect.

C. ethnocentrism.

D. categorization bias.

Answer B, Type DEF

72. Which of the following is true regarding the relationship between positive emotions and our thought processes?

A. Positive emotions and more complex thinking naturally go together.

B. Happy people seem to commit more effort to wrestling with differences.

C. Feeling very good may prime feelings of superiority.

D. Good moods necessarily reduce outgroup stereotyping.

Answer C, Type FAC

73. In general, the greater our familiarity with a social group, the more we see its

A. members as similar.

B. flaws rather than its strengths.

C. diversity.

D. strengths rather than its flaws.

Answer C, Type FAC

74. A Black in an otherwise White group, a man in an otherwise female group, or a woman in an otherwise male group seems

A. less prominent than the others in the group.

B. less responsible for what is happening in the group.

C. to have both fewer good and fewer bad qualities than others in the group.

D. None of the above.

Answer D, Type FAC

75. Kleck and Strenta had women who falsely believed they appeared disfigured by theatrical makeup interact with a female partner. Results indicated that women who thought they were disfigured

A. interacted for a longer period of time with their partners.

B. interacted for a shorter period of time with their partners.

C. rated their partners as more tense, distant, and patronizing.

D. rated their partners as warmer, more open, and friendlier.

Answer C, Type FAC

76. Mildred learns that ten Danerians were arrested for nonviolent crimes such as shoplifting and that ten Transylvanians were arrested for violent crimes such as rape. Mildred's tendency to estimate that more crimes were committed by Transylvanians than by Danerians best illustrates the effect of
   A.   group-serving bias.
   B.   authoritarianism.
   C.   the just-world phenomenon.
   D.   distinctive cases.
   Answer D, Type CON

77. Because we are sensitive to distinctive events, the simultaneous occurrence of two such events is especially noticeable. Our attentiveness to unusual occurrences can create
   A.   the group-serving bias.
   B.   authoritarianism.
   C.   the outgroup homogeneity effect.
   D.   illusory correlations.
   Answer D, Type DEF

78. Although most suspects in cases of incest, child molestation, and sexual abuse are heterosexual males, the local newspaper omits the word "heterosexual" in any related headline. In contrast, whenever a self-described gay male is arrested for a crime, the headline proclaims "homosexual arrested" in the case. The resulting prejudice that gay males are more likely to commit violent crimes can in part be blamed on
   A.   illusory correlation.
   B.   ingroup bias.
   C.   outgroup homogeneity effects.
   D.   group-serving bias.
   Answer A, Type CON

79. Hamilton and Rose's (1980) research in which students read sentences describing accountants, doctors, and salespeople reveals that
   A.   preexisting stereotypes lead us to "see" correlations that do not exist.
   B.   vivid information is irrelevant to occupational stereotypes.
   C.   positive information is better remembered if it describes doctors.
   D.   distinctive information is ignored in forming impressions.
   Answer A, Type FAC

80. Explaining away outgroup members' positive behaviors and attributing negative behaviors to their dispositions is known as
   A.   the scapegoat theory of prejudice.
   B.   the just-world bias.
   C.   Gause's Law.
   D.   group-serving bias.
   Answer D, Type DEF

81. Describing positive behaviors by an ingroup member in terms of a general disposition but describing the same behavior by an outgroup member as a specific isolated act has been called
   A.   the overgeneralization bias.
   B.   the ingroup homogeneity effect.
   C.   the outgroup specificity phenomenon.
   D.   the linguistic intergroup bias.
   Answer D, Type DEF

82. Jeremy's belief that earthquake victims are being punished by God for their own sins best illustrates
   A.   Gause's law.
   B.   the just-world phenomenon.
   C.   ingroup bias.
   D.   stereotype vulnerability.
   Answer B, Type CON

83. The just-world phenomenon can lead people to
   A.   think that the winners of a lottery actually deserved their good fortune.
   B.   think that judges have greater sensitivity to the problem of injustice than most people in the general population.
   C.   distrust those who are wealthy or well educated.
   D.   overestimate differences within an outgroup and underestimate differences within an ingroup.
   Answer A, Type CON

84. Research on whether stereotypes bias our judgments of individuals indicates that
   A.   we often evaluate individuals more positively than the groups they compose.
   B.   we may have strong gender stereotypes yet ignore them when judging a particular individual.
   C.   stereotypes sometimes bias our judgments of individuals by creating a contrast effect.
   D.   All of the above.
   Answer D, Type FAC

85. Although John knows a few successful, hardworking Black businessmen, he maintains his belief that Blacks are lazy and shiftless. His thinking best reflects
   A.   group-serving bias.
   B.   the fundamental attribution error.
   C.   regression toward the average.
   D.   subtyping.
   Answer D, Type CON

These items also appear in the Study Guide:

86. Prejudice is a negative _____, while discrimination is a negative _____.
   A.   belief; feeling
   B.   generalization; practice
   C.   attitude; behavior
   D.   stereotype; practice
   Answer C, Type DEF

87. Stereotypes are to discrimination as _____ are to _____.
   A.   categories; feeling
   B.   attitudes; actions
   C.   emotions; practice
   D.   beliefs; behavior
   Answer D, Type CON

88. Most Americans agree that
   A.   the activities of married women are best confined to the home and family.
   B.   they would probably move if Black people came to live in great numbers in their neighborhood.

C.   the two sexes are equally emotional.

D.   they would vote for a qualified woman whom their party nominated for president.

Answer D, Type FAC

89.   The group-serving bias seems to be less characteristic of groups that stress

A.   individualism.

B.   honesty.

C.   modesty.

D.   intelligence.

Answer C, Type FAC

90.   The stereotype of _____ is held by both men and women, by both feminists and nonfeminists.

A.   men as leaders

B.   men as decision makers

C.   women as homemakers

D.   women as mediators

Answer A, Type FAC

91.   According to the text, the authoritarian personality is an example of

A.   how conformity supports prejudice.

B.   a cognitive source of prejudice.

C.   how emotional needs contribute to prejudice.

D.   how social inequalities breed prejudice.

Answer C, Type FAC

92.   In one study, students were told that various members of "Group A" or "Group B" did either something desirable or something undesirable. While many more statements described members of Group A than Group B, both groups were associated with nine desirable behaviors for every four undesirable behaviors. Results indicated

A.   that students perceived members of Group B more negatively.

B.   that students perceived members of Group A more negatively.

C.   no differences in the students' perceptions of the groups.

D.   that authoritarian students viewed Group A more negatively.

Answer A, Type FAC

93.   Mr. Watson's belief that Blacks are lazy is an example of _____. His refusal to rent an apartment to a Black family is an example of _____.

A.   a stereotype; sexism

B.   discrimination; prejudice

C.   a stereotype; discrimination

D.   racism; prejudice

Answer C, Type CON

94.   According to the text, stereotypes are resistant to change because

A.   for the most part, they are accurate reflections of reality.

B.   our prejudgments influence how we interpret and process information.

C.   they are always based in an authoritarian attitude which is blind to disconfirming evidence.

D.   they are held by people with low intelligence.

Answer B, Type FAC

95.   Which of the following would you not expect to be true of the authoritarian personality?

A.   to discriminate against American Indians

B.   to want to achieve high social status

C. to be respectful of police

D. to be opposed to capital punishment

Answer D, Type CON

96. Which of the following would be an example of the group-serving bias?

A. Veryl believes that women are unemployed because of discrimination while men are unemployed because of low motivation.

B. Sue believes that members of her own family are prejudiced while her husband's family is tolerant.

C. Chuck believes that mistakes made by both men and women are due to low intelligence.

D. Bill believes that groups outperform individuals in solving problems.

Answer A, Type CON

97. The just-world phenomenon may lead us to believe that an unemployed person is

A. a victim of discrimination.

B. lazy.

C. in need of sympathy.

D. in need of a retraining program.

Answer B, Type CON

98. John has just failed a chemistry test. He goes back to his apartment and criticizes his roommate's choice of music. What term best describes John's behavior?

A. institutionalized aggression

B. just-world action

C. displaced aggression

D. authoritarian regression

Answer C, Type CON

99. Which of the following would be an example of racism as the term is defined in the text?

A. Mr. Jones' refusal to rent his apartments to Chinese

B. Mrs. Smith's prejudice toward Hispanics

C. a government regulation that prevents inner-city residents from being recruited to serve as Army officers

D. All of the above.

Answer D, Type CON

100. The results of one social-psychological study indicated that observers who discovered that a fellow worker had received a large prize as the result of a random drawing subsequently concluded that he had in fact worked especially hard. This is an example of

A. vivid, anecdotal information being more important than base-rate data.

B. disguised hostility.

C. outgroup bias.

D. the just-world phenomenon.

Answer D, Type CON

Critical Thinking Questions

101. Discuss the distinctions between prejudice, stereotypes, and discrimination. Do you think these distinctions are useful? Why or why not?

102. Research on the relation between religion and prejudice is nicely summarized by Gordon Allport (1958): "The role of religion is paradoxical. It makes prejudice and it unmakes prejudice." In your own opinion, why might this be true?

103. Based on the text's discussion of the social sources of prejudice, can you think of at least two ways to reduce prejudice in America?

104. Does the observation that prejudiced attitudes exist as a "by-product of normal thinking processes" justify the existence of prejudice? Why or why not?

105. What is the psychological benefit of believing in a "just world"? Who is most likely to receive this benefit?

Multiple Choice Questions

1.   According to the text, a dynamic salesperson who is self-assured, energetic, and "go-getting" on the sales floor should be described as
   A.   instrumental aggressive.
   B.   manipulative.
   C.   aggressive.
   D.   Assertive.
   Answer D, Type DEF

2.   Aggression is any physical or verbal behavior that
   A.   may result in physical or psychological damage.
   B.   springs from anger or hostility.
   C.   results in harm regardless of intent.
   D.   is intended to hurt someone.
   Answer D, Type DEF

3.   Which of the following would be an example of aggression as defined in the text?
   A.   Sam accidentally slams the car door too quickly, and it hits Tim's knee.
   B.   Luisa urges her classmates not to vote for Marcy for dormitory senator, citing some rumors about Marcy's social life.
   C.   Carla, a dentist, delivers a shot of novocaine before pulling her patient's diseased tooth.
   D.   Joe's eagerness and enthusiasm result in his being promoted to sales manager in a very short time.
   Answer B, Type CON

4.   Which of the following would be considered aggression as the term is defined in the text?
   A.   A motorist accidentally hits a child who has run into the path of his car.
   B.   An assertive salesperson manages to sell $200,000 worth of automobiles in one month.
   C.   A child attempts to hit her playmate with a rock but misses.
   D.   All of the above.
   Answer C, Type CON

5.   Tawanda is upset with Tina. During a social gathering she verbally cut Tina down in front of others. Tawanda's behavior was
   A.   assertive.
   B.   manipulative.
   C.   aggressive.
   D.   an example of displacement.
   Answer C, Type CON

6.   _____ aggression in humans appears to parallel _____ aggression in animals.
   A.   Hostile; silent
   B.   Hostile; social
   C.   Instrumental; social
   D.   Social; silent
   Answer B, Type FAC

7. Of the following, which is the best example of instrumental aggression?
   A. An angry football player tackles a quarterback after he has attempted a long pass.
   B. A jealous wife finds her husband with another woman and shoots them both.
   C. A group of mercenaries, hired to kill the dictator of a small country, arrange to poison him.
   D. A man smashes his TV set after he cannot make it work.
   Answer C, Type CON

8. The death penalty has not been shown to effectively deter homicide. One reason is that most murders are the result of
   A. hormonal influences.
   B. hostile aggression.
   C. instrumental aggression.
   D. a malfunctioning amygdala.
   Answer B, Type FAC

9. Cold, calculated mob murders should be classified as
   A. genetically based.
   B. hostile aggression.
   C. instrumental aggression.
   D. silent aggression.
   Answer C, Type DEF

10. In analyzing the causes of aggression, social psychologists have focused on three primary ideas. Which of the following is not one of them?
    A. Aggression is a variable trait; some humans rarely behave aggressively, while others cannot control aggressive impulses.
    B. There is an inborn aggressive drive among human beings.
    C. Aggression is a natural response to frustration.
    D. Like other social behaviors, aggression is learned.
    Answer A, Type FAC

11. Instinctive behavior is behavior that is
    A. survival-oriented and common to most members of a species.
    B. innate, unlearned, and shown by all members of a species.
    C. reflexive and automatic but easily overcome by learning.
    D. the way members of a species ought to behave.
    Answer B, Type DEF

12. Sigmund Freud argued that aggression ultimately springs from
    A. an innate sexual drive.
    B. a primitive death urge.
    C. observation of aggressive adult models.
    D. blocking of goal-directed behavior.
    Answer B, Type FAC

13. Who among the following argued that there is an inborn aggressive drive?
    A. Bandura
    B. Berkowitz
    C. Lorenz
    D. Dollard
    Answer C, Type FAC

14. In contrast to Freud's view of aggression, Lorenz argued that

A.   aggression is innate.
B.   we have innate mechanisms for inhibiting aggression.
C.   aggression is biologically influenced but is not instinctive.
D.   aggression is socially learned.
Answer B, Type FAC

15.   Instinct theories of aggression would have the most difficulty accounting for
A.   silent and social aggression in animals.
B.   wide variations in aggressiveness from culture to culture.
C.   biochemical influences on aggression.
D.   unprovoked outbursts of aggression.
Answer B, Type FAC

16.   Which theory is most susceptible to the criticism of trying to explain aggression by naming it?
A.   instrumental aggression theory
B.   instinct theory
C.   frustration-aggression theory
D.   social-learning theory
Answer B, Type FAC

17.   The study of neural influences on aggression has indicated that
A.   no one region of the brain controls aggression.
B.   activating the amygdala can facilitate aggressive outbursts in humans.
C.   activating certain brain regions can cause a tyrant monkey to be more docile.
D.   All of the above.
Answer D, Type FAC

18.   Which of the following has not been shown to be a <u>biochemical</u> influence on aggression?
A.   alcohol
B.   the amygdala
C.   testosterone
D.   serotonin
Answer B, Type FAC

19.   Which of the following statements about aggression is true?
A.   Animals of many species can be bred for aggressiveness.
B.   A fearless, impulsive, temper-prone child is at risk for violent behavior in adolescence.
C.   Identical twins are more likely than fraternal twins to agree on whether they have violent tempers.
D.   All of the above.
Answer D, Type FAC

20.   Research on alcohol and aggression has indicated that
A.   violent people are both more likely to drink and more likely to become aggressive when intoxicated.
B.   people who have been drinking commit about half of all violent crimes.
C.   in experiments, intoxicated people administer stronger shocks.
D.   All of the above.
Answer D, Type FAC

21.   Research has shown that violence-prone children and adults have
A.   high levels of estrogen.
B.   genes that predispose them toward alcoholism.
C.   low levels of serotonin.

D.	low levels of testosterone.
Answer C, Type FAC

22.	Studies of hormonal influences on aggression indicate that
A.	hormonal influences are as strong in humans as they are in lower animals.
B.	after age 25, testosterone and rates of violent crime decrease together.
C.	variations in testosterone seem to have no effect on behavior within the normal range of teen boys and adult men.
D.	All of the above.
Answer B, Type FAC

23.	Research on neural, genetic, and biochemical influences on aggression suggest that
A.	aggression is inevitable in some individuals.
B.	violent behavior is biologically programmed into human nature.
C.	biological influences predispose some people more than others to react aggressively to conflict.
D.	None of the above.
Answer C, Type FAC

24.	Jessie's car had a flat tire in the rain. After she managed to fix it, she arrived home late only to have a parking spot just in front of her apartment taken by a faster driver. Coming home, she kicks her pet cat who is waiting at the door. Jessie's behavior is perhaps most easily explained in terms of
A.	frustration-aggression theory.
B.	the adaptation-level phenomenon.
C.	Murphy's law.
D.	social learning theory.
Answer A, Type CON

25.	The blocking of goal-directed behavior is called
A.	instrumental aggression.
B.	hostile aggression.
C.	frustration.
D.	displacement.
Answer C, Type DEF

26.	Frustration grows when
A.	our motivation to achieve a goal is very strong.
B.	we expected gratification.
C.	we are completely blocked in attaining our goal.
D.	All of the above.
Answer D, Type DEF

27.	The redirection of aggression to a target other than the source of frustration is referred to as
A.	displacement.
B.	substitution.
C.	instrumental aggression.
D.	projection.
Answer A, Type DEF

28.	After arguing with her boyfriend Peter over the telephone, Roberta smashes down the receiver and then throws the phone across the room. This behavior most clearly demonstrates
A.	the weapons effect.
B.	displacement.

C.   instrumental aggression.

D.   Parkinson's second law.

Answer B, Type CON

29.   Frustration triggers the most aggression when we perceive the frustration as

A.   inevitable.

B.   deserved.

C.   unjustified.

D.   unwelcome.

Answer C, Type FAC

30.   In a revision of frustration-aggression theory, Berkowitz maintained that frustration most directly produces

A.   anger.

B.   aggression.

C.   relative deprivation.

D.   arousal.

Answer A, Type FAC

31.   In a revision of frustration-aggression theory, Berkowitz emphasized the importance of

A.   aggressive cues, such as weapons.

B.   the role of biochemical influences, such as alcohol.

C.   relative deprivation and the adaptation level phenomenon.

D.   catharsis as a reducer of frustration.

Answer A, Type FAC

32.   Berkowitz and LePage (1967) found that frustrated men delivered more shocks when

A.   guns happened to be in the room.

B.   badminton racquets happened to be in the room.

C.   they had just received a shot that lowers serotonin levels.

D.   they were initially depressed.

Answer A, Type FAC

33.   Research suggests that the sight of a weapon can

A.   elicit frustration.

B.   sensitize one to the danger of violence.

C.   amplify aggression.

D.   produce catharsis.

Answer C, Type FAC

34.   Although Seattle, Washington, and Vancouver, British Columbia, share similar populations, climates, economies, and rates of criminal activity, Vancouver has a much lower overall murder rate because

A.   it has more space per person.

B.   it carefully restricts handgun ownership.

C.   it punishes violent crime more quickly and surely.

D.   its police force is twice as large as Seattle's.

Answer B, Type FAC

35.   After the Detroit riots of the late 1960s, the National Advisory Commission on Civil Disorders concluded that when there occurs a "revolution of _____," frustrations can escalate even while conditions improve.

A.   poverty

B.   abstinence

C.   helplessness

D.   rising expectations

Answer D, Type FAC

36.   An important conclusion of research on the sources of social and civil unrest is that frustration arises from

A.   a mismatch between achievements and rewards.

B.   the gap between expectations and attainments.

C.   deprivation of elements essential to survival.

D.   learned helplessness and hopelessness.

Answer B, Type FAC

37.   The top-rated objective among entering collegians in 1993 was

A.   raising a family.

B.   helping others in difficulty.

C.   finding fulfilling work.

D.   being very well off financially.

Answer D, Type FAC

38.   Which of the following best represents the trend in the United States over the last 30 years?

A.   increasing wealth and increasing well-being

B.   increasing wealth without increasing well-being

C.   increasing wealth and decreasing health

D.   increasing wealth without increasing health

Answer B, Type FAC

39.   In 1957, 35 percent of Americans surveyed reported themselves "very happy"; in 1996, after years of improving affluence, _____ declared themselves to be "very happy."

A.   twice as many

B.   51 percent

C.   30 percent

D.   only 12 percent

Answer C, Type FAC

40.   According to the _____, feelings of success, failure, satisfaction, and dissatisfaction are relative to prior achievements.

A.   relative attainment hypothesis

B.   achievement motivation syndrome

C.   social prestige principle

D.   adaptation-level phenomenon

Answer D, Type DEF

41.   Donna has been short of money and worried about her job security. Yesterday she was surprised to find she was being promoted and given a 10 percent raise. The adaptation-level phenomenon suggests that she will

A.   soon be financially worried again.

B.   have much better self-esteem from now on.

C.   behave much less aggressively from now on.

D.   be a much more ambitious, achievement-oriented worker now that she sees that her past behavior has paid off.

Answer A, Type CON

42.   In a study of the experiences of lottery winners, Brickman and his colleagues found that

A.   over time, their self-reported overall happiness increased.

B.   the moment of winning the lottery was not much of an emotional high.

C.   over time, ordinary activities like reading and eating a good breakfast became more pleasurable for them.

D.   None of the above.

Answer D, Type FAC

43.   The perception that one is less well off than others to whom one compares oneself is referred to as

A.   the adaptation level phenomenon.

B.   relative deprivation.

C.   Parkinson's second law.

D.   the unjust-world principle.

Answer B, Type DEF

44.   Arvid didn't work very hard on his last class essay assignment, so he was relieved at first to find he'd gotten a C on it. But when he learned that most of his classmates had gotten B's and A's, he felt unhappy and angry about his grade. Arvid's experience is best explained in terms of

A.   the adaptation-level phenomenon.

B.   the relative deprivation principle.

C.   displacement.

D.   Parkinson's second law.

Answer B, Type CON

45.   Hennigan and colleagues suggest that the larceny theft rate in U.S. cities jumped after television was first introduced because the thieves

A.   observed too much crime on television.

B.   felt deprived relative to wealthy television characters and those portrayed in advertisements.

C.   became more removed from the socializing influence of home and school.

D.   wanted but could not afford the luxury of a television set.

Answer B, Type FAC

46.   Klein (1997) told participants that they had either a 30% or 60% lifetime chance of developing pancreatic disease. People in the _____ condition were least disturbed when told the average was _____.

A.   60%; 80%

B.   30%; 10%

C.   30%; 30%

D.   60%; 60%

Answer A, Type FAC

47.   Relative deprivation is the likely result of _____ comparison, especially for people with _____ self-esteem.

A.   upward; shaky

B.   upward; solid

C.   downward; shaky

D.   downward; solid

Answer A, Type FAC

48.   People who are facing a severe personal threat often search for a silver lining by

A.   analyzing the cloud.

B.   comparing upward.

C.   comparing downward.

D.   displacing aggression onto a scapegoat.
Answer C, Type FAC

49.   Jeremy instigates more and more fights with younger children on the school playground because it gains him the attention and respect of his friends. This most clearly suggests that his aggression is
A.   the result of frustration.
B.   instinctive.
C.   a learned response.
D.   the result of displacement.
Answer C, Type CON

50.   According to Albert Bandura, an important influence on one's tendency to be aggressive is
A.   hormonal factors.
B.   how much anger or frustration has built up inside.
C.   one's hereditary predisposition to be aggressive.
D.   observations of others' behavior.
Answer D, Type FAC

51.   In a famous experiment by Albert Bandura and colleagues, children watched an adult attack a Bobo doll with a mallet. They were then shown some attractive toys they were forbidden to play with. When they were taken to another room, they
A.   began to cry.
B.   attacked a Bobo doll.
C.   verbally attacked the adult experimenter.
D.   chose to watch a violent rather than a nonviolent film.
Answer B, Type FAC

52.   Research on the role of family influences on aggression indicates that
A.   most abused children become abusive parents.
B.   higher rates of violence occur where father care is minimal.
C.   an only child tends to be more aggressive in social situations outside the family.
D.   All of the above.
Answer B, Type FAC

53.   Compared to the national rate, abused children are _____ times _____ likely to abuse their own children.
A.   4; less
B.   4; more
C.   30; more
D.   40; more
Answer B, Type FAC

54.   Research with children suggests that observing aggressive behavior can
A.   lower their inhibitions against aggression.
B.   teach them ways to be aggressive.
C.   lead them to imitate directly aggressive behavior.
D.   All of the above.
Answer D, Type CON

55.   According to social-learning theory, aversive experiences lead directly to
A.   aggression.
B.   anticipated negative consequences.
C.   emotional arousal.

D.   constructive problem solving.
Answer C, Type FAC

56.   According to social learning theory, aggression is most likely when we _____ and _____.
     A.   are aroused; it seems safe and rewarding to aggress
     B.   feel hopeless; alternative strategies to achieve important goals have failed
     C.   are deprived; see others profiting from aggression
     D.   suffer a loss of self-esteem; want to impress others
Answer A, Type FAC

57.   Research in the laboratory and in real life suggests that pain, personal attacks, and overcrowding are _____ experiences that _____ the likelihood of aggression.
     A.   aversive; increase
     B.   aversive; decrease
     C.   frustrating; do not affect
     D.   frustrating; decrease
Answer A, Type FAC

58.   In view of research on the pain-attack response, Leonard Berkowitz now believes that _____ is the basic trigger of hostile aggression.
     A.   aversive stimulation
     B.   neural impulses
     C.   frustration
     D.   rage
Answer A, Type FAC

59.   In relation to aggression, the most studied environmental irritant is
     A.   pain.
     B.   cigarette smoke.
     C.   air pollution.
     D.   heat.
Answer D, Type FAC

60.   In an experiment by William Griffitt, students who answered questionnaires while they were _____ reported feeling more tired and aggressive and expressed more hostility toward a stranger than did participants in a control group.
     A.   distracted by loud noise
     B.   in an uncomfortably hot room
     C.   being closely observed
     D.   eating popcorn and peanuts
Answer B, Type FAC

61.   Which of the following aversive events can trigger an angry emotional outburst?
     A.   overcrowding
     B.   a dashed expectation
     C.   a personal insult
     D.   All of the above
Answer D, Type FAC

62.   In most studies of attack aggression, competing participants get to choose how much shock to give the loser after they beat him or her in one round of a contest. Which of the following axioms seems to guide the behavior of participants who have received escalating shocks from a programmed opponent?

A.   "Turn the other cheek."
B.   "The word is mightier than the sword."
C.   "A soft answer turneth away wrath."
D.   "An eye for an eye."
Answer D, Type CON

63.   Crowding is defined
A.   as too many people in one place.
B.   as too little space for a person to feel a sense of control.
C.   as a feeling of not enough space per person.
D.   in terms of an objective assessment of density.
Answer C, Type DEF

64.   In Schachter and Singer's classic study, participants injected with adrenaline were exposed to either an angry or a euphoric confederate. Participants who expected the injection to make them feel _____ became _____ when placed with the angry confederate.
A.   aroused; angry
B.   aroused; euphoric
C.   no side effects; angry
D.   no side effects; euphoric
Answer C, Type FAC

65.   The results of the Schachter and Singer experiment in which participants were injected with adrenaline prior to waiting with either a hostile or euphoric person support the idea that
A.   bodily arousal feeds one emotion or another depending on how we interpret the arousal.
B.   distinct physiological differences exist among the emotions.
C.   frustration is largely a function of our prior experience and of whom we compare ourselves with.
D.   every emotion triggers an opposing emotion.
Answer A, Type FAC

66.   Imagine that Steve is driving home when a car cuts him off on the highway. Under which of the following conditions is he most likely to be enraged by this incident?
A.   when he's on his way home from a 12-hour shift at work
B.   when he's on his way home from a lecture on stress reduction and relaxation techniques
C.   when he's on his way home from an electrifying rock concert
D.   when he's on his way home from his mother's house
Answer C, Type CON

67.   Which of the following has been found to be an effect of modeling sexual violence in movies and television?
A.   women are more likely to believe rape is a serious crime
B.   men become more accepting of violence against women
C.   women become more aggressive toward other women
D.   All of the above
Answer B, Type FAC

68.   John Court reports that as pornographic materials have become more widely available, the rate of reported rapes has generally been found to
A.   decrease.
B.   increase.
C.   remain the same.
D.   increase in the short run but decrease in the long run.

Answer B, Type FAC

69. Laboratory experiments confirm that exposure to violent pornography
    A. increases punitive behavior toward women.
    B. increases punitive behavior toward both men and women.
    C. increases men's sympathy toward female victimization.
    D. None of the above.
    Answer A, Type FAC

70. Check and Malamuth reported that students who read erotic rape stories and were then debriefed about the study's true purpose were
    A. more accepting of the "women enjoy rape" myth than other participants.
    B. less accepting of the "women enjoy rape" myth than other participants.
    C. more likely to overestimate the occurrence of rape in society than other participants.
    D. more likely to underestimate the occurrence of rape in society than other participants.
    Answer B, Type FAC

71. Which of the following statements about rape is true?
    A. Most stranger rapes and nearly all acquaintance rapes go unreported to police.
    B. In surveys of students and working women, researchers have found that over one-quarter of women reported an experience that meets the legal definition of rape or attempted rape.
    C. About one-third of college males admit there is the possibility that they would rape a woman if they thought no one would know and they would not be punished.
    D. All of the above.
    Answer D, Type FAC

72. Sexually aggressive men typically
    A. are sexually promiscuous.
    B. exhibit hostility toward women.
    C. desire dominance.
    D. All of the above.
    Answer D, Type FAC

73. "Watching violence on television gives people a harmless opportunity to vent their aggression." This statement is most clearly consistent with the _____ hypothesis.
    A. sensitization
    B. catharsis
    C. frustration-aggression
    D. social learning
    Answer B, Type CON

74. As an alternative to strict censorship of pornography portraying sexual violence, many psychologists favor
    A. federal registration of all those producing and distributing pornographic materials.
    B. a heavy tax on the sale and distribution of pornographic materials.
    C. media awareness training designed to promote critical viewing skills.
    D. more adequate control of who is allowed to purchase pornographic materials.
    Answer C, Type FAC

75. Research in the United States, Europe, and Australia has consistently found that
    A. the relation between TV viewing and violence seems to be explained by family size.
    B. more aggressive children become adults who prefer to watch violent TV.
    C. the more violent the content of a child's TV viewing, the more aggressive the child.

D.   TV has had no discernible effects on homicide rates.
Answer C, Type FAC

76.   Experimental evidence on the effects of viewing television violence leads to the conclusion that
    A.   an aggressive predisposition in children causes a preference for TV violence.
    B.   viewing TV violence increases violence.
    C.   viewing TV violence causes increased serotonin levels in adolescent boys.
    D.   viewing prime-time TV violence, but not cartoon violence, increases violence.
Answer B, Type FAC

77.   The conclusion of the Surgeon General and researchers on the relationship between violence in television and real-life aggressive behavior is best stated as the following:
    A.   Television is a primary cause of social violence.
    B.   Television is not correlated with social violence.
    C.   Television is a controllable cause of social violence.
    D.   Television violence and social aggression are correlated but are not causally linked.
Answer C, Type FAC

78.   Television violence can affect social behavior in all but which of the following ways?
    A.   Viewing violence produces a catharsis or release of aggressive energy.
    B.   Viewing violence produces arousal in viewers.
    C.   Viewing violence produces disinhibition in viewers.
    D.   Media portrayals of violence evoke imitation.
Answer A, Type FAC

79.   Fourteen-year-old Kevin frequently watches violent television programs. This will most likely lead him to
    A.   experience more distress at the sight of teens fighting on the streets.
    B.   underestimate the actual frequency of violent crimes in the world.
    C.   become more interested in resolving the conflict between two of his personal friends.
    D.   become more fearful of being criminally assaulted.
Answer D, Type CON

80.   Surveys of children and adolescents indicate that heavy viewers of TV violence
    A.   become desensitized to violence.
    B.   exaggerate the frequency of violence in the world.
    C.   are more fearful of being personally assaulted.
    D.   All of the above.
Answer D, Type FAC

81.   According to the text, groups can amplify aggressive reactions through the processes of
    A.   groupthink and minority influence.
    B.   social loafing and social facilitation.
    C.   crowding and conservative shift.
    D.   diffusion of responsibility and polarization.
Answer D, Type FAC

82.   Researchers have found that in both the laboratory and real world contexts, increased aggression is predicted by
    A.   the presence of weapons.
    B.   male actors.
    C.   group interaction.
    D.   All of the above.
Answer D, Type FAC

83. It is the near consensus among social psychologists today that the catharsis hypothesis of aggressive expression, as Freud, Lorenz, and their followers supposed,
    A. has not been confirmed.
    B. works with aggressive action but not with aggressive fantasy.
    C. works for women but not for men.
    D. is well supported in most conditions and circumstances.
    Answer A, Type FAC

84. The social-learning approach suggests that to reduce aggression we should
    A. model cooperative, nonaggressive behavior.
    B. reward cooperative, nonaggressive behavior.
    C. ignore aggressive behavior.
    D. All of the above.
    Answer D, Type FAC

85. Which of the following would be the best advice to give parents who are concerned about the frequent aggressive outbursts of their 8-year-old daughter?
    A. "Encourage your daughter to express her anger by attacking an old piece of furniture specifically set aside for that purpose."
    B. "Spank your daughter for temper tantrums as well as for fighting with her brother."
    C. "Make a point of rewarding and praising your daughter whenever she is socially cooperative and helpful."
    D. "Encourage your daughter to view the devastating consequences of violence portrayed on television."
    Answer C, Type CON

The following items also appear in the Study Guide:

86. The murders committed by mobster "hit men" provide an example of
    A. emotional aggression.
    B. silent aggression.
    C. how catharsis can reduce aggression.
    D. instrumental aggression.
    Answer D, Type FAC

87. Which of the following is false?
    A. Animals' social aggression and silent aggression seem to involve the same brain region.
    B. Alcohol enhances violence by reducing people's self-awareness.
    C. Low levels of serotonin are often found in the violence-prone
    D. "Hostile" aggression springs from emotions such as anger.
    Answer A, Type FAC

88. Compared to prisoners convicted of nonviolent crimes, those convicted of unprovoked violent crimes tend to
    A. be first-borns.
    B. have authoritarian attitudes.
    C. be older.
    D. have higher testosterone levels.
    Answer D, Type FAC

89. To know whether people are frustrated, we need to know
    A. their expectations and their attainments.
    B. their level of deprivation and their power.
    C. their wants and their intelligence.

D.   their needs and their age.
Answer A, Type FAC

90.   The fact that affluent people often feel as frustrated as those who have less can be understood in terms of
A.   the catharsis hypothesis.
B.   the weapons effect.
C.   displacement.
D.   the adaptation-level phenomenon.
Answer D, Type FAC

91.   Emotional arousal plus anticipated consequences provides the formula for aggression according to
A.   ethological theory.
B.   catharsis theory.
C.   frustration-aggression theory.
D.   social learning theory.
Answer D, Type DEF

92.   Which of the following is false?
A.   Pain heightens aggressiveness in animals but not in humans.
B.   Being insulted by another is especially conducive to aggression.
C.   In laboratory experiments heat triggers retaliative actions.
D.   According to social learning theory, aggression is most likely when we are aroused and it seems safe and rewarding to aggress.
Answer A, Type FAC

93.   Living three to a room in a college dorm seems to
A.   diminish one's sense of control.
B.   lead to the establishment of stronger friendships.
C.   lead to more hostile but less instrumental aggression.
D.   improve grades because students are more likely to study in the library.
Answer A, Type FAC

94.   According to the author of the text, television's most influential effect may be that it
A.   desensitizes people to violence around them.
B.   is the major cause of social violence.
C.   presents an unreal picture of the world.
D.   replaces other activities that people might engage in.
Answer D, Type FAC

95.   Which of the following would be an example of aggression as defined in the text?
A.   A wife deliberately belittles her husband in front of friends after he burns the pot roast.
B.   A golfer accidentally hits another player with a golf ball.
C.   A nurse gives a penicillin shot to a child.
D.   A salesman tops his previous record by selling 50 cars in one month.
Answer A, Type CON

96.   A person kicking a cat after losing a game of checkers is an example of
A.   regression.
B.   displacement.
C.   relative deprivation.
D.   the weapons effect.
Answer B, Type CON

97. A 65-degree day seems warm in February but cold in July. This is best explained in terms of
    A.   relative deprivation.
    B.   the adaptation-level phenomenon.
    C.   displacement.
    D.   Parkinson's second law.
    Answer B, Type CON

98. John has just received a 5 percent increase in salary. However, after learning that his coworkers have all received 10 percent increases, John becomes angry with his employer. We can understand John's feelings in terms of
    A.   relative deprivation.
    B.   the adaptation-level phenomenon.
    C.   Parkinson's second law.
    D.   the hydraulic model of aggression.
    Answer A, Type CON

99. As part of therapy, a clinical psychologist encourages her patients to install a punching bag in their homes to release hostility. The therapist apparently believes in
    A.   social learning theory.
    B.   Parkinson's second law.
    C.   the catharsis hypothesis.
    D.   the adaptation-level phenomenon.
    Answer C, Type CON

100. Which of the following is the best example of instrumental aggression?
    A.   An angry football player tackles a quarterback after he has completed a long pass.
    B.   A jealous wife finds her husband with another woman and shoots both of them.
    C.   A group of former soldiers kill the dictator of a small country for $10,000.
    D.   A man smashes his television set after he finds it does not work
    Answer C, Type CON

Critical Thinking Questions

101. What is aggression? Based on your own experiences, give an example of hostile aggression and an example of instrumental aggression.

102. Compare and contrast the frustration-aggression theory and the social learning theory of aggression.

103. Discuss the relationship between physiological arousal and emotion.

104. Research suggests that catharsis neither occurs nor effectively reduces aggression, yet the notion of catharsis and its therapeutic effects is widely believed. Why?

105. Given what we know about the causes of aggression and the factors that contribute to its expression, suggest five strategies for reducing aggression in our society.

Multiple Choice Questions

1. A motivation to bond with others in relationships that provide ongoing, positive interactions is the definition for
   A. association anxiety.
   B. the need for attachment.
   C. the need to belong.
   D. affiliative predisposition.
   Answer C, Type DEF

2. One factor that will increase the likelihood that a friendship will develop is
   A. the degree to which their interests compliment yours.
   B. how often your paths cross.
   C. avoiding repetitious exposure.
   D. All of the above.
   Answer B, Type FAC

3. Research on proximity and social attraction generally supports the view that
   A. familiarity breeds contempt.
   B. familiarity leads to liking.
   C. proximity leads to affection and animosity with equal frequency.
   D. distance makes the heart grow fonder.
   Answer B, Type FAC

4. Functional distance refers to
   A. the natural geographic route between two locations.
   B. the distance between residences "as the crow flies."
   C. how often people's paths cross.
   D. the direction and route of travel one undertakes when deliberately seeking out a given person.
   Answer C, Type DEF

5. If you are new in the office and want to make new friends, your best bet is to get a desk
   A. that is smaller than that of anyone else.
   B. in the quietest corner of the office.
   C. near the coffeepot.
   D. next to the air conditioner.
   Answer C, Type CON

6. Research suggests that randomly assigned college roommates
   A. will most likely become friends.
   B. will likely be unhappy about the assignment and come to dislike each other.
   C. are as likely to become enemies as they are to become friends.
   D. will show initial attraction that fades over time.
   Answer A, Type CON

7. Penny has just arrived as a new student on campus and does not know anyone. All else being equal, is she most likely to become friends with Joni who lives next door, with Crissy who lives

two doors down, with Beth who lives three doors down, or with Helda who lives in the room directly above?
A. Joni
B. Crissy
C. Beth
D. Helda
Answer A, Type CON

8. Darley and Berscheid gave university women ambiguous information about two other women. Asked how much they liked each other, the participants reported feeling more attracted to the person whom they
A. expected they would probably not meet.
B. expected they would eventually meet.
C. had read about first.
D. had read about second.
Answer B, Type FAC

9. The text suggests that our tendency to like people with whom we need to have continuing interactions even though we may not have chosen them
A. short-circuits critical thinking.
B. leads to inefficient use of time.
C. is adaptive.
D. demonstrates how the need to belong becomes dysfunctional.
Answer C, Type FAC

10. Anticipatory liking—expecting that someone will be pleasant and compatible—increases the chance of
A. becoming involved in an inequitable relationship.
B. a dysfunctional, co-dependent relationship.
C. being exploited in the early stages of a relationship.
D. a rewarding relationship.
Answer D, Type FAC

11. The tendency for novel stimuli to be liked more after repeated exposure to them is referred to as
A. the mere exposure effect.
B. the novelty phenomenon.
C. display liking.
D. proactive stimulation.
Answer A, Type DEF

12. Robert Zajonc found that the mere exposure effect works with which of the following stimuli?
A. nonsense syllables
B. people's faces
C. musical selections
D. All of the above.
Answer D, Type FAC

13. The mere exposure effect will be stronger
A. when people perceive stimuli without awareness.
B. if the repetitions are incessant rather than distributed over time.
C. if one's initial reactions to the stimulus are negative.
D. for animate than for inanimate objects.
Answer A, Type FAC

14. In experiments by Robert Zajonc and his coworkers, participants were exposed to brief novel passages of music while they focused their attention on other tasks. Results indicated that mere exposure leads to liking
    A. only when the exposed stimulus is task-related.
    B. only when people are consciously attending to the exposed stimulus.
    C. even when people are unaware of what they have been exposed to.
    D. unless background stimuli create a distraction and interfere with the processing of the task.
    Answer C, Type FAC

15. On the basis of his research on the mere exposure effect, Robert Zajonc argues that our emotions are often more _____ than our thinking.
    A. sophisticated
    B. instantaneous and primitive
    C. slowly aroused
    D. complex
    Answer B, Type FAC

16. Zajonc has demonstrated that the more times people see a foreign word, the more likely they are
    A. to say it means something good.
    B. to say it means something bad.
    C. to dislike the word once they find out what it means.
    D. to like the word, but only after they find out what it means.
    Answer A, Type FAC

17. When Mita, Dermer, and Knight showed women and their close friends photographs of the women and asked them to state their preferences among them, they found that the women themselves liked the _____ photographs best.
    A. black-and-white
    B. color
    C. mirror-image
    D. true-image
    Answer C, Type FAC

18. The fact that people prefer letters appearing in their own name illustrates
    A. the belongingness effect.
    B. the proximity effect.
    C. the mere exposure effect.
    D. the matching effect.
    Answer C, Type FAC

19. A political campaign booklet seems to be applying the _____ when it says, "Repetition breeds familiarity and familiarity breeds trust."
    A. matching phenomenon
    B. mere exposure effect
    C. equity principle
    D. disclosure reciprocity effect
    Answer B, Type CON

20. A young woman's physical attractiveness is a moderately good predictor of
    A. how frequently she dates.
    B. her ultimate educational level.
    C. her marital happiness.

D.   All of the above.
Answer A, Type FAC

21.   Researchers provide men and women students with various pieces of information about someone of the other sex, including a picture of the person or a brief introduction, and later ask them how interested they are in dating the participant. Results show that
A.   women are as influenced by a man's looks as men are by a woman's.
B.   men are somewhat more influenced by a woman's looks than women are by a man's.
C.   women are somewhat more influenced by a man's looks than men are by a woman's.
D.   men are influenced by a woman's looks, while women are not influenced at all by a man's looks.
Answer B, Type FAC

22.   Elaine Hatfield and her coworkers matched University of Minnesota freshmen for a Welcome Week computer dance. When the students were asked to evaluate their dates, what determined whether they liked each other?
A.   similarity of values
B.   similarity of academic competence
C.   physical attractiveness
D.   common family background
Answer C, Type FAC

23.   Men who place a personal ad that emphasizes their income and education
A.   receive more responses to their ads.
B.   receive fewer responses to their ads.
C.   are rated as less desirable by women.
D.   are more likely to attract unattractive women.
Answer A, Type FAC

24.   Researchers have found that people tend to pair off with partners who are about as attractive as themselves. This is known as
A.   physical equity.
B.   the matching phenomenon.
C.   the reciprocity effect.
D.   the attractiveness stereotype.
Answer B, Type DEF

25.   When Gregory White studied some UCLA dating couples, he found that those who were most similar in physical attractiveness were most likely, nine months later, to have
A.   fallen more deeply in love with each other.
B.   broken up.
C.   less passionate but more companionate relationships.
D.   ingratiating but inequitable relationships.
Answer A, Type FAC

26.   When people describe themselves in personal ads seeking partners of the other sex, women often offer _____ and seek _____.
A.   companionship; attractiveness
B.   attractiveness; status
C.   status; companionship
D.   commitment; excitement
Answer B, Type FAC

27.   The preference for those who are physically attractive is evident among

    A.   adults judging adults and children.

    B.   children judging other children.

    C.   babies gazing at faces.

    D.   All of the above.

Answer D, Type FAC

28.   Clifford and Hatfield showed fifth-grade teachers identical information about a boy or girl, with the photograph attached of an attractive or unattractive child. The teachers judged _____ as being _____.

    A.   attractive children; more honest and concerned about others

    B.   unattractive children; more independent and assertive

    C.   attractive children; more intelligent and successful in school

    D.   unattractive children; less popular but probably harder workers and better students

Answer C, Type FAC

29.   Which of the following best expresses the meaning of the physical attractiveness stereotype?

    A.   What is beautiful is good.

    B.   What is beautiful is unpredictable.

    C.   What is beautiful is superficial.

    D.   What is beautiful is untouchable.

Answer A, Type FAC

30.   Kalick had Harvard students indicate their impressions of eight women, judging from photos taken before or after cosmetic surgery, and found that

    A.   presurgery women were judged to be more genuine, honest, and appealing.

    B.   postsurgery women were judged to be kinder and more likable.

    C.   presurgery women were judged to be more intelligent and competent.

    D.   postsurgery women were judged to be more independent and insensitive.

Answer B, Type FAC

31.   Which of the following traits is not assumed of physically attractive people?

    A.   intelligence

    B.   happiness

    C.   sexual warmth

    D.   honesty

Answer D, Type FAC

32.   According to the text, attractiveness probably most affects

    A.   long-term romantic relationships.

    B.   first impressions.

    C.   the likelihood of academic success.

    D.   co-habiting couples rather than married couples.

Answer B, Type FAC

33.   Small average differences between attractive and unattractive people in areas like self-confidence and social skills are probably the result of

    A.   self-fulfilling prophecies.

    B.   personality traits that are genetically linked with physical appearance.

    C.   psychological reactance to social expectations.

    D.   social and economic differences in family background.

Answer A, Type FAC

34.   People judge men as more attractive if they have features that suggest

    A.   dominance.

B.   sociability.
C.   baby-faced youth.
D.   nondominance.
Answer A, Type FAC

35.   Studies of computer composites of faces show that
A.   perfectly average is quite attractive.
B.   perfectly average is quite unattractive.
C.   modest caricatures of attractive features are quite unattractive.
D.   None of the above.
Answer A, Type FAC

36.   The evolutionary view of physical attractiveness is supported by research showing that men in
       many cultures worldwide prefer female characteristics that signify
A.   high energy.
B.   sociability.
C.   reproductive potential.
D.   maturity and dominance.
Answer C, Type FAC

37.   To men who have recently been viewing pornographic material, average women seem _____
       attractive, confirming the _____.
A.   more; contrast effect
B.   more; mere exposure effect
C.   less; contrast effect
D.   less; mere exposure effect
Answer C, Type FAC

38.   Commenting on the relationship between love and perceived attractiveness, Miller and Simpson
       note, "The grass may be greener on the other side, but happy gardeners are
A.   less likely to notice."
B.   not interested in grass."
C.   always flitting from flower to flower."
D.   the most critical gardeners of all."
Answer A, Type FAC

39.   At a party, Ellie meets Rob and Blake. The three get involved in a philosophical discussion that
       lasts through the evening. By the end of the evening she has discovered that she and Blake see
       things eye-to-eye, whereas she and Rob see things differently. All else equal, Ellie will probably
A.   like Rob better.
B.   like Blake better.
C.   like Rob and Blake equally.
D.   like a stranger she merely anticipates meeting more than either Rob or Blake.
Answer B, Type CON

40.   In a classic study, Newcomb found that among students who lived together in a boardinghouse
       for many weeks, the ones who were most likely to have formed close friendships were those who
A.   were most similar in level of physical attractiveness.
B.   had the highest initial agreement on attitudes.
C.   had opposite but complementary personality characteristics.
D.   came from the same region or state.
Answer B, Type FAC

41.   Which of the following proverbs finds greatest support in the research on social attraction?

A. "Familiarity breeds contempt."
B. "Absence makes the heart grow fonder."
C. "You can't tell a book by its cover."
D. "Birds of a feather flock together."
Answer D, Type CON

42. When Sprecher and Duck put 83 student couples together on a blind get-acquainted date, the 16 who saw each other again were especially likely to
A. see themselves as having different but complementary personality needs.
B. have engaged debate over some important issue on their first date.
C. have lived in a multicultural setting as children.
D. see themselves as similar to one another.
Answer D, Type FAC

43. Brent is a White man who has been given a choice to work with Darwin or Ken. Darwin is a Black man who shares many of Brent's values and attitudes. Ken is a White man who shares little in common with Brent. Who will Brent like most and want to work with?
A. Darwin
B. Ken
C. All else equal, his liking will be equally high for both Darwin and Ken.
D. All else equal, his liking will be equally low for both Darwin and Ken.
Answer A, Type CON

44. According to the _____ hypothesis, people are attracted to those whose needs are different in ways that complete each other.
A. accentuation
B. matching
C. complementarity
D. reciprocity
Answer C, Type DEF

45. Which of the following proverbs is clearly not supported by the research findings?
A. "Opposites attract."
B. "Familiarity breeds fondness."
C. "Out of sight, out of mind."
D. "Even virtue is fairer in a fair body."
Answer A, Type CON

46. The tendency for opposites to mate or marry
A. has only been documented among teenage couples.
B. has increased in the United States since 1960.
C. is just as powerful as the similarity-attraction connection.
D. has never been reliably demonstrated.
Answer D, Type FAC

47. Berscheid and colleagues asked students how much they liked people who had evaluated them. They found that students liked a rater who had said eight positive things about them _____ compared to another rater who had said seven positive things and one negative thing about them.
A. much less
B. slightly less
C. about the same
D. more
Answer D, Type FAC

48. _____ includes strategies, such as flattery, by which people seek to gain another's favor.
    A.   Social elicitation
    B.   Self-disclosure
    C.   Social penetration
    D.   Ingratiation
    Answer D, Type DEF

49. Our tendency to like those we perceive as liking us is influenced by which of the following factors?
    A.   our attributions for why they seem to like us
    B.   the degree of complementarity that exists between us and them
    C.   the degree of exposure to them
    D.   their demographic uniqueness
    Answer A, Type FAC

50. Hatfield gave university women evaluations, affirming the self-esteem of some and wounding others with negative evaluations. Each participant was then asked to evaluate a man who had earlier asked her for a date. Women whose evaluations had been _____ expressed _____ the man.
    A.   positive; more liking of
    B.   negative; more liking of
    C.   positive; more hostility toward
    D.   negative; more hostility toward
    Answer B, Type FAC

51. Research by Aronson and Linder (1965) suggests that more often than not, we like people more if they
    A.   consistently evaluate us positively.
    B.   reverse an earlier criticism and come to evaluate us positively.
    C.   consistently give us ingratiating feedback.
    D.   consistently give us constructive criticism.
    Answer B, Type FAC

52. According to Elliot Aronson, "as a relationship ripens toward greater intimacy, what becomes increasingly important is
    A.   the absence of conflict."
    B.   consistent praise."
    C.   autonomy."
    D.   authenticity."
    Answer D, Type FAC

53. The fact that we like those people whom we associate with good feelings is most clearly consistent with the _____ theory of attraction.
    A.   cognitive dissonance
    B.   reward
    C.   two-factor
    D.   James-Lange
    Answer B, Type DEF

54. In research at the University of Warsaw, Lewicki asked students to choose which person in two photographs looked friendlier and found that their choices were almost always influenced by whether or not the photographs
    A.   were of men or women.

B.   looked like their own friends.
C.   were in color or black-and-white.
D.   reminded them of friendly or unfriendly experimenters.
Answer D, Type FAC

55.   The advice to continue having romantic dinners, trips to the theatre, and vacations once married would most probably be offered by
A.   mere exposure theory.
B.   the triangle theory.
C.   equity theory.
D.   reward theory.
Answer D, Type CON

56.   Which theory provides the best explanation for the effects of proximity, similarity, and attractiveness on liking?
A.   triangle theory
B.   reward theory
C.   disclosure theory
D.   attachment theory
Answer B, Type FAC

57.   According to the text, the first step in scientifically studying romantic love is to
A.   define and measure it.
B.   manipulate it.
C.   control all other factors that might influence it.
D.   study the factors that might influence it.
Answer A, Type FAC

58.   Psychologist Robert Sternberg views love as a triangle whose three sides include all but which of the following?
A.   attachment
B.   passion
C.   commitment
D.   intimacy
Answer A, Type FAC

59.   Eros is to _____ as storge is to _____.
A.   game playing; passion
B.   passion; game playing
C.   friendship; game playing
D.   passion; friendship
Answer D, Type CON

60.   Which of the following is one of the three components assessed by Zick Rubin's Love Scale?
A.   respect
B.   caring
C.   commitment
D.   friendship
Answer B, Type DEF

61.   Hatfield defines _____ as a state of intense longing for union with another.
A.   attraction anxiety
B.   storge
C.   passionate love

D.   intimate attraction

Answer C, Type DEF

62.   The two-factor theory of emotion suggests that passionate love can be increased by
A.   mere exposure.
B.   the matching phenomenon.
C.   secure attachment.
D.   physical arousal.

Answer D, Type DEF

63.   Dutton and Aron had interviewers approach men crossing bridges in a scenic state park, ask them to complete questionnaires, and give them their phone numbers in case the men wanted to call them. Results showed that participants were most likely to call the interviewer if they had been interviewed by a
A.   woman on a low, secure bridge.
B.   woman on a high, wobbly bridge.
C.   man on a low, secure bridge.
D.   man on a high, wobbly bridge.

Answer B, Type FAC

64.   Which theory suggests that love is a function of physiological arousal along with the label that we give to our arousal?
A.   triangle theory
B.   two-factor theory
C.   correspondent inference theory
D.   reward theory

Answer B, Type DEF

65.   Snyder and Simpson report that, compared to low self-monitors, high self-monitors are more
A.   affected by a prospective date's physical appearance.
B.   willing to end a relationship in favor of a new partner.
C.   sexually promiscuous.
D.   All of the above.

Answer D, Type FAC

66.   In comparison to women, men fall in love more _____ and out of love more
_____.
A.   readily; readily
B.   slowly; slowly
C.   readily; slowly
D.   slowly; readily

Answer C, Type FAC

67.   The subjective experience of passionate love is most influenced by which of the following factors?
A.   similarity
B.   proximity
C.   gender
D.   complementarity

Answer C, Type FAC

68.   The affection we feel for those with whom our lives are deeply intertwined is called
A.   companionate love.
B.   storge.

C.   secure attachment.

D.   committed friendship.

Answer A, Type DEF

69.   A study of 50 couples in India found that after five years of marriage those in love-based marriages reported _____ feelings of love and those in arranged marriages showed _____ feelings of love.

A.   stable; decreasing

B.   decreasing; increased

C.   increased; stable

D.   stable; increased

Answer B, Type FAC

70.   Simpson, Campbell, and Berscheid (1986) suspect that the rising divorce rate over the past 20 to 30 years is at least partly due to

A.   the growing importance of passionate love in people's lives.

B.   the growing importance of companionate love in people's lives.

C.   the decreasing importance of passionate love in people's lives.

D.   the decreasing importance of storge love in people's lives.

Answer A, Type FAC

71.   Twelve-month-old Joshua enters an unfamiliar laboratory playroom with his mother. When she leaves, he gets distressed. When she returns, he runs to her and hugs her close. After this intense reunion he returns to playing. Joshua demonstrates the characteristics of _____ attachment.

A.   secure

B.   insecure

C.   avoidant

D.   ambivalent

Answer A, Type CON

72.   Which adult attachment style is marked by individuals being less invested in relationships and more likely to engage in one-night stands?

A.   secure

B.   insecure

C.   anxious-ambivalent

D.   avoidant

Answer D, Type FAC

73.   When benefits are proportional to contributions in a relationship,

A.   equality necessarily exists.

B.   mutuality exists.

C.   equity exists.

D.   companionate love exists.

Answer C, Type DEF

74.   Melanie believes that her boyfriend enjoys far more benefits from their relationship than she does, even though she invests more time, effort, and resources in their friendship. Clearly Melanie believes that her relationship with her boyfriend lacks

A.   equity.

B.   attachment.

C.   disclosure reciprocity.

D.   loyalty.

Answer A, Type CON

75. Margaret and Leah have invested in a small business venture together. Their initial capital investment totaled $15,000, with Margaret putting up $10,000 and Leah supplying $5,000. In their first year they net $21,000 profit. Which of the following distributions of their profits is equitable?
    A.   It depends on Margaret and Leah's respective needs.
    B.   Margaret gets $14,000 and Leah gets $7,000.
    C.   Margaret and Leah each get $10,500.
    D.   An equitable distribution is not possible because they invested different amounts to begin with.
    Answer B, Type CON

76. Those involved in relationships marked by long-term equity
    A.   depend on tit-for-tat exchanges.
    B.   are unconcerned with short-term equity.
    C.   make sure they reciprocate favors as soon as possible.
    D.   None of the above.
    Answer B, Type FAC

77. In studies at the University of Maryland, Clark, and Mills found that tit-for-tat exchanges _____ people's liking for each other when _____.
    A.   boosted; their relationship was relatively formal
    B.   diminished; they sought true friendship
    C.   Both A and B.
    D.   None of the above.
    Answer C, Type FAC

78. A survey of several hundred married couples revealed that spouses who perceived inequity in the marriage felt more
    A.   depressed.
    B.   hostility.
    C.   altruistic satisfaction.
    D.   motivated to work on the marriage.
    Answer A, Type FAC

79. Self-disclosure involves
    A.   protecting oneself by closing off part of oneself from others.
    B.   stopping oneself from getting involved in an intimate relationship.
    C.   revealing intimate aspects of oneself to others.
    D.   closing down emotionally.
    Answer C, Type DEF

80. The tendency for one person's intimacy of self-disclosure to match that of a conversational partner is referred to as
    A.   the matching phenomenon.
    B.   disclosure reciprocity.
    C.   reciprocal exchange.
    D.   mutual self-revelation.
    Answer B, Type DEF

81. In a recent experiment, researchers found that compared to students who engaged in 45 minutes of small talk, those engaged in 45 minutes of escalating self-disclosure felt _____ at the end of the study.

A. vulnerable and exposed
B. isolated and lonely
C. dislike for their conversation partner
D. remarkably close to their conversation partner

Answer D, Type FAC

82. In addition to love and satisfaction, close relationships that last are rooted in
    A. fear of the costs of ending the relationship.
    B. a sense of moral obligation to the relationship.
    C. inattention to possible alternative partners.
    D. All of the above.

    Answer D, Type FAC

83. Compared to those in collectivistic cultures, couples in individualistic cultures are more likely to
    A. emphasize passion and romance in a marriage.
    B. expect personal fulfillment in a marriage.
    C. get divorced.
    D. All of the above.

    Answer D, Type FAC

84. John Gottman's observation of 2000 couples led him to conclude that healthy marriages are marked by
    A. an absence of conflict.
    B. an ability to reconcile differences and to overbalance criticism with affection.
    C. success in maintaining the passion of initial romance.
    D. both parties having fulfilling work as well as friends and relatives who provide social support.

    Answer B, Type FAC

85. According to the text, sustained satisfaction in close relationships depends on
    A. the time and effort people put into them.
    B. maintaining equality of each partner's inputs.
    C. a certain amount of complementarity between partners.
    D. the religiosity of the partners.

    Answer A, Type FAC

The following items also appear in the Study Guide:

86. The need to belong and to form close interpersonal relationships
    A. is at the core of our existence and thus is characteristic of people everywhere.
    B. is largely a 20th century motive that is most evident in industrialized societies.
    C. is a learned motive serving our more fundamental need for self-esteem.
    D. conflicts with our more basic need to survive.

    Answer A, Type FAC

87. Which of the following principles is supported by the research on social attraction?
    A. Familiarity breeds fondness.
    B. Opposites attract.
    C. Beauty times brains equals a constant.
    D. Absence makes the heart grow fonder.

    Answer A, Type FAC

88. Based on research presented in the text, if you go out on a blind date you would be most influenced by your date's

A.   open-mindedness.
B.   sense of humor.
C.   physical attractiveness.
D.   sincerity.
Answer C, Type FAC

89.   In terms of adult attachment styles, _____ individuals seem to be possessive and jealous, while _____ individuals are less invested in relationships and more likely to leave them.
A.   secure; insecure
B.   anxious-ambivalent; avoidant
C.   avoidant; anxious-ambivalent
D.   insecure; apathetic
Answer B, Type FAC

90.   People seem to have a lower risk of divorce if they
A.   had parents who divorced.
B.   live in a large city.
C.   cohabited before marriage.
D.   are religiously committed.
Answer D, Type FAC

91.   Which of the following is true?
A.   Companionate love typically leads to romantic love.
B.   Self-disclosure reduces feelings of romantic love.
C.   Companionate love is more likely to endure when both partners feel it to be equitable.
D.   Spouses who pray together are more likely to report conflict in their marriage.
Answer C, Type FAC

92.   An employee who feels underpaid may demand an increase in wages or exert less effort at his or her task. This behavior is an
A.   attempt to restore equity.
B.   attempt to achieve complementarity.
C.   example of the matching phenomenon.
D.   example of the overexposure effect.
Answer A, Type CON

93.   Tom, who tends to be extraverted, has just moved into the dormitory at Federal College. He is most likely to make friends with
A.   Bill, his next-door neighbor.
B.   John, a chemistry major who lives across campus.
C.   Michael, an introvert who lives on the next floor.
D.   Stuart, a student who lives off campus and who loves dogs.
Answer A, Type CON

94.   Mary, who is attractive, very intelligent, and high in social status, marries Tom, who is also attractive, very intelligent, and high in social status. Their relationship is best understood as an example of
A.   the ingratiation effect.
B.   complementarity.
C.   the mere-exposure effect.
D.   the matching phenomenon.
Answer D, Type CON

95. Some years ago, a mysterious student enveloped in a big, black bag began attending a speech class at a state university. While the teacher knew "Black Bag's" identity, the other students did not. As the semester progressed, the students' attitude toward Black Bag changed from hostility to curiosity to friendship. What may best explain the students' change in attitude?
    A. Exposure breeds liking.
    B. Stress produces affiliation.
    C. Boredom breeds a liking for the novel.
    D. Similarity attracts.
    Answer A, Type CON

96. Mary, a talkative, extraverted young woman, is strongly attracted to Ronald, a quiet, introverted, middle-aged man. Mary's attraction to Ronald would be best explained by
    A. exchange theory.
    B. the matching phenomenon.
    C. the equity principle.
    D. the complementarity hypothesis.
    Answer D, Type CON

97. You overhear a casual acquaintance express approval of you in the coffee shop. You are most likely to think well of that acquaintance if
    A. you had learned an hour earlier that you had received an average grade on a history test.
    B. you had learned an hour earlier that you had failed a chemistry test.
    C. the acquaintance is unattractive.
    D. the acquaintance is engaged to be married.
    Answer B, Type CON

98. Joe, a college sophomore, has dated several women for short periods of time. His dating preferences are strongly influenced by physical appearance and he quickly ends a relationship in favor of a new partner. Joe is probably
    A. high in self-monitoring.
    B. low in self-monitoring.
    C. low in authoritarianism.
    D. high in authoritarianism.
    Answer A, Type CON

99. Bill and Sara's relationship becomes progressively more intimate as each engages in a bit more self-revelation in response to the other's self-disclosure. Their relationship is marked by the _____ effect.
    A. disclosure reciprocity
    B. mutual disinhibition
    C. reciprocal disinhibition
    D. reciprocal intimacy
    Answer A, Type CON

100. A stranger rides the same bus you do to school every day. According to the mere exposure effect, as the days pass you will come to view the stranger
    A. merely as another student.
    B. more unfavorably.
    C. more critically.
    D. more favorably.
    Answer D, Type CON

Critical Thinking Questions

101. List and briefly explain the four factors that lead to initial attraction.

102. In your opinion, why is the complementarity hypothesis so widely believed despite the fact that attraction research repeatedly fails to confirm it?

103. What are the similarities and differences between what Sternberg (1988) and the text refer to as companionate love and what Sternberg calls consummate love?

104. Explain equity theory of attraction. How does it apply differently to initial relationships compared to long-term relationships?

105. Apply the attitudes-follow-behavior principle to explain how couples can increase their chances of maintaining a close relationship.

CHAPTER TWELVE
ALTRUISM: HELPING OTHERS

Multiple Choice Questions

1. The motive to increase another's welfare without conscious regard for one's self-interests defines
    A. the social responsibility norm.
    B. egoism.
    C. social-exchange theory.
    D. altruism.
    Answer D, Type DEF

2. According to the text, _____ provides the classic illustration of altruism.
    A. the parable of the Prodigal Son
    B. the parable of the Good Samaritan
    C. the Kitty Genovese case
    D. the Sylvia Likens case
    Answer B, Type FAC

3. The notion that humans interact in such a way as to minimize costs and maximize rewards to self defines the heart of
    A. social exchange theory.
    B. egoism.
    C. the reciprocity norm.
    D. self-theory.
    Answer A, Type DEF

4. According to social exchange theory, we use a _____ strategy in deciding when and whether to help others.
    A. social comparison
    B. compensatory
    C. minimax
    D. marginal utility
    Answer C, Type FAC

5. Before agreeing to help out at the local homeless shelter, Sharon weighs the costs (e.g., getting up at dawn) and benefits (e.g., feeling good about herself) of doing so. This strategy would be predicted by
    A. the empathy-altruism hypothesis.
    B. social-exchange theory.
    C. the social responsibility norm.
    D. social comparison theory.
    Answer B, Type CON

6. According to social exchange theory, the rewards that motivate helping are
    A. internal or external.
    B. internal only.
    C. external only.
    D. consciously recognized before the act of helping.
    Answer A, Type FAC

7. Social exchange theorists argue that we are most likely to help someone
    A. who is dependent on us.
    B. who is less attractive than we are.
    C. who deserves to be helped.
    D. whose approval is important to us.
    Answer D, Type FAC

8. The executives of a major corporation contribute to charitable causes only when they are certain their gift will be well publicized, improve their public image, and ultimately translate into increased profits. The corporation's charitable acts are most easily explained in terms of
    A. the empathy-altruism hypothesis.
    B. Latané and Darley's decision tree.
    C. social exchange theory.
    D. the moral exclusion principle.
    Answer C, Type CON

9. Researcher Dennis Krebs found that Harvard University men whose physiological responses revealed the most distress in response to another's distress
    A. gave the most help to the person.
    B. became self-focused and gave little help to the person.
    C. were more likely to rationalize the other's distress as deserved.
    D. tended to be majoring in the humanities rather than in the natural sciences.
    Answer A, Type FAC

10. Researchers have identified a number of motivations that explain why people volunteer. Which of the following is <u>not</u> one of those motivations?
    A. to learn new skills
    B. to convert those helped to a particular religious belief system
    C. to enhance one's career opportunities by gaining experience and contacts
    D. to boost self-worth and confidence
    Answer B, Type FAC

11. A major weakness of social exchange theory is that it
    A. is impossible to test experimentally.
    B. fails to account for the reciprocal exchange of favors.
    C. easily degenerates into explaining-by-naming.
    D. ignores the role of internal self-rewards in motivating altruism.
    Answer C, Type FAC

12. The doctrine of psychological egoism maintains that
    A. self-esteem is a more important motive than social approval.
    B. self-interest motivates all behavior.
    C. our self-concept is determined by others' evaluation of us.
    D. the healthy personality has a strong ego.
    Answer B, Type DEF

13. Altruism is to _____ as egoism is to _____.
    A. Gouldner; Batson
    B. reciprocity; social justice
    C. evolutionary theory; social norms theory
    D. another's welfare; one's own welfare
    Answer D, Type CON

14. According to the text, the notion of egoism has fallen into disrepute because

A.   it fails to take into account people's internal motives.

B.   it is vulnerable to the criticism of circular explanation.

C.   it defines rewards and costs independently of altruistic behavior.

D.   None of the above.

Answer B, Type FAC

15.   According to Daniel Batson, when witnessing another person's distress triggers empathy and compassion, the act of helping is motivated by

A.   egoism.

B.   altruism.

C.   the social responsibility norm.

D.   anxiety-reduction.

Answer B, Type FAC

16.   When witnessing another person's distress triggers anxiety and distress, the act of helping is most likely to be motivated by

A.   egoism.

B.   altruism.

C.   empathy.

D.   the norm of reciprocity.

Answer A, Type FAC

17.   Batson and his colleagues had university women watch another woman suffer a series of painful shocks. Some participants were led to feel empathy for her and were then asked if they would trade places, taking her remaining shocks. The results indicated that

A.   most participants agreed to help but only if they knew they would otherwise continue to see her suffer.

B.   most participants agreed to help even if they knew that their part in the experiment was complete and that they would no longer have to see her suffer.

C.   most participants downplayed the victim's suffering or convinced themselves that she deserved to be shocked.

D.   most participants refused to trade places but expressed sympathy and sought compensation for the victim from the experimenters.

Answer B, Type FAC

18.   Schaller and Cialdini told participants who felt sad over a suffering victim that their sadness was going to be relieved by listening to a comedy tape. Under these conditions, participants who felt empathy for the victim

A.   were not especially helpful.

B.   became distressed at the attempt to turn their attention away from victim.

C.   were even more likely to offer aid to the victim.

D.   asked the experimenters to include the victim in the mood-boosting experience.

Answer A, Type FAC

19.   The finding that people will sometimes persist in wanting to help a suffering person even when they believe their distressed mood has been temporarily frozen by a "mood-fixing" drug suggests that

A.   egoism is a strong motivator of helping behavior.

B.   social-exchange theory is a powerful predictor of helping behavior.

C.   empathy is a poor predictor of helping behavior.

D.   genuine altruism may exist.

Answer D, Type FAC

20. Researchers studying helping behavior
    A. agree that some acts are truly altruistic and are performed only to increase another's welfare.
    B. agree that all helpful acts are either obviously or subtly egoistic.
    C. debate whether some acts are truly altruistic and performed simply to increase another's welfare.
    D. agree that all helpful acts are unconsciously motivated by gene survival.
    Answer C, Type FAC

21. Despite ongoing theoretical and empirical debate, research may never show that empathy-based helping is a source of genuine altruism because
    A. neither empathy nor altruism can be adequately defined.
    B. no experiment rules out all possible egoistic explanations for helpfulness.
    C. personal survival overrides all other human motives.
    D. psychological egoism has been convincingly demonstrated in all other forms of social behavior.
    Answer B, Type FAC

22. If you find a lost wallet, you ought to return it to its owner or turn it in to the proper authorities. Such a prescription for appropriate behavior is an example of a
    A. norm.
    B. template.
    C. moral schema.
    D. natural law.
    Answer A, Type CON

23. Two social norms that can motivate helping behavior are
    A. reciprocity and social responsibility.
    B. kin selection and moral inclusion.
    C. social exchange and reciprocity.
    D. social responsibility and kin selection.
    Answer A, Type FAC

24. Sociologist Alvin Gouldner has contended that the norm of reciprocity
    A. is the ultimate basis for feelings of empathy.
    B. is stronger in females than in males.
    C. is as universal as the incest taboo.
    D. has little application in close relationships such as marriage.
    Answer C, Type FAC

25. After Mr. Walters's neighbor helped him paint his house, Mr. Walters felt obligated to offer to help the neighbor remodel his kitchen. Mr. Walters's sense of obligation most likely resulted from the
    A. door-in-the-face phenomenon.
    B. social responsibility norm.
    C. reciprocity norm.
    D. equal status norm.
    Answer C, Type CON

26. Mail surveys and solicitations sometimes try to boost response rates by including a small gift (e.g., greeting cards). This strategy is based on
    A. altruistic motives.
    B. the social responsibility norm.

C.   the norm of reciprocity.

D.   the door-in-the-face technique.

Answer C, Type FAC

27.   The social responsibility norm refers to the expectation that

A.   people will help when necessary in order to receive help themselves later.

B.   leaders should help more than regular group members.

C.   people will help those dependent upon them.

D.   to receive help, people have the responsibility to ask for it.

Answer C, Type DEF

28.   Devon and Yvonne are from England, James is from France, and Tikh is a man from India. Which one of these people is most likely to support and act on the norm of social responsibility?

A.   Yvonne

B.   Devon and James are equally likely to act on it and more likely than Yvonne or Tikh

C.   Devon and Yvonne are equally likely to act on it, and more likely than James or Tikh

D.   Tikh

Answer D, Type CON

29.   According to the text, the social responsibility norm gets selectively applied according to the following principle:

A.   Give but require repayment with interest.

B.   Give people what they deserve.

C.   Give away only what you will never use.

D.   Do unto others as they have done unto you.

Answer B, Type FAC

30.   If victims seem to have created their own problems by laziness or lack of foresight, we are less willing to offer help. Helping responses are thus closely tied to

A.   the overjustification effect.

B.   attributions.

C.   self-concept.

D.   empathy.

Answer B, Type FAC

31.   When people need our help, we are most likely to provide assistance if we attribute their need to

A.   a lack of motivation.

B.   circumstances beyond their control.

C.   poor planning or foresight.

D.   their mood or disposition.

Answer B, Type FAC

32.   A classmate of Bianca's wants to borrow Bianca's notes to study for an upcoming exam. Research suggests that Bianca is most likely to agree if the woman says she needs the notes because she

A.   takes inadequate notes.

B.   doesn't like this class as well as her other courses.

C.   has been absent due to illness.

D.   has not been able to concentrate in class.

Answer C, Type CON

33.   Evolutionary psychology contends that the essence of life is

A.   gene survival.

B.   self-actualization.

C.   holistic health.

D.   the discovery of meaning.

Answer A, Type DEF

34.   According to evolutionary theory, genetic selfishness predisposes us toward helping based on

A.   reciprocity.

B.   social responsibility.

C.   social justice.

D.   egoism.

Answer A, Type FAC

35.   The idea that evolution has selected altruism toward one's close relatives to enhance the survival of mutually shared genes is referred to as

A.   evolutionary kinship.

B.   altruistic selection.

C.   kin selection.

D.   self-serving helpfulness.

Answer C, Type DEF

36.   Which theory specifically predicts that we will be more altruistic toward our relatives than toward close friends?

A.   evolutionary psychology

B.   social norms theory

C.   social exchange theory

D.   self-presentation theory

Answer A, Type FAC

37.   Evolutionary psychology is to _____ as social exchange theory is to _____.

A.   reciprocity; empathy

B.   kin selection; rewards and costs

C.   social responsibility norm; the reciprocity norm

D.   empathy; rewards and costs

Answer B, Type FAC

38.   Evolutionary psychologists would have greatest difficulty explaining why

A.   Jill agrees to donate bone marrow to save the life of a stranger.

B.   Milly agrees to drive her neighbor to the doctor.

C.   Simon donates a kidney to save the life of his son.

D.   Rick helps his best friend paint his house.

Answer A, Type CON

39.   The reciprocity norm should be strongest for which of the following?

A.   Kent, a London resident

B.   Julia, a New York city resident

C.   Missy, a resident of a small, rural farm town

D.   Tam, a Tokyo resident

Answer C, Type CON

40.   People who live in _____ are least likely to relay a phone message, mail lost letters, cooperate with survey interviewers, do small favors, or help a lost child.

A.   big cities

B.   small towns

C.   rural environments

D.   apartments

Answer A, Type FAC

41. According to Donald Campbell, the reason that humans sometimes demonstrate nonreciprocal altruism toward strangers is that
    A. unique circumstances have created a genetic predisposition to be selfless in rare individuals.
    B. human societies have evolved ethical rules such as "Love your neighbor."
    C. improved communication has made the world smaller and thus everyone is our kin.
    D. helpers misperceive strangers as either close kin or capable of reciprocity.
    Answer B, Type FAC

42. According to your text, the _____ theory of altruism proposes two types of prosocial behavior: a tit-for-tat reciprocal exchange and a more unconditional, intrinsic helpfulness.
    A. social norms
    B. social exchange
    C. evolutionary
    D. All of the above.
    Answer D, Type FAC

43. According to the text, which theory of altruism provides a coherent scheme for summarizing a variety of observations?
    A. social norms
    B. social exchange
    C. evolutionary
    D. All of the above.
    Answer D, Type FAC

44. In observing people's responses to staged emergencies, John Darley and Bibb Latané found that _____ greatly decreased intervention.
    A. social alienation
    B. a lack of empathy
    C. the presence of other bystanders
    D. self-concern
    Answer C, Type FAC

45. By 1980, about four dozen studies of bystander non-intervention involving nearly 6000 people showed that bystanders were most likely to offer help if they were
    A. alone.
    B. female.
    C. self-forgetful.
    D. part of a group.
    Answer A, Type FAC

46. Darley and Latané describe a sequence of decisions a bystander must make before he or she will intervene in an emergency. Which of the following is not one of the specific steps?
    A. noticing the incident
    B. interpreting the incident as an emergency
    C. assessing the victim's desire for help
    D. assuming personal responsibility for intervening
    Answer C, Type FAC

47. A stranger has collapsed on a city sidewalk due to a heart attack. According to Darley and Latané, what is the first thing that must happen before you will help in this emergency?
    A. You must recognize the event as life-threatening.

B.   You must assume responsibility for helping.
C.   You must notice the stranger.
D.   You must make sure the victim is alone and truly in need of help.
Answer C, Type CON

48.   Latané and Darley had university students complete questionnaires in a small room, and then had smoke pour into the room from a wall vent. Students who were working _____ tended to notice the smoke _____.
A.   in groups; less than five seconds
B.   alone; less than five seconds.
C.   on a challenging task; about 20 seconds
D.   on a rote task; less than five seconds
Answer B, Type FAC

49.   The fact that a bystander may be less likely to interpret an incident as an emergency when other unresponsive bystanders are present provides an example of
A.   normative influence.
B.   informational influence.
C.   diffusion of responsibility.
D.   social loafing.
Answer B, Type FAC

50.   Which of the following contribute to the fact that we are slower to interpret an ambiguous event as an emergency when other people are present?
A.   informational influence
B.   the illusion of transparency
C.   pluralistic ignorance
D.   All of the above
Answer D, Type FAC

51.   The finding that a person is less likely to help in an emergency when other people are present is called
A.   the bystander effect.
B.   pluralistic ignorance.
C.   the self-interest effect.
D.   the suppression of responsibility effect.
Answer A, Type DEF

52.   Takooshian and Bodinger (1982) staged hundreds of car burglaries in 18 cities. They found that fewer than 1 in 10 passers-by
A.   called the police.
B.   interpreted the event as a burglary.
C.   tried to stop them.
D.   even questioned their activity.
Answer D, Type FAC

53.   In staging physical fights between a man and a woman, Shotland and Straw found that bystanders intervened only 19 percent of the time when the woman shouted,
A.   "Get away from me, I don't know you!"
B.   "Get away from me, I don't know why I ever married you!"
C.   "Get away from me, I have a gun!"
D.   "Get away from me, you're drunk!"
Answer B, Type FAC

54. Darley and Latané set up an experiment in which participants listening over headphones heard another participant suffering a seizure and crying for help. Of participants who believed there were _____ other witnesses, _____ sought to help the victim.
   A.   no; none
   B.   no; 85 percent
   C.   no; 31 percent
   D.   four; 85 percent
   Answer B, Type FAC

55. According to Darley and Latané, even if people notice an event that they realize to be an emergency, _____ in the presence of other bystanders can inhibit helping.
   A.   pluralistic ignorance
   B.   diffusion of responsibility
   C.   self-presentation concerns
   D.   anxiety
   Answer B, Type FAC

56. When Irving Piliavin and his colleagues staged an emergency--a staggering, collapsing man--on 103 subway trips, they found that the victim was promptly offered assistance almost every time, even when he appeared to be drunk rather than disabled. Further research seems to confirm that bystander helpfulness was due to
   A.   subway passengers' fear of street crime.
   B.   the sophistication and experience of the observers in offering first aid.
   C.   the fact that the situation was unambiguous.
   D.   the fact that subway riders were not in very large groups.
   Answer C, Type FAC

57. Interviews with participants in studies of bystander intervention reveal that
   A.   people are typically unaware of the influence of others on their decision to help.
   B.   people are typically aware that the presence of others inhibits helping.
   C.   people are typically willing to admit that they look to others for information about how to respond.
   D.   people are typically angry about being deceived by the experimenter.
   Answer A, Type FAC

58. Which of the following seem to contribute to the fact that people in bigger, more densely populated cities are less likely to help?
   A.   compassion fatigue
   B.   diffusion of responsibility
   C.   sensory overload from encountering so many people in need
   D.   All of the above
   Answer D, Type FAC

59. In the experimental studies of bystander non-intervention, researchers have
   A.   always first obtained the participant's informed consent.
   B.   been careful to debrief their laboratory participants.
   C.   subsequently found that most research participants believe the laboratory experiments have little, if any, application to everyday life.
   D.   All of the above.
   Answer B, Type FAC

60. Research evidence indicates that prosocial models
   A.   presented on television have virtually no effect on children.

B.   promote altruism in children but not in adults.

C.   promote altruism in the observers.

D.   in the long run decrease helping because observers seem to believe that aid is less necessary.

Answer C, Type FAC

61.   Which of the following factors is likely to increase helping behavior?

A.   the presence of others who offer help

B.   the presence of others who do nothing

C.   time pressure

D.   being non-religious

Answer A, Type FAC

62.   In an enactment of the Good Samaritan situation, Darley and Batson studied the helpfulness of Princeton seminarians in order to assess whether helping behavior is influenced by

A.   religious education.

B.   age differences.

C.   social responsibility.

D.   time pressures.

Answer D, Type FAC

63.   Darley and Batson had Princeton seminary students think about a talk they were about to have recorded in an adjacent building. Participants who had been _____ were most likely to stop and offer aid to a "victim" they encountered en route to the recording studio.

A.   asked to talk about career opportunities

B.   asked to talk about the Good Samaritan parable

C.   given extra time to reach the studio

D.   told they were already late in departing for the studio

Answer C, Type FAC

64.   Experiments have induced guilt by having people deliver shock, lie, cheat, or destroy property. Such studies consistently show that people who feel guilty

A.   typically displace their frustration by justifying others' suffering.

B.   are more likely to help an undeserving person than an innocent victim.

C.   will do whatever they can to expunge the guilt and restore their self-esteem.

D.   tend to be distracted and thus are less likely to notice others' need for help.

Answer C, Type FAC

65.   In a study by McMillen and Austin, participants were induced to feel guilty by denying that they had been tipped off by an accomplice about how to answer test questions. After the test, the experimenter asked participants if they had any spare time to volunteer. Results showed that

A.   guilty participants wanted to leave immediately.

B.   guilty participants volunteered significantly more time than nonguilty participants did.

C.   nonguilty participants volunteered significantly more time than guilty participants did.

D.   guilty participants agreed to stay but distraction over their guilt feelings kept them from performing the task adequately.

Answer B, Type FAC

66.   A negative mood is more likely to boost helping in _____ than in _____.

A.   children; adults

B.   adults; children

C.   men; women

D.   women; men

Answer B, Type FAC

67. The mood-enhancing effects of altruism appear to be the result of
    A.   genetic predispositions.
    B.   informational influence.
    C.   socialization.
    D.   evolutionary processes.
    Answer C, Type FAC

68. Which of the following negative moods is most likely to enhance helping behavior?
    A.   guilt
    B.   anger
    C.   profound grief
    D.   depression
    Answer A, Type FAC

69. Studies of the effects of mood on helping suggest that adults who feel _____ are more likely than those in a neutral control condition to help.
    A.   guilty
    B.   sad
    C.   happy
    D.   All of the above
    Answer D, Type FAC

70. Few findings have been more consistent than the fact that _____ people are helpful people.
    A.   happy
    B.   well-rested
    C.   well-educated
    D.   easy-going
    Answer A, Type FAC

71. Who of the following is most likely to respond favorably to an unexpected request for a charitable donation to a local hospital?
    A.   Melvin's older sister, who is hurrying to get to her scheduled appointment with the family doctor.
    B.   Melvin's mother, who just received a very favorable job evaluation from her employer.
    C.   Melvin's younger brother, who is depressed over receiving a D on a physics exam.
    D.   Melvin's father, who is annoyed over the newspaper boy's trampling of his flower bed.
    Answer B, Type CON

72. Preliminary indications of research on personality traits are that those high in _____ are most likely to be concerned and helpful.
    A.   femininity, assertiveness, and dominance
    B.   emotionality, empathy, and self-efficacy
    C.   masculinity, sympathy, and nurturance
    D.   sensitivity, compassion, and introversion
    Answer B, Type FAC

73. Compared to low self-monitoring people, high self-monitoring people are especially helpful if they think that
    A.   no one is watching them.
    B.   helping will be effective.
    C.   helpfulness will be socially rewarded.
    D.   no one else is likely to help.

Answer C, Type FAC

74. Research on the relation between personality traits and helping behavior reveals that
   A. personality traits have little to no influence on helping.
   B. the person and the situation interact to predict helping.
   C. assertiveness strongly predicts helping across a variety of situations.
   D. gender is the only person characteristic that predicts helping better than situational factors.
   Answer B, Type FAC

75. Most altruism studies explore spontaneous acts of helping. Researchers who have explored planned or sustained helping report that when people make intentional choices about long-term altruism, _____ predicts altruism.
   A. age
   B. gender
   C. religiosity
   D. intelligence
   Answer C, Type FAC

76. Which of the following statements about the relationship between gender and helping is true?
   A. Male helpers are more likely to help female victims than male victims.
   B. Female helpers are equally likely to help female and male victims.
   C. Women are more likely to seek help.
   D. All of the above.
   Answer D, Type FAC

77. Confederates who were dressed either conservatively or in counterculture garb approached either "straight" or "hip" college students and asked for change to make a phone call. Results of this experiment confirmed a _____ bias in helping.
   A. familiarity
   B. similarity
   C. credibility
   D. complementarity
   Answer B, Type FAC

78. A racial bias in helping is least likely to emerge when
   A. norms for appropriate behavior are well-defined.
   B. norms for appropriate behavior are ambiguous.
   C. the victim is well-dressed.
   D. the situation is ambiguous.
   Answer A, Type FAC

79. Bystanders increase their helpfulness as they become more
   A. self-aware.
   B. depressed.
   C. anxious.
   D. self-accepting.
   Answer A, Type FAC

80. A charitable organization telephones to ask Mary to contribute $100 to send delinquent youth to a summer camp. After she refuses, the solicitor asks if she would be willing to give just $10. Mary agrees. Mary was influenced by the _____ technique.
   A. foot-in-the-door
   B. face-in-the-mirror

C.   overjustification

D.   door-in-the-face

Answer D, Type CON

81.   Regarding people who are different as within one's circle of moral concern is called

     A.   moral exclusion.

     B.   moral inclusion.

     C.   exclusive altruism.

     D.   ingroup moralism.

     Answer B, Type DEF

82.   Both European Christians who risked their lives to rescue Jews during the Nazi era and civil rights activists of the 1950s report that

     A.   they came from families who themselves had been victims of some form of social injustice.

     B.   they had warm, close relationships with parents who were committed to humanitarian causes.

     C.   their efforts were in part a reaction to having been raised in a troubled family environment in which parents and children were in frequent conflict.

     D.   they were firstborn or only children whose parents had taught them courage and independence.

     Answer B, Type FAC

83.   Which of the following is an effective way to increase helping behavior?

     A.   reduce the ambiguity of the situation

     B.   model prosocial behavior

     C.   make people feel guilty

     D.   All of the above

     Answer D, Type FAC

84.   What principle or concept suggests that rewarding people for their helpfulness may, in the long run, undermine their self-motivated altruism?

     A.   the door-in-the-face principle

     B.   moral exclusion

     C.   the overjustification effect

     D.   the insufficient justification effect

     Answer C, Type FAC

85.   Findings suggest that students who have learned about the research on the bystander effect are subsequently more

     A.   likely to suspect that victims in emergency situations may be part of a social psychological experiment.

     B.   likely to offer help to victims in emergency situations.

     C.   sensitive to the ethical dilemmas faced by psychologists working with human participants.

     D.   likely to actively support the passage of Good Samaritan laws.

     Answer B, Type FAC

The following items also appear in the Study Guide:

86.   According to social-exchange theory we will help when

     A.   the benefits are external and the costs are internal.

     B.   the benefits are greater than the costs.

     C.   the benefits and costs are proportional.

D.   the benefits are smaller than the costs.

Answer B, Type FAC

87.   The social-responsibility norm is an expectation that people will

    A.   help those dependent on them.

    B.   help those who have helped them.

    C.   assume responsibility for helping their parents.

    D.   assume responsibility for correcting past mistakes.

Answer A, Type DEF

88.   Since we are born selfish, evolutionary psychologists propose that we attempt to

    A.   develop a drug that will encourage altruism.

    B.   develop an "altruistic gene."

    C.   teach altruism.

    D.   live only in small, isolated communities.

Answer C, Type FAC

89.   Latané and Darley attempted to explain people's failure to intervene in cases like that of Kitty Genovese in terms of

    A.   a situational influence.

    B.   a personality trait.

    C.   a mood factor.

    D.   selfish genes.

Answer A, Type FAC

90.   Which of the following is not one of the steps in Darley and Latané's decision tree?

    A.   noticing the incident

    B.   interpreting the incident as an emergency

    C.   weighing the costs and benefits of helping

    D.   assuming responsibility for intervening

Answer C, Type FAC

91.   According to the text, people in a hurry may be less willing to help because

    A.   they have weighed the costs of helping and have decided they are too high.

    B.   they never fully grasp the situation as one requiring their assistance.

    C.   they tend to be selfish and primarily concerned with meeting their own needs.

    D.   they tend to be in a negative mood state and therefore are less likely to help.

Answer B, Type FAC

92.   Researchers who have investigated the relationship between empathy and altruism

    A.   agree that empathy leads to genuine altruism.

    B.   agree that empathy leads to helping that is egoistically motivated.

    C.   agree that empathy leads to pure altruism in females but not in males.

    D.   debate whether empathy leads to pure altruism.

Answer D, Type FAC

93.   Which of the following negative moods is most likely to motivate altruism?

    A.   depression

    B.   anger

    C.   guilt

    D.   grief

Answer C, Type FAC

94.   What does research indicate regarding the role of gender difference in predicting helping?

    A.   Gender is unrelated to helping.

B.   Males are more helpful than females.

C.   Females are more helpful than males.

D.   Gender difference interacts with the situation.

Answer D, Type FAC

95.   You trip over a fallen branch and sprain your ankle. According to research on the bystander effect, a stranger who sees your plight will be most likely to offer aid if there are _____ others present.

A.   no

B.   two

C.   four

D.   ten

Answer A, Type CON

96.   Who of the following is least likely to help an injured pedestrian?

A.   Peter, who has just found $10 in a grocery store.

B.   Anita, who is five minutes late for a committee meeting.

C.   Carol, who has just lost a dollar bill in a poker game.

D.   Ralph, who is five minutes early for work.

Answer B, Type CON

97.   Your roommate asks you to loan her twenty-five dollars to buy her boyfriend a birthday present, and you refuse. She then asks for three dollars to purchase a new notebook. You loan her the three dollars. Your roommate has successfully used the

A.   overjustification effect.

B.   insufficient justification effect.

C.   door-in-the-face technique.

D.   foot-in-the-door technique.

Answer C, Type CON

98.   From an evolutionary perspective it would be most difficult to explain why

A.   John paid his son's hospital bill.

B.   Phyllis helps her mother clean the house.

C.   William helps his next-door neighbor paint his house.

D.   Ruth risked her life to save a stranger from being murdered.

Answer D, Type CON

99.   Which of the following techniques should elementary schoolteachers use if they hope to promote enduring altruistic tendencies in students?

A.   Show them films of heroes who risked their own welfare to help others.

B.   Offer a new bicycle to the boy or girl who is most helpful to other students in a two-week period.

C.   Reprimand and punish any overt aggression.

D.   Instill a sense of patriotism.

Answer A, Type CON

100.   The reciprocity norm applies most strongly to our interactions with our

A.   superiors.

B.   inferiors.

C.   equals.

D.   None of the above—the norm's application is totally independent of others' relative social status.

Answer C, Type FAC

Critical Thinking Questions

101.   Compare and contrast the three theories of helping: social exchange, social norms, and evolutionary.

102.   Explain the relation between the norm of social responsibility and attributions about those in need.

103.   Describe the various effects of feelings on helping.

104.   Identify the steps in Darley and Latané's "decision tree" of helping. Based on this model, how could you increase your chances of getting someone to help you in an emergency?

105.   In addition to reducing the ambiguity of the situation and increasing personal responsibility, explain at least two other ways to increase helping behavior.

CHAPTER THIRTEEN
CONFLICT AND PEACEMAKING

Multiple Choice Questions

1. Dean and Mary have been saving money since they got married. Now Dean wants to buy a new car, but Mary wants to continue saving for a new house. Dean and Mary
   A. are experiencing conflict.
   B. are experiencing dissonance.
   C. have mirror-image perceptions.
   D. are developing superordinate goals.
   Answer A, Type CON

2. The occurrence of conflict in any relationship
   A. is usually a sign of lack of motivation.
   B. can stimulate improved relations.
   C. is a necessary evil of human interaction.
   D. necessarily signifies an incompatibility of goals.
   Answer B, Type FAC

3. Conflict is defined as
   A. perceived incompatibility of actions or goals.
   B. dissatisfaction with relationship outcomes.
   C. hostility that results from frustrating interaction.
   D. competition for mutually exclusive goals.
   Answer A, Type DEF

4. According to your text, in its most positive sense peace is
   A. nothing more than the suppression of open conflict.
   B. the result of creatively managed conflict.
   C. the appearance of calm.
   D. None of the above.
   Answer B, Type FAC

5. Which of the following is not one of the ingredients of conflict explored in the chapter on Conflict and Peacemaking?
   A. competition
   B. social dilemmas
   C. instinctive hostility
   D. misperceptions
   Answer C, Type FAC

6. Pursuing one's self-interest to the collective detriment of one's community or society is the central pattern in
   A. mirror-image perception.
   B. the jigsaw problem.
   C. perceived injustice.
   D. a social dilemma.
   Answer D, Type FAC

7.   In the Prisoner's Dilemma, if both prisoners confess, each will _____; if neither confesses, each will _____.
     A.   get a moderate sentence; get a light sentence
     B.   get a severe sentence; get a light sentence
     C.   get a severe sentence; go free
     D.   get a moderate sentence; get a severe sentence
     Answer A, Type FAC

8.   In playing the laboratory version of the Prisoner's Dilemma, you would personally obtain the best payoff on any given trial if you _____ and the other person _____ .
     A.   defect; cooperates
     B.   defect; defects
     C.   cooperate; defects
     D.   cooperate; cooperates
     Answer A, Type FAC

9.   In the Prisoner's Dilemma, taking the non-cooperative strategy of confession leads to a worse outcome if the other person _____.
     A.   also confesses
     B.   does not confess
     C.   cooperates
     D.   None of the above
     Answer A, Type FAC

10. As the text points out, threatening an enemy with "big sticks" doesn't deter war. Yet arms spending continues. This fact is partly explained by the laboratory observation that
     A.   participants with "big sticks" control the severity of the conflict.
     B.   competition (e.g., armament) often breeds peaceful resolution.
     C.   unconditional cooperation (e.g., disarmament) often gets exploited.
     D.   unconditional cooperation (e.g., disarmament) often leads to peaceful resolutions.
     Answer C, Type FAC

11. In the tragedy of the commons, the "commons" refers to
     A.   disputed border territory.
     B.   stolen goods or winnings.
     C.   any jointly used, finite resource.
     D.   private property that repeatedly changes ownership.
     Answer C, Type DEF

12. In real life, which of the following parallels the tragedy of the commons?
     A.   pollution of rivers and streams
     B.   littering in public places
     C.   use and overuse of natural resources
     D.   All of the above.
     Answer D, Type FAC

13. In the common's dilemma people often consume more than they realize when
     A.   others take on a cooperative strategy.
     B.   resources are not partitioned.
     C.   the "commons" is divided into equal parts.
     D.   everyone cooperates.
     Answer B, Type FAC

14.   Despite official government warning of a severe water shortage, most citizens fail to conserve in the belief that their personal water consumption will have little effect on the community's total water supply. The eventual depletion of the community's water resources provides an example of
    A.   mirror-image perceptions.
    B.   individualistic calamity.
    C.   the tragedy of the commons.
    D.   rational disaster.
    Answer C, Type CON

15.   Julian Edney's Nuts Game best illustrates the dynamics of
    A.   the Commons Dilemma.
    B.   the Prisoner's Dilemma.
    C.   integrative agreements.
    D.   inequitable relationships.
    Answer A, Type FAC

16.   In Julian Edney's Nuts Game, each player seated beside a bowl of nuts wants to accumulate as many nuts as possible, and every 10 seconds the bowl's total is doubled. Most of Edney's groups
    A.   wait until the bowl's contents have multiplied many times and then divide this larger sum equally among themselves.
    B.   wait until the bowl's contents have multiplied many times and then compete for the lion's share of the nuts.
    C.   go through about two replenishment periods before emptying the bowl.
    D.   empty the bowl before even the first 10-second replenishment.
    Answer D, Type FAC

17.   Kaori Sato gave Japanese students opportunities to harvest trees in a simulated forest for money. When the students shared equally the costs of planting the forest, the result was that
    A.   most of the trees were left to grow too tall for harvesting because the students bickered about the criterion to be used in sharing profits.
    B.   most of the trees were harvested before they had grown to the most profitable size.
    C.   none of the trees were harvested because the collectivist students did not want to be the first to ask for his or her share.
    D.   students made maximum profit not only for themselves individually but for the group.
    Answer B, Type FAC

18.   In both the Prisoner's Dilemma and the Commons Dilemma, people are tempted to explain their own behavior _____ and others' behavior _____.
    A.   situationally; situationally
    B.   dispositionally; dispositionally
    C.   situationally; dispositionally
    D.   dispositionally; situationally
    Answer C, Type FAC

19.   Which of the following is not a feature of the Prisoner's Dilemma and Commons Dilemma?
    A.   One party's wins necessarily equals the other party's losses.
    B.   Participants tend to commit the fundamental attribution error.
    C.   Participants' motives change in the course of the entrapment.
    D.   Both are non-zero-sum games.
    Answer A, Type FAC

20.   In a non-zero-sum game
    A.   both can win and both can lose.

B.   one side wins and the other loses.

C.   one's gains equals another's losses.

D.   altruistic motives dominate.

Answer A, Type DEF

21.   According to theorist Garrett Hardin, _____ in a commons brings ruin to all.

A.   regulation

B.   freedom

C.   unrest

D.   competition

Answer B, Type FAC

22.   Facing the recurring dilemma of cookie-jar depletion within 24-hours of its being re-stocked, Mom decides to do something to reduce this weekly tragedy of the commons. What strategy will be most effective in protecting the commons?

A.   scold Dad for eating too many and then ask him to scold the children

B.   give each family member just three cookies a day and keep the rest hidden

C.   stop buying cookies for a month to illustrate the personal consequences of destroying the commons

D.   call a family meeting and scold everyone all at once for eating too many cookies

Answer B, Type CON

23.   Which of the following is cited in the text as a method for resolving social dilemmas?

A.   communication

B.   punishment

C.   GRIT

D.   All of the above.

Answer A, Type FAC

24.   Which of the following is not cited in the text as a method for resolving social dilemmas?

A.   regulation

B.   changing payoffs

C.   communication

D.   GRIT

Answer D, Type FAC

25.   The smaller the commons, the more

A.   responsibility each person feels for it.

B.   intense the conflict among individual members.

C.   apathetic people are about its preservation.

D.   the more likely communication will take the form of intimidation and deception.

Answer A, Type FAC

26.   In research by both Edney and Dawes on social dilemmas, it was found that

A.   group discussion polarized competitive tendencies.

B.   group discussion had no effect on the outcome.

C.   group discussion led to greater cooperation and better outcomes for all participants.

D.   group discussion led to escalated conflict and tension.

Answer C, Type FAC

27.   Which of the following is cited in the text as an example of changing payoffs to resolve social dilemmas?

A.   allowing carpoolers to drive in the faster, freeway lane

B.   requiring carpool cars and vans to park in special, larger parking lots farther away from the office building

C.   lowering the price of gasoline well below $1 per gallon

D.   All of the above.

Answer A, Type FAC

28.   According to research, it seems that just knowing about the dire consequences of noncooperation in a social dilemma

A.   is sufficient to convince people to behave cooperatively.

B.   leads to greater mistrust of others.

C.   tends to foster greater self-interest and competition.

D.   has little real effect on people's behavior.

Answer D, Type FAC

29.   Ross and Ward (1969) had participants play a variation of the Prisoner's Dilemma game. When the simulation was labeled _____, two-thirds of the participants cooperated.

A.   "Community Game"

B.   "Wall Street Game"

C.   "War Games"

D.   "The Prisoner's Dilemma"

Answer A, Type FAC

30.   Jeffrey Scott Mio and colleagues found that after reading about the commons dilemma, theater patrons

A.   littered less.

B.   demanded reserved seats.

C.   were more likely to assist a handicapped person find a seat.

D.   spent more for theater refreshments.

Answer A, Type FAC

31.   Competition can contribute to the conflict between which of the following?

A.   the United States and Iraq

B.   Hispanics and Blacks in Los Angeles

C.   Darrin and Maria

D.   All of the above

Answer D, Type CON

32.   Despite the fact that, as Sherif noted, the behavior of the boys in the warring camps seemed "wicked, disturbed, and vicious," what actually triggered their evil behavior was

A.   their leaders' modeling of aggression.

B.   their delinquent backgrounds.

C.   their ethnic identities.

D.   an evil situation.

Answer D, Type FAC

33.   Equity exists when

A.   rewards are distributed in proportion to individuals' contributions.

B.   partners share equally in the rewards of collective effort.

C.   rewards are distributed in relation to individuals' needs or deservingness.

D.   group members decide among themselves how rewards are to be distributed.

Answer A, Type DEF

34.   Before they married, Melinda and Michael, who are both employed full time and collect the same pay, agreed to share equally in routine household tasks such as cleaning and grocery

shopping. In reality, Melinda is now doing about 80 percent of the household work. This situation is an example of
A. an integrative disaster.
B. an inequitable relationship.
C. a social dilemma.
D. a zero-sum relationship.
Answer B, Type CON

35. "From each according to his abilities, to each according to his needs" is a motto that would most likely be found in
A. a relationship characterized by equity.
B. a capitalist culture.
C. a noncapitalist culture.
D. a relationship characterized by injustice.
Answer C, Type FAC

36. What does your text refer to as the "golden rule" of social justice?
A. "Equity for strangers, equality for friends."
B. "An eye for an eye, a tooth for a tooth."
C. "Care most for those in greatest need."
D. "Whoever has the gold makes the rules."
Answer D, Type DEF

37. Research indicates that the more people value their inputs, the more likely they are to
A. feel incompetent and unworthy.
B. feel that a given outcome from a relationship is sufficient.
C. tolerate exploitation from others without any retaliation.
D. feel underbenefitted in a relationship and inclined to retaliate.
Answer D, Type FAC

38. Compared to Americans, people socialized in China and India are more likely to favor _____ as the basis for justice when rewards are distributed to those within their groups.
A. equity
B. equality
C. achievement
D. whatever the group leader pronounces
Answer B, Type FAC

39. Individualistic cultures are to _____ as collectivistic cultures are to _____.
A. equity; equality
B. need; equality
C. achievement; aptitude
D. equality; need
Answer A, Type CON

40. Justice can be defined as
A. the distribution of rewards in proportion to individual contributions.
B. the equal distribution of rewards.
C. the distribution of rewards according to individual needs.
D. All of the above.
Answer D, Type DEF

41. What do self-serving bias, group polarization, and negative stereotypes have in common?
A. They illustrate the power of the situation.

B.   They are potential seeds of misperception.

C.   They illustrate that we are cognitive misers.

D.   None of the above.

Answer B, Type FAC

42.   The misperceptions of those who are in conflict with each other, such as two nations who regard each other with suspicion and hostility, are usually

A.   nonreciprocal.

B.   unilateral.

C.   mutual.

D.   inequitable.

Answer C, Type FAC

43.   Studies of political statements reveal that during the cold war years people in both the United States and the Soviet Union held which of the following attitudes?

A.   They preferred mutual disarmament to all other outcomes.

B.   They wanted above all not to disarm while the other side armed.

C.   They perceived the other side as preferring to achieve military superiority.

D.   All of the above.

Answer D, Type FAC

44.   The reciprocal views that parties in conflict often hold of one another are referred to as

A.   mirror-image perceptions.

B.   stereotypic reciprocation.

C.   complementary images.

D.   reciprocal illusions.

Answer A, Type DEF

45.   The Republic of Fredonia believes its long-time enemy, the kingdom of Franistan, is aggressive, greedy, and impulsive. On the other hand, Franistan believes Fredonia is hostile, selfish, and unpredictable. This is an example of

A.   an inequitable relationship.

B.   a zero-sum relationship.

C.   mirror-image perceptions.

D.   the tragedy of the commons.

Answer C, Type CON

46.   In times of tension, as during an international crisis,

A.   views of the opposing side become more simplistic.

B.   political statements acknowledge that each country's motives are complex.

C.   judgments about action are prolonged and postponed by time-consuming reevaluations.

D.   All of the above.

Answer A, Type FAC

47.   When two sides have clashing perceptions, at least one of them is misperceiving the other, and when that is the case, according to Urie Bronfenbrenner, "It is characteristic of such images that they are _____."

A.   self-defeating

B.   self-confirming

C.   self-handicapping

D.   self-monitoring

Answer B, Type FAC

48.   Destructive mirror-image perceptions operate in conflicts between

A.   countries.
B.   small groups.
C.   individuals.
D.   All of the above.
Answer D, Type FAC

49.   In a study by executives who were asked to describe a recent conflict, Thomas and Pondy found that 12 percent described the opposing party as _____ and 74 percent perceived themselves as _____.
A.   cooperative; cooperative
B.   intelligent; intelligent
C.   cooperative; competitive
D.   rational; competent
Answer A, Type FAC

50.   The management of a large manufacturing company believes that recent worker unrest at its plant is the result of a few union leaders who are manipulating and intimidating employees who are basically loyal to the company and content with existing working conditions. The management's view is likely an example of
A.   mirror-image perception.
B.   a superordinate attributional error.
C.   an evil leader-good people illusion.
D.   a self-fulfilling misperception.
Answer C, Type CON

51.   One aspect of mirror-image perception is that one side tends to
A.   exaggerate the other's position.
B.   see itself reflected in the way others see it.
C.   see the situation as the reflection of evil leadership.
D.   None of the above.
Answer A, Type FAC

52.   Your text offers what advice when in conflict?
A.   assume the other does not share your values
B.   assume the other sees events exactly as you see them
C.   compare perceptions, assuming the other sees the situation differently
D.   simplify your thinking about the other
Answer C, Type FAC

53.   Which of the following is not one of the four C's of peacemaking identified in the text?
A.   contact
B.   correction
C.   conciliation
D.   communication
Answer B, Type FAC

54.   Findings showing that "attitudes follow behavior" and that proximity boosts liking suggest the possibility that _____ may reduce conflict.
A.   contact
B.   conciliation
C.   mediation
D.   a superordinate goal
Answer A, Type FAC

55. In 1986 social psychologist Walter Stephan reviewed studies of the effects of school desegregation and concluded that
    A. school desegregation is the only real success story in efforts to change racial attitudes in the United States.
    B. school desegregation has had little effect on racial attitudes in the United States.
    C. the effect of school desegregation has been consistently positive but gradual.
    D. such programs have caused significant deterioration in race relations nationwide.
    Answer B, Type FAC

56. Surveys of nearly 4000 Europeans reveal that an important factor determining whether attitudes toward a minority group will become more favorable is whether
    A. one has a friend who is a member of that minority group.
    B. the minority group tends to be submissive.
    C. the minority group has a history of significant accomplishment.
    D. the language of the minority group can be easily mastered.
    Answer A, Type FAC

57. For Blacks, the most noticeable consequence of desegregated schooling has been
    A. very short-term improvement of interracial relations.
    B. reduced likelihood of attending primarily White colleges.
    C. increased likelihood of living and working in integrated settings.
    D. a more favorable self-image.
    Answer C, Type FAC

58. When interracial contact is _____, improved relations should not be expected.
    A. unequal
    B. competitive
    C. unsupported by authorities
    D. All of the above
    Answer D, Type FAC

59. In order for contact between opposing racial groups to reduce conflict, the contact must
    A. occur in a zero-sum context.
    B. be structured to confer equal status on both races.
    C. temporarily award superior status to the minority group.
    D. be mediated by a third party.
    Answer B, Type FAC

60. Sondra is a Black ninth-grade student whose family has just moved into a new school district. Her last school was academically inferior, but her new school is a predominantly White middle-class neighborhood school. Chances are that Sondra will
    A. achieve and be quickly accepted in this vastly improved environment.
    B. achieve some improvement but likely at the expense of holding back several of her White classmates.
    C. be perceived by both her classmates and herself as having lower academic status.
    D. will not do very well in class but will be readily accepted by the White, middle-class students.
    Answer C, Type CON

61. In the typical school classroom, desegregated or not, students' behavior can best be described as
    A. apprehensive and inhibited.
    B. diverse but equal.
    C. competitive and unequal.

D.   interdependent and cohesive.
Answer C, Type FAC

62.   Keesha, Ayako, and Maria were strangers before the plane they were on crashed into the Gulf of
        Mexico. Having survived the ordeal together, they now keep in close touch. Their experience
        illustrates the power of _____ to unite.
        A.   a shared threat
        B.   submerged goals
        C.   fear and anxiety
        D.   competition for limited resources
        Answer A, Type CON

63.   Being especially conscious of who "they" are can serve to intensify
        A.   ingroup pride.
        B.   outgroup pride.
        C.   intergroup sharing.
        D.   intergroup conciliation.
        Answer A, Type FAC

64.   Leaders who focus their group on a threatening external enemy can expect the group to
        A.   become distracted and less productive.
        B.   become divisive.
        C.   rebel against that leader.
        D.   become more cohesive.
        Answer D, Type FAC

65.   Conflict between groups tends to promote _____ within groups.
        A.   instability
        B.   quiet reflection
        C.   unity
        D.   debate
        Answer C, Type FAC

66.   Through the use of _____, Muzafer Sherif made enemies into friends.
        A.   contact
        B.   superordinate goals
        C.   bargaining
        D.   conciliation
        Answer B, Type FAC

67.   After their town was ravaged by a disastrous tornado, two rival community groups set aside their
        differences and worked together on repairing the damage. This cooperation best illustrates the
        importance of
        A.   mediation.
        B.   the GRIT strategy.
        C.   superordinate goals.
        D.   the jigsaw technique.
        Answer C, Type CON

68.   Blake and Mouton (1979) studied executives' behavior in several series of experiments that
        paralleled Sherif's boys' camp paradigm and concluded that
        A.   superordinate goals do not reduce conflict among Type A personalities.
        B.   cooperative strategies fail to reduce conflicts between groups of adults with competitive
                histories.

C.   adult reactions parallel those of Sherif's participants.

D.   adults maintain competitive attitudes, hold grudges longer, and are less willing to cooperate than children.

Answer C, Type FAC

69.   In experiments with University of Virginia students, Stephen Worchel and his associates found that _____ boosts groups' attraction for one another.

A.   any effort to cooperate, whether successful or not,

B.   a successful cooperative experience

C.   cooperation on physical but not on mental tasks

D.   cooperation among females but not among males

Answer B, Type FAC

70.   Elliot Aronson's jigsaw technique involved having elementary school children

A.   study in small, racially mixed teams and then compete with other teams in a class tournament.

B.   form academically and racially diverse groups with each member of the group becoming an expert in one area.

C.   role-play being members of another race for two-week periods.

D.   take turns telling each other about their family backgrounds in small-group discussions.

Answer B, Type FAC

71.   By emphasizing the contribution Jackie Robinson might make to the Brooklyn Dodgers' winning the 1947 pennant, Branch Rickey used _____ to reduce racial prejudice and conflict among team members.

A.   a superordinate goal

B.   an integrative agreement

C.   arbitration

D.   the GRIT strategy

Answer A, Type FAC

72.   A "practical, proven method for implementing contact theory in the desegregated classroom," says Slavin (1985) is

A.   academic competitions between different schools.

B.   after-school classes on race relations.

C.   peer support groups.

D.   cooperative learning.

Answer D, Type FAC

73.   Which of the following conditions makes it more likely that we will generalize a newly formed positive attitude toward a member of another group to the whole outgroup?

A.   if we see another ingroup member modeling friendship with outgroup members

B.   if we perceive our new outgroup friend as an atypical member of that group

C.   if we think of our new outgroup friend as an individual, not as a group member

D.   All of the above.

Answer A, Type FAC

74.   Darren grew up learning to dislike and mistrust Whites. When he left his all-Black high school to go to a mixed-race college he became good friends with Todd—a White member of the basketball team. Darren will most likely generalize his positive attitude toward Todd to Whites as a whole if

A.   he acknowledges that Todd is a member of the White outgroup.

B.   he continues to minimize the importance of race.

C.   he continues to have success on the basketball team.

D.   None of the above.

Answer A, Type CON

75.   Someone who identifies with both his or her ethnic culture and the larger culture is said to have a
_____ identity.

A.   schizophrenic

B.   multiple

C.   bicultural

D.   subcultural

Answer C, Type DEF

76.   Low self-esteem is often observed among

A.   the grandchildren of immigrants.

B.   people who have neither an ethnic nor a mainstream identity.

C.   people who affirm both their ethnic and their mainstream identities.

D.   people who affirm their ethnic identity but disavow their mainstream identity.

Answer B, Type FAC

77.   _____ occurs when conflicted parties seek an agreement through direct negotiation.

A.   Bargaining

B.   Amelioration

C.   Mediation

D.   Arbitration

Answer A, Type DEF

78.   A mediator seeks to achieve a mutually beneficial resolution by having the parties adopt a _____
orientation.

A.   carefree

B.   win-lose

C.   win-win

D.   submissive

Answer C, Type FAC

79.   Mediators seek to establish _____ that reconcile both parties' interests to their mutual benefit.

A.   arbitrated agreements

B.   integrative agreements

C.   mirror-image agreements

D.   zero-sum agreements

Answer B, Type DEF

80.   According to conflict researchers, you are more likely to divulge your needs and concerns if your
relationship with your partner includes

A.   mediation.

B.   trust.

C.   passion.

D.   the threat of withdrawal.

Answer B, Type FAC

81.   A mediator may try to improve relationship communication by having conflicting parties restrict
their arguments to statements of

A.   the opposing side's underlying motives.

B.   how they feel or think in response to the other's actions.

C.   personal analysis of the probable causes of the conflict.

D.   proposed solutions or conditions for reconciliation.

Answer B, Type FAC

82.   David and Julie fought over what to name their new puppy, until finally they went to Mom to get her to decide on a settlement. David and Julie relied on _____ to resolve their conflict.

A.   mediation
B.   bargaining
C.   conciliation
D.   arbitration

Answer D, Type CON

83.   Charles Osgood's GRIT strategy is an alternative that best fits into the _____ category of the "four C's of peacemaking."

A.   contact
B.   conciliation
C.   communication
D.   correction

Answer B, Type FAC

84.   Which of the following is not one of the steps in Charles Osgood's GRIT strategy?

A.   Build up first-strike capability to negotiate from a position of strength.
B.   Announce your conciliatory intent.
C.   Carry out several verifiable conciliatory acts.
D.   Maintain retaliatory capability.

Answer A, Type FAC

85.   Conflict expert Morton Deutsch captures the spirit of GRIT in advising negotiators to be

A.   strong-willed and sober.
B.   poker-faced and stoic.
C.   firm, fair, and friendly.
D.   soft, smiling, and sympathetic.

Answer C, Type FAC

The following items also appear in the Study Guide:

86.   Which of the following is true of conflict?

A.   Without conflict, people seldom face and resolve their problems.
B.   Conflict always involves a real incompatibility of goals.
C.   Social psychologists have studied interpersonal but not international conflict.
D.   Social psychologists have not been able to study conflict in a laboratory setting.

Answer A, Type FAC

87.   Edney's Nuts Game

A.   is a non-zero-sum game played between two persons.
B.   demonstrates how mirror-image perceptions can increase conflict.
C.   demonstrates how conciliation reduces conflict.
D.   illustrates the tragedy of the commons.

Answer D, Type FAC

88.   Research on laboratory dilemmas reveals that cooperation is facilitated if

A.   one person is 100 percent cooperative.
B.   the opponents can communicate with one another.
C.   the game is changed into a zero-sum game.
D.   the size of the payoffs is increased.

Answer B, Type FAC

89. Bargaining tough is likely to backfire
    A. when the conflict is over a pie of fixed size.
    B. when the conflict is over a pie that can shrink.
    C. when females bargain tough with males.
    D. in virtually every situation.
    Answer B, Type FAC

90. The "Kennedy experiment" was an application of_____ to international tension reduction.
    A. equal status contact
    B. the jigsaw technique
    C. arbitration
    D. the GRIT model
    Answer D, Type FAC

91. Two gas station owners in Roseville cut their gas prices in order to capture a portion of their competitor's business. However, neither gained any of the other's customers and in the long run both operated at a loss. This outcome best illustrates the dynamics of
    A. a social dilemma.
    B. he GRIT strategy.
    C. an inequitable relationship.
    D. mirror-image perceptions.
    Answer A, Type CON

92. Rodney and Ralph are twin brothers who each contributed $75 to purchase a new bicycle. Rodney rides it 75 percent of the time. This would be an example of
    A. an inequitable relationship.
    B. the tragedy of the commons.
    C. a zero-sum relationship.
    D. mirror-image perceptions.
    Answer A, Type CON

93. John believes he is hardworking but his wife Rachel is lazy. Rachel believes she is hardworking but John is lazy. This is an example of
    A. an inequitable relationship.
    B. mirror-image perception.
    C. a superordinate goal.
    D. a social trap.
    Answer B, Type CON

94. Which of the following best illustrates a superordinate goal?
    A. A college student who has been failing English gets an "A" on a paper.
    B. A woman beats her husband at tennis.
    C. Apartment dwellers install a television antenna they can all use.
    D. An obese person loses 20 pounds in two weeks.
    Answer C, Type CON

95. According to the text, contact between two conflicting racial groups can often improve relationships and correct misperceptions. Which kind of contact is, however, least likely to have that effect?
    A. placing Black and White athletes on the same baseball team
    B. having Black and White employees work together in small groups in an industrial plant

C.   placing White policemen on duty in predominantly Black residential neighborhoods

D.   having Blacks and Whites move into the same apartment building

Answer C, Type CON

96.   Sherif's studies of conflict in summer camp should lead one to suggest which of the following to a couple having marital difficulties?

A.   play poker, keeping a cumulative score

B.   encounter each other: express your true feelings

C.   work together on something

D.   take separate vacations

Answer C, Type CON

97.   Factory workers want a pay rate of $15 per hour and management offers $12 per hour. After weeks of conflict they agree to have a third party set the pay scale. After hearing both sides the third party sets the rate at $14. This is an example of resolving conflict through

A.   bargaining.

B.   arbitration.

C.   mediation.

D.   conciliation.

Answer B, Type CON

98.   The GRIT model could be applied to the reduction of conflict between

A.   individuals.

B.   groups.

C.   nations.

D.   All of the above.

Answer D, Type CON

99.   Compared to compromises, integrative agreements are

A.   more enduring and lead to better ongoing relationships.

B.   only reached through mediation or arbitration.

C.   only possible when perceived injustice is the cause of conflict.

D.   less likely to lead to a permanent settlement.

Answer A, Type FAC

100.   Kevin and Joel, two teenage brothers, are fighting over the evening newspaper. Knowing Kevin only wants the sports section and Joel only wants the latest stock quotations, their mother takes the paper and gives each boy the section containing the news of interest. In this case the mother arrived at a(n)

A.   mutual compromise.

B.   cooperative settlement.

C.   enlightened consensus.

D.   integrative agreement.

Answer D, Type CON

Critical Thinking Questions

101.   Compare and contrast the Prisoner's Dilemma and the Tragedy of the Commons.

102.   What is your ideal definition of justice in an intimate relationship? Is it the same as your ideal definition of justice in the realm of economics? Why or why not?

103.   When will desegregation be most likely to lead to improved race relations and when will it not?

104.   Why do common external threats and superordinate goals both lead to greater cooperation between conflicting parties?

105. According to the text, the goal of a third-party mediator is to "enable conflicting parties to make concessions and still save face." Based on the text's discussion, what are the strategies that a mediator can use to achieve this goal?

Multiple Choice Questions

1. _____ psychology is the study, assessment, and treatment of people with psychological difficulties.
    A.   Psychometric
    B.   Health
    C.   Medical
    D.   Clinical
    Answer D, Type DEF

2. According to the text, professional clinical judgment is vulnerable to
    A.   illusory correlations.
    B.   overconfidence bred by hindsight.
    C.   self-confirming diagnosis.
    D.   All of the above.
    Answer D, Type FAC

3. Chapman and Chapman had college students and professional clinicians study the relationship between patients' test performances and diagnoses. They found that
    A.   if students or clinicians expected a particular association, they perceived it, regardless of whether the data was supportive.
    B.   students and clinicians only saw relationships that were indeed supported by the data.
    C.   professional clinicians were more accurate than students in assessing relationships.
    D.   students and clinicians only recognized positive relationships if the actual correlations were greater than .75.
    Answer A, Type FAC

4. Our tendency to notice confirming instances but not disconfirming instances of an expected relationship contributes to
    A.   illusory correlation.
    B.   perceptual connectivity.
    C.   the attention heuristic.
    D.   the ultimate attribution error.
    Answer A, Type DEF

5. Following the suicide of a friend or family member, feelings of guilt are often magnified by
    A.   illusory thinking.
    B.   the fundamental attribution error.
    C.   hindsight bias.
    D.   confirmation bias.
    Answer C, Type FAC

6. Dr. Phillips, a psychotherapist, is plagued by doubt and guilt after a client commits suicide. These guilt feelings probably stem from _____ on the part of the therapist.
    A.   self-serving bias
    B.   the ultimate attribution error
    C.   self-handicapping
    D.   hindsight bias

Answer D, Type CON

7. Clinician David Rosenhan and his colleagues faked schizophrenic symptoms to infiltrate mental hospitals. Once they had been admitted and no longer complained of any fake symptoms,
    A. professional clinicians quickly distinguished them from the real patients and released them from hospitalization.
    B. the clinicians sought and found evidence in their histories and behavior to confirm their admitting diagnoses.
    C. the pseudopatients were ostracized by the hospital's real patients.
    D. the pseudopatients absorbed their "sick" roles and developed additional symptoms in the course of their treatment.
    Answer B, Type FAC

8. In the Rosenhan study, clinicians who dealt with pseudopatients who had faked symptoms to get into mental hospitals demonstrated the error of
    A. self-serving bias.
    B. hindsight bias.
    C. self-handicapping.
    D. overjustification.
    Answer B, Type FAC

9. Snyder and Swann gave interviewers some hypotheses to test concerning individuals' traits, and found that people often test for a trait by
    A. asking those being tested for a general self-evaluation.
    B. looking for information that will contradict it.
    C. looking for information that will confirm it.
    D. All of the above.
    Answer C, Type FAC

10. Darnell is a personnel officer instructed to probe job candidates for signs of ambition and self-motivation. If given the following list of questions to use in interviewing candidates, which question is Darnell most likely to choose?
    A. "In what kinds of situations are you most likely to feel discouraged and ready to give up?"
    B. "What do you believe is the single most important quality to have for this job?"
    C. "Can you give me examples of how you have taken initiative in the past and shown yourself to be a self-starter?"
    D. "Who is the person you most admire?"
    Answer C, Type CON

11. Annette is going out on a first date with Tony, whom her best friend says is funny and fun-loving. On the date, Annette predictably asks Tony, "What is the most fun-loving thing you've ever done?" What is the likely effect of such questioning on Tony?
    A. He will act more fun-loving on the date than if not asked such questions.
    B. He will act more reserved and shy than if not asked such questions.
    C. He will resent such questions and become annoyed.
    D. He will try to explain that there are times when he is not fun-loving.
    Answer A, Type CON

12. Research indicates that when interviewers are instructed to test for a trait, they tend to ask questions that show evidence of
    A. the confirmation bias.
    B. the illusion of control.

C.   negative attributional style.

D.   illusory correlation.

Answer A, Type FAC

13.   Confirmation bias has been demonstrated to occur when

A.   college student research participants are given a hypothesis (e.g., "this person is extraverted") to test.

B.   experienced psychotherapists are given a hypothesis to test.

C.   people evaluate themselves in response to questions such as "are you happy with your social life?"

D.   All of the above.

Answer D, Type FAC

14.   Snyder and his colleagues found that they could get interviewers to search for behaviors that would disconfirm the trait they were testing for by

A.   telling them that it was relevant and informative to find out ways in which the person might not be like the stereotype.

B.   promising $25 to the interviewer who developed the set of questions that told the most about the interviewee.

C.   Both A and B resulted in interviewers overcoming their confirmation bias.

D.   None of the above worked in overcoming the confirmation bias of the interviewers.

Answer A, Type FAC

15.   Freudian therapists who expect to find evidence of early childhood traumas are likely to uncover such experiences among clients who are

A.   gay males.

B.   real victims of childhood sex abuse.

C.   healthy, successful adults.

D.   All of the above.

Answer D, Type FAC

16.   Some researchers believe that psychotherapists' susceptibility to confirmation bias may explain

A.   their patients' recovered memories of sex abuse.

B.   the occurrence of transference in therapy.

C.   the sadder-but-wiser effect in depressed patients.

D.   the beneficial effects of patients' optimism.

Answer A, Type FAC

17.   When researchers pit statistical prediction--such as predicting graduate school success on a formula including grades and aptitude scores--against interviewers' intuitive prediction,

A.   statistical prediction is usually superior to expert intuition.

B.   expert intuition is usually superior to statistical intuition.

C.   statistical prediction and expert intuition do equally well.

D.   both methods usually fare no better than chance.

Answer A, Type FAC

18.   Research suggests that the prediction of someone's future academic success is best when the prediction is based on

A.   statistics.

B.   the judgments of trained admissions officers.

C.   statistics plus the judgments of trained admissions officers.

D.   letters of recommendation.

Answer A, Type FAC

19. Robyn Dawes suggests that clinicians and interviewers express more confidence in their intuitive assessments than in statistical data because of
   A.   unreliability in statistical predictions.
   B.   the lack of validity in standardized tests like the SAT or GRE.
   C.   cognitive conceit.
   D.   the fundamental attribution error.
   Answer C, Type FAC

20. According to research evidence, professional clinicians
   A.   often overestimate the predictive powers of their clinical intuition.
   B.   are frequently the victims of illusory correlation.
   C.   are fooled by hindsight analysis and self-confirming diagnoses.
   D.   All of the above.
   Answer D, Type FAC

21. According to the text, an important implication of the research on illusory thinking is that
   A.   intuition really has no legitimate place in doing science.
   B.   the scientific method is the only legitimate way to answer significant human questions.
   C.   research psychologists must test their preconceptions before propounding them as truth.
   D.   the conventional wisdom is almost always wrong.
   Answer C, Type FAC

22. Alloy and Abramson had depressed and nondepressed students observe whether their pressing a button was linked with a light blinking and found that depressed students
   A.   were too self-focused to complete the task.
   B.   were quite accurate at assessing their control.
   C.   exaggerated the extent of their control of the light.
   D.   underestimated the extent of their control of the light.
   Answer B, Type FAC

23. The work of Alloy and Abramson in studying how depressives view the extent of their personal control over events provides evidence of the phenomenon known as
   A.   optimistic well-being.
   B.   pessimistic exaggeration.
   C.   depressive realism.
   D.   learned helplessness.
   Answer C, Type DEF

24. The tendency of mildly depressed people to make accurate rather than self-serving judgments is referred to as
   A.   accurate explanatory style.
   B.   the Barnum effect.
   C.   realistic pessimism.
   D.   depressive realism.
   Answer D, Type DEF

25. Jane, a college senior, is mildly depressed. Asked to describe herself, she notes both her positive and negative qualities. She recalls both past successes and failures and takes personal responsibility for both. Jane clearly illustrates the _____ effect.
   A.   rose-colored-glasses
   B.   sadder-but-wiser
   C.   head-in-the-clouds
   D.   feet-on-the-ground

Answer B, Type CON

26. Compared to depressed people, normal people
    A.   exaggerate their control of events around them.
    B.   have realistic perceptions of the good and bad things the future holds.
    C.   readily accept responsibility for both success and failure.
    D.   describe themselves with a fairly even mix of positive and negative qualities.
    Answer A, Type FAC

27. "Explanatory style" refers to
    A.   the complexity of one's persuasive arguments.
    B.   one's habitual way of explaining life events.
    C.   the pitch and speed with which one communicates.
    D.   whether one relies primarily on reason or emotion in debating an issue.
    Answer B, Type DEF

28. Explaining life events in terms of factors that are stable, global, and internal is a _____ explanatory style.
    A.   negative
    B.   positive
    C.   realistic
    D.   repressive
    Answer A, Type DEF

29. Maxwell, a college junior, suffers from chronic depression. After learning that he has performed poorly on his chemistry test, he is most likely to say,
    A.   "The test was not a fair assessment of what I actually know."
    B.   "My chemistry professor does not grade his tests fairly."
    C.   "I'm incompetent and probably always will be."
    D.   "I am sure most people did poorly on the test."
    Answer C, Type CON

30. Which of the following attributions regarding a failure or a setback illustrates the global quality of a depressed person's explanatory style?
    A.   "It's my fault."
    B.   "It's going to last forever."
    C.   "The whole world is against me."
    D.   "It's going to affect everything I do."
    Answer D, Type CON

31. Which of the following best illustrates an internal attribution for a failure or setback?
    A.   "I'll never succeed."
    B.   "This ruins everything."
    C.   "It's my fault."
    D.   "The whole world is against me."
    Answer C, Type CON

32. Depressed moods can lead to
    A.   memories for negative events.
    B.   bleak assessments of one's future performance.
    C.   reciprocal depression in others.
    D.   All of the above.
    Answer D, Type FAC

33. Strack and Coyne found that depressed people were realistic in thinking that other people

A. possessed more accurate self-concepts.
B. did not appreciate their behavior.
C. would welcome their friendship and trust.
D. were less influenced by fear of social disapproval.
Answer B, Type FAC

34. College students who have depressed roommates tend to become
    A. somewhat depressed themselves.
    B. more accepting of people suffering psychological disorder.
    C. more optimistic about their own lives.
    D. more studious and committed to achieving academic success.
    Answer A, Type FAC

35. When given a choice whether to read a favorable or unfavorable assessment of their personality,
    _____ percent of depressed people elect to see unfavorable information.
    A. 100
    B. 82
    C. 25
    D. 12
    Answer B, Type FAC

36. The vicious cycle of depression is usually triggered by negative experiences that lead directly to
    A. self-focus and self-blame.
    B. depressed mood.
    C. further negative experiences.
    D. blaming others for the negative experience.
    Answer A, Type FAC

37. Which of the following explains the relation between depression and negative thinking?
    A. depressed moods cause negative thinking
    B. negative thinking causes depressed moods
    C. depression and negative thinking are unrelated in laboratory experiments
    D. both a and b are true
    Answer D, Type FAC

38. In North America, today's young adults are _____ as likely as their grandparents ever to
    have suffered depression.
    A. one-half
    B. twice
    C. three times
    D. five times
    Answer C, Type FAC

39. According to researcher Martin Seligman, near-epidemic levels of depression in America today,
    ironically, can be blamed in part on the promotion of attitudes that say,
    A. "Everybody needs somebody sometime."
    B. "You can make it on your own."
    C. "You're nobody if nobody loves you."
    D. "Eat, drink, and be merry, for tomorrow we die."
    Answer B, Type FAC

40. According to Martin Seligman's analysis of the attitudes that promote near-epidemic levels of
    depression in America, most of us feel that, if we don't "make it" in today's world, we can blame
    A. our parents.

B.   the government.

C.   the alienation of the modern world.

D.   only ourselves.

Answer D, Type FAC

41.   In comparison to those in Western cultures, depressed people in Japan are more likely to report feeling

      A.   guilt and self-blame over personal failure.

      B.   shame over letting down their family or co-workers.

      C.   sad about social problems such as poverty and discrimination.

      D.   All of the above.

Answer B, Type FAC

42.   Loneliness is best described as a state created by the awareness that you

      A.   are alone most of the time.

      B.   have lost a significant relationship.

      C.   have less numerous or meaningful social relationships than you desire.

      D.   are not really respected even though you have many acquaintances.

Answer C, Type DEF

43.   When beeped by an electronic pager at various times during a week and asked to record what they were doing and how they felt, _____ were most likely to report feeling lonely when alone.

      A.   children

      B.   adolescents

      C.   adults

      D.   women

Answer B, Type FAC

44.   According to Dill and Anderson (1998), chronic depression, loneliness, and shyness are primarily related in which of the following ways?

      A.   depression causes loneliness which causes shyness

      B.   shyness is causally unrelated to loneliness, but loneliness causes depression

      C.   shyness is a cause of both loneliness and depression, but loneliness and depression are unrelated

      D.   shyness is a cause of both loneliness and depression, and loneliness is a cause of depression

Answer D, Type FAC

45.   Chronically lonely people seem to have the same _____ as chronically depressed people.

      A.   unrealistic vision of the future

      B.   need to achieve perfection

      C.   illusion of control

      D.   negative explanatory style

Answer D, Type FAC

46.   Which of the following statements about lonely people is true?

      A.   They perceive others in negative ways.

      B.   They tend to be low in self-esteem.

      C.   When talking with strangers, they spend more time talking about themselves and take less interest in the other person.

      D.   All of the above.

Answer D, Type FAC

47.   According to self-presentation theory, we will feel social anxiety when we are

A.   motivated to impress others but doubt our ability to do so.
B.   motivated and able to impress others, but they ignore us.
C.   in any circumstance in which we can be observed.
D.   depressed.
Answer A, Type DEF

48.   Which of the following theories most clearly predicts that we will feel anxious when we are motivated to impress others but doubt our ability to do so?
A.   social learning theory
B.   self-presentation theory
C.   self-perception theory
D.   cognitive dissonance theory
Answer B, Type DEF

49.   According to the text, shyness is a form of _____ characterized by self-consciousness and worry about what others think.
A.   loneliness
B.   social anxiety
C.   depression
D.   social incompetence
Answer B, Type DEF

50.   Shy people tend to
A.   make a bad first impression.
B.   over-personalize social situations.
C.   become well-liked over time.
D.   All of the above.
Answer D, Type FAC

51.   According to the text, labeling oneself as shy, depressed, or under the influence of alcohol can serve _____ function.
A.   an anger-reducing
B.   a self-handicapping
C.   a concurrence-seeking
D.   a group-identification
Answer B, Type FAC

52.   Brodt and Zimbardo found that shy women who were bombarded with loud noise and told that it would leave them _____ were subsequently _____ in interacting with a handsome male.
A.   with a pounding heart; no longer so shy
B.   unaffected; no longer so shy
C.   with a pounding heart; even more shy
D.   unaffected; even more shy
Answer A, Type FAC

53.   Psychology's contribution to the interdisciplinary field of behavioral medicine is _____.
A.   clinical psychology
B.   psychiatry
C.   behavioral analysis
D.   health psychology
Answer D, Type DEF

54.   Which of the following statements is true?

A. Most of us are not good at judging our own heart rate, blood pressure, or blood sugar level.

B. One's actual blood pressure is closely related to how one feels—making judgments of blood pressure easy and fairly accurate.

C. Most of us are quite good at judging our own heart rate, blood pressure, and blood-sugar level.

D. Early signs of illnesses such as cancer and heart disease are easily recognized.

Answer A, Type FAC

55. According to the text and research evidence, premenstrual syndrome (PMS)

A. occurs in 6 of 10 women.

B. leads to premenstrual dysphoric disorder in 3 of 10 women.

C. is a socially constructed disorder.

D. is a myth perpetuated by men.

Answer C, Type FAC

56. Which of the following statements is false?

A. People more often seek treatment if they believe their symptoms have a physical rather than a psychological cause.

B. Women are more often sick.

C. Women are more likely than men to visit a physician.

D. Men use fewer prescription and nonprescription drugs.

Answer B, Type FAC

57. Which of the following has been linked with a greater vulnerability to illness?

A. an anger-prone personality

B. depression

C. pessimism

D. All of the above.

Answer D, Type FAC

58. Experiments that subject animals to mild but uncontrollable electric shocks, loud noises, or crowding have shown that such experiences

A. directly cause diseases like cancer.

B. lower the body's resistance to disease.

C. strengthen the animals' capacity to deal with future stressors.

D. lead to the animals becoming more aggressive in interacting with members of their own species.

Answer B, Type FAC

59. A growing body of evidence reveals that people who undergo highly stressful experiences become

A. more resistant to low-level illnesses like colds and flu.

B. become more vulnerable to disease.

C. less self-disclosing and more socially isolated.

D. stronger and more socially skilled than unstressed people.

Answer B, Type FAC

60. Research has reported that newlywed couples who become angry while discussing problems

A. experience catharsis and better long-term relationships with their spouses.

B. are subsequently more susceptible to problems of depression and loneliness.

C. suffer more immune system suppression the next day.

D. are more prone to develop colon cancer in the subsequent six months.

Answer C, Type FAC

61. A large Swedish study has found that, compared with unstressed workers, those with a history of workplace stress
    A. are better prepared to deal with stress in their family lives.
    B. tend to have a more pessimistic explanatory style.
    C. are at much greater risk of developing colon cancer.
    D. develop stronger immune defenses.
    Answer C, type FAC

62. Which of the following is <u>not</u> an example of one of the components of a pessimistic explanatory style?
    A. "This is all my fault."
    B. "I've learned my lesson."
    C. "This is going to ruin everything."
    D. "Things are going to be terrible from now on."
    Answer B, Type CON

63. Peterson and Seligman analyzed the press quotes of baseball Hall of Famers and found that those who routinely offered pessimistic explanations for bad events, like losing big games, were more likely to
    A. earn lower salaries.
    B. experience divorce.
    C. play aggressively.
    D. die at younger ages.
    Answer D, Type FAC

64. Research by Scheier and Carver indicates that people who agree with statements like _____ are less often bothered by various illnesses and even recover faster from operations like coronary bypass surgery.
    A. "My fate is out of my hands."
    B. "Human life is fragile."
    C. "I usually expect the best out of life."
    D. "I rarely count on good things happening to me."
    Answer C, Type FAC

65. A study of 86 women undergoing breast cancer therapy found that survival time was nearly doubled among those who
    A. participated in morale-boosting weekly support groups.
    B. were involved in some competitive team sport.
    C. developed a new hobby that captured their interest.
    D. participated in daily relaxation exercises.
    Answer A, Type FAC

66. Julie has been recently diagnosed as having breast cancer and is receiving the best medical treatment available. Research suggests that her chances of survival may also be enhanced if her attitude is
    A. disciplined and cooperative.
    B. realistic and impassive.
    C. hopeful and determined.
    D. pessimistic and combative.
    Answer C, Type CON

67. Research investigating the nature of the connection between explanatory style and health has shown that people who routinely use the pessimistic style
   A. have weaker bodily immune defenses.
   B. boost the morale of others via a contrast effect.
   C. also tend to be impulsive and resistant to influence.
   D. complain more but are not really sicker than optimists.
   Answer A, Type FAC

68. Both assertiveness training and rational-emotive therapy are cited in the text as examples of psychotherapeutic techniques that
   A. utilize social support to change behavior.
   B. utilize the attitudes-follow-behavior principle.
   C. encourage changes in explanatory style.
   D. use counter-conditioning strategies.
   Answer B, Type FAC

69. Mendonca and Brehm found that overweight children were more likely to lose weight and keep it off after an eight-week program if they
   A. felt responsible for choosing their weight-loss program.
   B. were regularly monitored and penalized for breaking rules.
   C. were praised and rewarded for even minor weight loss.
   D. had been assigned to their "least preferred" treatment program and thus exercised the greatest effort in losing weight.
   Answer A, Type FAC

70. Axom and Cooper put women who wanted to lose weight through some supposedly therapeutic tasks, such as making perceptual judgments. Results indicated that those who
   _____ lost the most weight.
   A. were most authoritarian
   B. committed the most effort to the tasks
   C. felt the most social pressure to perform the tasks
   D. found the tasks most interesting
   Answer B, Type FAC

71. A study by Haemmerlie and Montgomery enticed shy college men to participate in laboratory exercises in which they were able to perceive themselves as socially competent after they
   A. were taught specific communication skills.
   B. took a short course on positive thinking.
   C. delivered self-laudatory speeches to strangers.
   D. had several successful conversations with women.
   Answer D, Type FAC

72. Research by Haemmerlie and Montgomery supports the notion that social skills training can lead shy men to
   A. become dependent on their therapist.
   B. develop more positive self-perceptions.
   C. concentrate on their social incompetence.
   D. become more shy 6 months after treatment.
   Answer B, Type FAC

73. Haemmerlie and Montgomery conclude that the success of their social skills training with shy men may very well have occurred because their program

A. employed skilled counselors who took responsibility for inspiring the men to feel confident and competent.

B. included no counseling, so the participants had to act on their own.

C. protected the men from having to participate in actual conversations until they had been extensively trained first.

D. paved the way for conversational success by providing many external reasons for initiating conversation.

Answer B, Type FAC

74. The vicious cycles that maintain depression, loneliness, and shyness can be broken by
    A. training in more effective social skills.
    B. positive experiences that alter self-perceptions.
    C. changing negative thought patterns.
    D. All of the above.

Answer D, Type FAC

75. Improvements achieved through changing thought or behavior patterns are most likely to endure if people
    A. redesign their behavioral contexts.
    B. are required to report back to their therapist on a regular basis.
    C. attribute such changes to factors under their own control.
    D. recognize that success depends on a power beyond themselves.

Answer C, Type FAC

76. Bill, a middle-aged insurance salesman, has recently managed to lose 50 pounds while on a weight-control program. Research suggests that he is most likely to maintain the weight loss if he
    A. attributes his changed eating behavior to the program.
    B. credits his success to his own efforts at self-control.
    C. successfully persuades several friends to participate in the same treatment program.
    D. subsequently participates in an assertiveness training program.

Answer B, Type CON

77. According to the text, which of the following is a social-psychological principle that can be applied to the treatment of psychological difficulties?
    A. attitudes-follow-behavior
    B. we are cognitive misers
    C. acceptance breeds compliance
    D. None of the above.

Answer A, Type FAC

78. Warr and Payne (1982) asked British adults what had emotionally strained them and what had brought them emotional pleasure the day before. Their most frequent answers were _____ and _____, respectively.
    A. family; hobbies
    B. work; friends
    C. family; family
    D. work; family

Answer C, Type FAC

79. A common conclusion reached by six studies involving thousands of people is that
    A. close relationships promote health.
    B. close relationships promote stress and some forms of illness.

C.   family relationships are unrelated to health.

D.   physical health is not linked to social support.

Answer A, Type FAC

80.   Ginny was sexually abused as a child, but she has never told anyone. Robin was also abused, but she has been able to talk about it as an adult. According to research, Ginny is more likely to

A.   suffer from health problems.

B.   want psychotherapy.

C.   have been a firstborn child.

D.   seek out a large circle of supportive friends.

Answer A, Type CON

81.   Within individualistic cultures, who is more likely to report greater life satisfaction?

A.   individualists

B.   materialists

C.   those with a competitive approach to life

D.   those with a group-centered approach to life

Answer D, Type FAC

82.   When asked what makes their lives meaningful or happy, most people mention _____ before anything else.

A.   satisfying close relationships

B.   their health

C.   their work

D.   money

Answer A, Type FAC

83.   Which of the following is the best predictor of overall happiness?

A.   a satisfying job

B.   satisfaction with finances

C.   satisfaction with one's community

D.   satisfaction with marriage

Answer D, Type FAC

84.   According to the text, marriage enhances happiness for which of the following reasons?

A.   it provides regular sex to both partners

B.   it provides financial security

C.   it provides multiple roles (e.g., spouse, parent) that can contribute to self-esteem

D.   it provides companionship

Answer C, Type FAC

85.   According to the text, how can you enhance your own happiness?

A.   act happy

B.   give priority to close relationships

C.   sleep

D.   All of the above.

Answer D, Type FAC

The following items also appear in the Study Guide:

86.   According to the text, social psychology has contributed to all of the following except

A.   our understanding of psychological disorders.

B.   the treatment of psychological disorders.

C.   improving the process of clinical judgment and prediction.

D.   the definition of psychological disorder.
Answer D, Type FAC

87.   The text suggests that clinicians may continue to have confidence in uninformative or ambiguous tests because of human susceptibility to
A.   the inoculation effect.
B.   learned helplessness.
C.   the representativeness heuristic.
D.   illusory correlation.
Answer D, Type FAC

88.   According to the text, the pervasiveness of illusory thinking points to the need for a _____ study of thought and behavior.
A.   psychohistorical
B.   literary
C.   scientific
D.   humanistic
Answer C, Type FAC

89.   Which of the following attributions regarding a failure or setback illustrates the stable quality of a depressed person's explanatory style?
A.   "It's all my fault."
B.   "It's going to last forever."
C.   "The whole world is against me."
D.   "It's going to affect everything I do."
Answer B, Type FAC

90.   Compared to nondepressed people, depressed people are more likely to attribute their failures and setbacks to causes that are
A.   unstable
B.   specific
C.   internal
D.   situational
Answer C, Type FAC

91.   Brodt and Zimbardo found that shy women were no longer shy when they
A.   were provided an alternative explanation for their social anxiety.
B.   were provided alcohol before interacting with others.
C.   discovered most people feel shy.
D.   were taught to blame their failures on circumstances beyond their control.
Answer A, Type FAC

92.   Which of the following is not given as an example of a therapy that utilizes the "attitudes-follow-behavior" principle?
A.   assertiveness training
B.   rational-emotive therapy
C.   self-help groups
D.   psychoanalysis
Answer D, Type FAC

93.   Robyn Dawes, writing in House of Cards: Psychology and Psychotherapy Built on Myth, reports that interviewers' ratings of medical school applicants were highly predictive of the applicants'
A.   likelihood of receiving the M.D.
B.   eventual performance in their first year of residency.

C.   likelihood of graduating from medical school with honors.

D.   None of the above.

Answer D, Type FAC

94.   Chronically lonely people tend to blame _____ for their poor social relationships.

A.   their parents and early childhood experiences

B.   the uncaring attitudes of those presently around them

C.   themselves

D.   cultural patterns

Answer C, Type FAC

95.   Dr. Jones is a psychologist who specializes in the causes and control of stress. Dr. Jones is most likely a(n) _____ psychologist.

A.   consumer

B.   educational

C.   forensic

D.   health

Answer D, Type CON

96.   Philip suffers from chronic depression. How is he likely to respond when told that he failed the test to renew his driver's license?

A.   "Yesterday was just my unlucky day."

B.   "I imagine very few people have passed that same test."

C.   "The person giving the test is incompetent."

D.   "I am a poor driver and always will be."

Answer D, Type CON

97.   Mary wants advice on how to cope with the stress of a new job. She would be best advised to approach her new job with a sense of

A.   skepticism and humility.

B.   ambition and competitiveness.

C.   urgency and time-consciousness.

D.   control and optimism.

Answer D, Type CON

98.   As a result of participating in a program to help him quit smoking, Bill has not had a cigarette for three weeks. He is least likely to return to smoking if he attributes his success in quitting the habit to

A.   his own motivation.

B.   the therapist who helped him quit.

C.   the support of his friends.

D.   the unique nature of the therapeutic program.

Answer A, Type CON

99.   Valerie is a mildly depressed college student. From research presented in the text on depression she

A.   probably suffers from the better-than-average phenomenon.

B.   assumes that her behavior is well-accepted by others.

C.   demonstrates the sadder-but-wiser effect.

D.   is below average in intelligence.

Answer C, Type CON

100.   Gayle, a Freudian analyst, finds that, without exception, her patients report dreams closely related to their emotional problems and that are easily understood in terms of Freud's theory of

personality. From research presented in the text, what may best explain why the dreams and problems of Gayle's patients are so consistent with Freudian theory?

A.   Freud's theory is the oldest and most comprehensive of all the theories of personality.

B.   Freud's theory is more ambiguous than any other theory, and thus any problem fits into its framework.

C.   The patients are perhaps induced to give information that is consistent with Gayle's theoretical orientation.

D.   Freudian psychotherapists are "true believers" and Gayle's report is an attempt to convert other therapists to her orientation.

Answer C, Type CON

Critical Thinking Questions

101.   Discuss how the hindsight bias and the confirmation bias can lead clinicians to be overconfident in their clinical judgments.

102.   Discuss the goal of explanatory style therapy for depression.

103.   How are chronic shyness, loneliness, and depression related?

104.   Identify and explain two social-psychological principles that may be usefully applied to the treatment of psychological difficulties.

105.   Married people are happier people, partly because they are less likely to suffer loneliness. Why else, according to the text, does marriage promote happiness?

Multiple Choice Questions

1. The text identifies all of the following questions or topics as pertinent to both social psychology and the law except
    A. How is the judicial function of a government related to its legislative function?
    B. How do a culture's norms and traditions influence its legal decisions?
    C. What legal procedures strike people as fair?
    D. In cases of civil liability, why do clients and their attorneys spend such enormous sums on legal fees before reaching settlements?
    Answer A, Type FAC

2. At the University of Washington, Elizabeth Loftus found that eyewitnesses in a hypothetical robbery-murder case were influential
    A. unless their testimony was shown to be useless.
    B. even when their testimony was discredited.
    C. only if other evidence supported their story.
    D. only if they were similar to those making judgment.
    Answer B, Type FAC

3. Loftus found that when an eyewitness who had testified against the defendant in a hypothetical robbery-murder case was discredited because of having poor vision
    A. about half the jurors switched their votes from guilty to innocent.
    B. the majority of jurors still voted for conviction.
    C. jurors regarded the eyewitness testimony as useless and it had no impact on their verdict.
    D. a boomerang effect occurred with all jurors now voting for acquittal.
    Answer B, Type FAC

4. A prosecuting attorney is uncertain whether her eyewitness will seem credible to the jury. The eyewitness's testimony could help win a conviction, but the witness might be discredited by the defense attorney. What advice should the prosecutor accept?
    A. Put the witness on the stand, since even a discredited eyewitness is more convincing than no eyewitness at all.
    B. Don't put the witness on the stand, since a discredited eyewitness is worse than no eyewitness at all.
    C. Put the eyewitness on the stand but admit your reservations about the witness's credibility before the defense attorney raises the issue.
    D. Put the witness on the stand only if he or she is attractive and similar to the jurors.
    Answer A, Type CON

5. Wells, Lindsay, and their colleagues staged the theft of a calculator hundreds of times before eyewitnesses. In attempting to determine whether people could spot erroneous testimony, the researchers had mock jurors observe the eyewitnesses being questioned. Results indicated that the jurors believed correct eyewitnesses _____ percent of the time and incorrect eyewitnesses _____ percent of the time.
    A. 60; 40
    B. 60; 20
    C. 80; 40

D.   80; 80
Answer D, Type FAC

6.   Lindsay, Wells, and Rumpel staged the same calculator theft under conditions that sometimes gave witnesses a clear view of the thief and sometimes didn't. When conditions were so poor that most witnesses misidentified an innocent person, _____ of the jurors believed the witness.
A.   none
B.   fewer than half
C.   more than half
D.   almost all
Answer C, Type FAC

7.   Studies of eyewitness testimony indicate that
A.   jurors have very good ability at discerning whether eyewitnesses have mistakenly identified an innocent person.
B.   when witnessing conditions are shown to have been poor, jurors do not usually believe eyewitness testimony.
C.   eyewitnesses who are shown to have poor eyesight have little effect on the juror's judgment.
D.   None of the above are true.
Answer D, Type FAC

8.   Jurors think that an eyewitness who can recall trivial details such as how many pictures were hanging in the room probably
A.   gained information about these details by a second visit to the crime scene and thus is less credible.
B.   was paying better attention than one who recalls no details.
C.   was not paying attention to the culprit or the crime itself.
D.   is no more accurate in recalling important information than witnesses with no memory for details.
Answer B, Type FAC

9.   Research indicates that eyewitnesses who remember trivial details of a crime scene
A.   also tend to overestimate the degree of harm or damage done as a result of the crime.
B.   also tend to be particularly suspicious of all unfamiliar faces.
C.   are less likely to have paid attention to the culprit's face.
D.   are more likely to have paid attention to the culprit's face.
Answer C, Type FAC

10.   City police find that Mr. Caldwell, an eyewitness to a murder in a local bank, correctly remembers many trivial details of the crime scene, including the specific time on the clock and the paintings on the wall. Research findings suggest that Mr. Caldwell's recall of trivial details means
A.   it is more likely that he can also correctly identify the murderer.
B.   it is less likely that he can also correctly identify the murderer.
C.   nothing in terms of his ability to correctly identify the murderer.
D.   it is more likely that he can also correctly identify the murderer, provided Mr. Caldwell is also highly educated.
Answer B, Type CON

11.   A prosecuting attorney learns that a crucial eyewitness to a grocery store robbery correctly remembers trivial details of the crime scene. If the prosecutor hopes to convince the jury that the eyewitness is credible, research suggests

A.	he should make the jury aware of the witness's ability to remember trivial details.

B.	he should deliberately avoid making the jury aware of the witness's ability to remember trivial details.

C.	it will make no difference whether the jury knows that the witness can remember trivial details.

D.	he should make the jury aware of the witness's ability to remember trivial details only if the jury is composed of all males.

Answer A, Type CON

12.	Wells and his colleagues report that it's the _____ eyewitness whom jurors find to be most believable.

A.	older

B.	younger

C.	confident

D.	emotional

Answer C, Type FAC

13.	Of the following eyewitnesses to a crime, who would probably appear most believable to a jury?

A.	Billy, a fifth-grader whose father is a lawyer

B.	Paul, a radio announcer who appears very confident about what he saw

C.	Moira, a retired teacher who has traveled widely to visit other countries

D.	Joyce, a shy student who smiles and speaks very softly

Answer B, Type CON

14.	Which of the following statements about eyewitness testimony is false?

A.	Eyewitnesses' certainty about what they have seen is closely related to their accuracy.

B.	Confident witnesses are more believable to jurors than those lacking confidence.

C.	Incorrect witnesses are virtually as confident as correct witnesses.

D.	In the United States alone, some 80,000 trials a year hinge on eyewitness testimony.

Answer A, Type FAC

15.	In 1972 the U.S. Supreme Court declared that among the factors to be considered in determining eyewitness accuracy is " the level of _____ demonstrated by the witness."

A.	impartiality

B.	interest

C.	certainty

D.	fluency

Answer C, Type FAC

16.	Which of the following statements is true?

A.	eyewitnesses can be highly inaccurate and yet sincerely confident

B.	confident eyewitnesses are more accurate than uncertain eyewitnesses

C.	both the gender and race of the eyewitness have been shown to influence their degree of accuracy

D.	eyewitnesses who pay attention to details are most likely to pay attention to the culprit's face

Answer A, Type FAC

17.	Mistaken eyewitnesses tend to be less _____ than accurate witnesses.

A.	willing to testify

B.	confident

C.	persuasive

D.	None of the above.

Answer D, Type FAC

18. In a classic 1947 experiment, Allport and Postman showed participants a picture of a White man brandishing a razor while arguing with a Black man. After six tellings of the story, participant to participant, the last version of the story said that
    A. the Black man held the razor.
    B. both the White man and the Black man held razors.
    C. both men were Black and fighting each other.
    D. both men were White and conversing with each other.
    Answer A, Type FAC

19. Loftus and her associates' studies of the misinformation effect provide a dramatic demonstration of
    A. memory construction.
    B. repressed memory.
    C. proactive interference.
    D. state-dependent memory.
    Answer A, Type FAC

20. In research by Loftus and colleagues, University of Washington students were shown slides depicting successive stages of an automobile-pedestrian accident. Results showed that
    A. most witnesses did not notice the difference between a stop sign and a yield sign.
    B. eyewitnesses were unable to determine whether the driver or the pedestrian had been at fault.
    C. when the information was presented slowly, eyewitnesses' accuracy of recall became nearly flawless.
    D. asking misleading questions caused distortion of eyewitnesses' memories.
    Answer D, Type FAC

21. The process of witnessing an event, receiving misleading information about it, and then incorporating the misleading information into one's memory of the event is referred to as the _____ effect.
    A. false memory
    B. misinformation
    C. inoculation
    D. interference
    Answer B, Type DEF

22. In the process known as the misinformation effect, individuals
    A. give misleading testimony in court.
    B. receive wrong information about an event and then incorporate that information into their memory for the event.
    C. give wrong information to police.
    D. fail to remember any information following a traumatic event.
    Answer B, Type DEF

23. After hearing a television report falsely indicating that drugs may have contributed to a recent auto accident, several eyewitnesses of the accident began to remember the driver as traveling at a faster rate of speed than was actually the case. This provides an example of
    A. flashbulb memory.
    B. state-dependent memory.
    C. the serial position effect.
    D. the misinformation effect.

Answer D, Type CON

24. Which of the following statements about asking eyewitnesses suggestive questions is true?
    A. After suggestive questioning, witnesses may believe that a red light was green or a clean-shaven robber had a mustache.
    B. Witnesses are most likely to incorporate misleading information into their memories if they think the questioner is well informed.
    C. Young children are more susceptible than adults to leading questions.
    D. All of the above.

Answer D, Type FAC

25. The tendency for witnesses to incorporate misleading information into their memories is especially strong when
    A. suggestive questions are repeated.
    B. the questioner is female rather than male.
    C. the event was a traffic incident rather than a violent crime.
    D. the witness is low in need for cognition.

Answer A, Type FAC

26. Research on the memories of young children indicates that
    A. they are better at remembering verbal than visual details.
    B. they tend to fabricate stories about their own victimization even when asked open-ended questions.
    C. they are especially susceptible to misinformation.
    D. None of the above.

Answer C, Type FAC

27. After Ceci and Bruck produced false memories in a group of preschool children, the children were interviewed by a professional psychologist. Following the interview,
    A. children realized that their memories were false.
    B. children were less anxiety-prone than before the interview.
    C. the psychologist could not reliably separate real from false memories.
    D. the psychologist could reliably identify the false memories.

Answer C, Type FAC

28. Ceci believes that young children's susceptibility to the misinformation effect raises the distinct possibility that
    A. some people have been falsely accused in sex abuse cases.
    B. many educators overestimate the competence of their students.
    C. repression leads children to forget that they were physically abused.
    D. many children are simply unable to experience empathy for dissimilar others.

Answer A, Type FAC

29. Which of the following statements is true?
    A. Retelling events accurately makes people less resistant to the misinformation effect.
    B. Rehearsing answers before taking the witness stand decreases the confidence of those who are wrong.
    C. Retelling events commits people to their recollections, accurate or not.
    D. All of the above.

Answer C, Type FAC

30. Wells, Ferguson, and Lindsay had eyewitnesses to a staged theft rehearse their answers to questions before taking the witness stand. Doing so
    A. increased the accuracy of the eyewitness testimony.

B.   decreased the confidence of those who were correct.
C.   increased the confidence of those who were wrong.
D.   increased the confidence of those who were correct and decreased the confidence of those who were wrong.
Answer C, Type FAC

31.   Sheppard and Vidmar had some students serve as witnesses to a fight, while others took the roles of lawyers and judges. When they had been interviewed by the defense lawyer, the witnesses
A.   gave testimony condemning the defendant as guilty.
B.   gained self-confidence and claimed to remember more details.
C.   gave testimony that was favorable to the defendant.
D.   were less susceptible to the misinformation effect.
Answer C, Type FAC

32.   Eyewitness testimony can be distorted or biased by which of the following?
A.   suggestive questions
B.   an eyewitness' own retelling of events
C.   whether they are an eyewitness for the defendant or the plaintiff
D.   All of the above
Answer D, Type FAC

33.   An eyewitness gains confidence from which of the following sources?
A.   knowing that another person identified the same person
B.   being asked the same question repeatedly
C.   preparing for cross-examination
D.   All of the above
Answer D, Type FAC

34.   Stan was initially uncertain about the man he identified as the burglar in a police lineup. His confidence increased, however, after
A.   learning that he was the only eyewitness in the case.
B.   being asked the same question repeatedly.
C.   viewing a thousand police mug shots.
D.   None of the above—his uncertainty remained.
Answer B, Type CON

35.   In Wells and Bradfield (1998), participants were asked to identify a gunman they had seen, on video, entering a store. After making a false identification but receiving confirming feedback, _____ percent rated their initial certainty as very high.
A.   100
B.   58
C.   10
D.   2
Answer B, Type FAC

36.   Which of the following statements about Wells and Bradfield (1998) is false?
A.   Participants were well aware of the influence of feedback on their initial confidence ratings.
B.   The effect of the experimenter's feedback was huge.
C.   The results illustrate the I-knew-it-all-along phenomenon.
D.   All of the above.
Answer A, Type FAC

37. Which of the following is <u>not</u> one recommended strategy for increasing the accuracy of eyewitnesses and jurors?
    A. Train police interviewers to elicit unbiased accounts.
    B. Educate jurors about the limitations of eyewitness testimony.
    C. Ask witnesses to scan a lineup of several suspects or mug shots simultaneously rather than one at a time.
    D. Have police acknowledge that the offender may not even be in the lineup.
    Answer C, Type FAC

38. The "cognitive interview" procedure for questioning eyewitnesses involves which of the following?
    A. allowing eyewitnesses to offer their own unprompted recollections
    B. guiding eyewitnesses to visualize the scene
    C. guiding eyewitnesses to imagine how they were feeling at the time
    D. All of the above
    Answer D, Type FAC

39. When Fisher and his colleagues trained detectives to use the "cognitive interview" procedure for questioning eyewitnesses,
    A. accuracy and confidence of eyewitnesses increased.
    B. the amount of information elicited from eyewitnesses increased 50%.
    C. false memory rate increased 50%.
    D. false memory rate increased slightly, but confidence increased dramatically.
    Answer B, Type FAC

40. Whose eyewitness testimony is probably the most reliable?
    A. Millie's report given immediately after a grocery store robbery. She was simply asked to tell the police what she saw.
    B. Fred's report given in court about a bank robbery a month ago. He has been interviewed several times by the defense attorney before appearing in court.
    C. Sue's report given immediately after observing an attempted rape. She was asked very specific questions by the police, who had identified a suspect immediately after the assault.
    D. All of the above are equally reliable.
    Answer A, Type CON

41. A police interrogator questioning a robbery eyewitness hopes to learn whether the assailant was wearing a bright green hat similar to one seen in another robbery. According to research, which of the following questions will elicit the most detailed, undistorted recall from the eyewitness?
    A. "Did you see whether the robber was wearing a hat?"
    B. "Can you describe the hat the robber was wearing?"
    C. "What color was the robber's hat?"
    D. "How was the robber dressed?"
    Answer D, Type CON

42. Researchers have found that eyewitnesses' accuracy can improve when
    A. interrogators delay the interview at least one week.
    B. the witnesses scan a group of mug shots or a composite drawing before reviewing a lineup.
    C. they are presented with a sequence of individual people, one by one, instead of being presented with a group of photos or a lineup.
    D. the seriousness of the crime is highlighted.

Answer C, Type FAC

43. Which of the following has been suggested as a strategy for reducing misidentifications in police lineups?
    A. giving eyewitnesses a "blank" lineup that contains no suspects and screening out those who make false identifications
    B. minimizing false identifications with instructions which acknowledge that the offender may not be in the lineup
    C. composing the lineup of one suspect and several known innocent people rather than a group of several suspects
    D. All of the above.
    Answer D, Type FAC

44. Which of the following is the best strategy for weeding out eyewitnesses who are just guessing?
    A. compose a lineup of several people known to be innocent, including just one suspect
    B. compose a lineup of several suspects and dress them all alike
    C. compose a lineup of several suspects who look very different from one another
    D. None of the above.
    Answer A, Type FAC

45. Which of the following is not one of the explanations experts offer to educate jurors to evaluate eyewitness testimony better?
    A. Eyewitnesses often perceive events selectively.
    B. Research using staged crimes shows that witnesses often choose the wrong person in a lineup.
    C. The most confident eyewitness usually turns out to be the most accurate.
    D. Eyewitnesses are especially prone to error when trying to identify someone of another race.
    Answer C, Type FAC

46. Which of the following is the most agreed upon phenomenon by experts on eyewitness testimony?
    A. Attitudes and expectations may not influence eyewitness memory.
    B. Eyewitness confidence is a reasonable, but not perfect, predictor of identification accuracy.
    C. Information obtained after the event will have minimal effects on memory.
    D. Question wording will likely affect eyewitness testimony about an event.
    Answer D, Type FAC

47. Clarence Darrow argued that "facts regarding the crime are relatively unimportant." Research suggests that
    A. Darrow was right.
    B. Darrow was partly right—the facts seem to matter about 10% of the time.
    C. Darrow was too cynical—facts do matter.
    D. None of the above.
    Answer C, Type FAC

48. A study of more than 3500 criminal cases and some 4000 civil cases found that _____ the judge agreed with the jury's decision.
    A. two times in three
    B. three times in four
    C. four times in five
    D. nine times in ten

Answer C, Type FAC

49. The more lenient treatment juries often give to _____ defendants suggests jurors' judgments continue to be contaminated by cultural bias.
    A. young
    B. high-status
    C. repentant
    D. poor
    Answer B, Type FAC

50. Which of the following factors is <u>not</u> likely to lead to a lighter sentence for the person convicted?
    A. high status
    B. baby-faced features
    C. height
    D. physical attractiveness
    Answer C, Type FAC

51. When a researcher gave students a description of a case of student cheating and showed them a photograph of either an attractive or unattractive person accused of the crime, he found that attractive defendants were
    A. recommended for least punishment.
    B. more likely to be judged as guilty.
    C. liked or respected.
    D. perceived as more dangerous.
    Answer A, Type FAC

52. Who among the following is likely to receive the most severe sentence for drunk driving?
    A. Kim, a good looking real estate agent
    B. Tim, an unattractive auto mechanic with long hair
    C. Ken, a clean-cut businessman
    D. Carol, an attractive single mother
    Answer B, Type CON

53. If convicted, _____ people strike people as more dangerous, especially if they are sexual offenders.
    A. cute or baby-faced
    B. attractive .
    C. unattractive
    D. underage
    Answer C, Type FAC

54. In researching over 1700 defendants appearing in Texas misdemeanor cases, Downs and Lyons found that the judges _____ less attractive defendants.
    A. set lower bails for
    B. set greater fines for
    C. spent less time reviewing the cases of
    D. spent more time questioning
    Answer B, Type FAC

55. Which of the following factors has been shown to influence either the likelihood of conviction or the severity of punishment?
    A. status
    B. attractiveness
    C. similarity to the jurors

D.   All of the above
Answer D, Type FAC

56.   Research shows that when people play the role of juror, they are more sympathetic to a defendant who
A.   shares their religion.
B.   is of another race.
C.   speaks a different language.
D.   is of the other gender.
Answer A, Type FAC

57.   When Paul Amato had Australian students read evidence concerning a left- or right-wing person accused of a politically motivated burglary, they judged him less guilty if
A.   he claimed to have no religious preferences.
B.   his political views were similar to their own.
C.   he claimed he had been hired to commit the crime.
D.   he proved he had not profited by the burglary.
Answer B, Type FAC

58.   According to the text, what factor helps explain why in acquaintance rape trials, men more often than women judge the defendant not guilty?
A.   similarity
B.   height
C.   status
D.   attractiveness
Answer A, Type FAC

59.   Research shows that when a judge rules evidence to be inadmissible and admonishes the jury to ignore it,
A.   jurors are generally able to follow the judge's instructions.
B.   jurors have a hard time ignoring the evidence and its influence on their deliberations.
C.   jurors do so if the evidence damages the defendant's case but not if it hurts the prosecution's case.
D.   the evidence typically becomes the focus of debate in jury deliberations.
Answer B, Type FAC

60.   Jurors have difficulty "erasing" the impact of inadmissible evidence
A.   when it's a criminal trial as opposed to a civil trial.
B.   when the inadmissible evidence is presented by the defense as opposed to the prosecution.
C.   especially when the inadmissible evidence has an emotional impact.
D.   when a witness, as opposed to a trial lawyer, blurts out the inadmissible evidence.
Answer C, Type FAC

61.   As a result of the judge's admonition that a jury disregard evidence ruled inadmissible, the stricken evidence may have even greater impact on the jury's decision than if it had not been ruled out. This is probably due to _____ in the jurors.
A.   reactance
B.   disinhibition
C.   self-efficacy
D.   self-monitoring
Answer A, Type FAC

62.   The concept of reactance has been used to explain why

A.   jurors show sympathy for an attractive defendant.
B.   a judge's instructions to a jury to ignore certain testimony can actually add to its impact.
C.   a severe potential punishment makes juries less likely to convict.
D.   experienced jurors' judgments differ from those of novice jurors.
Answer B, Type FAC

63. Which of the following statements is true?
A.   Most people will admit that pretrial publicity has influenced their ability to be impartial.
B.   The effect of pretrial publicity on jury members can be removed by a judge's instructions to disregard such publicity.
C.   A judge's orders to ignore inadmissible testimony can boomerang—adding to the impact of the testimony.
D.   Getting jurors to publicly pledge their impartiality eliminates the effect of pretrial publicity.
Answer C, Type FAC

64. To minimize the effects of inadmissible testimony, the text suggests that judges are best advised to
A.   wait until jurors have heard the testimony before ruling it inadmissible, so jurors specifically know what they are to disregard.
B.   forewarn jurors that certain types of evidence may be irrelevant and could be ruled inadmissible.
C.   meet with jurors during their deliberations after the trial to insure that inadmissible testimony is not influencing their judgments.
D.   immediately follow the trial by seeking a verbal pledge from each juror to ignore inadmissible evidence.
Answer B, Type FAC

65. Research suggests that the <u>victim's</u> characteristics can affect juror's judgments
A.   as long as the defendant was aware of those characteristics.
B.   even when the defendant was not aware of those characteristics.
C.   as long as the victim is similar to the jurors.
D.   as long as the defendant is similar to the jurors.
Answer B, Type FAC

66. From research findings, which of the following statements appears to be true?
A.   A severe potential punishment makes jurors less willing to convict.
B.   Experienced jurors' judgments differ from those of novice jurors.
C.   Defendants are judged more harshly when the victim is attractive.
D.   All of the above.
Answer D, Type FAC

67. In studying the thought processes of mock jurors, researchers have found that
A.   jurors construct a story that makes sense of all the evidence.
B.   verbal instructions are well understood.
C.   evidence in the form of statistical probabilities is the most convincing.
D.   All of the above.
Answer A, Type FAC

68. Research indicates that jurors are more likely to be persuaded when attorneys present evidence
A.   in the order of a narrative story.
B.   in the form of testing a hypothesis in an experiment.
C.   by numerically listing their specific arguments.

D. without interpretation or drawing conclusions from it.
Answer A, Type FAC

69. In a Nevada study of people's ability to comprehend judicial instructions, viewers of videotaped criminal instructions could answer _____ percent of the 89 questions posed to them about what they had heard.
A. 15
B. 30
C. 50
D. 65
Answer A, Type FAC

70. Research suggests that statistical information will have its maximal impact on jurors
A. who are men.
B. when the numbers are supported by a convincing story.
C. when trivial narrative details are left out and "just the facts" are presented.
D. None of the above.
Answer B, Type FAC

71. According to the text, giving jurors transcripts of court proceedings can
A. lead to stimulus overload and, in the long run, result in fewer people being willing to serve on juries.
B. aid the processing of complex information.
C. short-circuit their interest in the case and reduce their motivation to reach the best verdict.
D. help them review the evidence less emotionally and thus suffer less burnout.
Answer B, Type FAC

72. Individual differences in racial prejudice
A. potently predict jurors' verdicts in civil cases.
B. are relevant only in racially charged cases.
C. influence the sentencing phase but not the conviction phase of a trial.
D. are relevant only in rape cases.
Answer B, Type FAC

73. In experiments, jurors' personalities and general attitudes have been found to have the greatest effect on the verdict when
A. the evidence is clearly prodefendant.
B. the evidence is clearly antidefendant.
C. the evidence is ambiguous.
D. the crime is one that could warrant the death penalty.
Answer C, Type FAC

74. Death-qualified jurors are
A. more likely to be women.
B. less likely to convict in criminal cases.
C. more likely to convict in criminal cases.
D. more concerned with due process of law than with crime control.
Answer C, Type FAC

75. Evidence from social science research clearly indicates that
A. death-qualified jurors are more sympathetic to defendants than non-death-qualified jurors.
B. the death penalty is not a significant deterrent to crime.

C.   the death penalty undoubtedly is a significant deterrent to crime.

D.   None of the above.

Answer B, Type FAC

76.   Research suggests that jury deliberations can be influenced by all of the following processes except

A.   group polarization.

B.   minority influence.

C.   deindividuation.

D.   informational influence.

Answer C, Type FAC

77.   Research suggests that a hung jury is likely unless at least _____ of the jurors agree at the outset of deliberation.

A.   one-half

B.   two-thirds

C.   three-quarters

D.   90 percent

Answer B, Type FAC

78.   Research suggests that jurors in the minority will be most persuasive when they

A.   are consistent.

B.   are self-confident.

C.   win defections from the majority.

D.   All of the above.

Answer D, Type FAC

79.   Bray and Noble found that as a result of group deliberation low authoritarians recommended a _____ prison term and high authoritarians recommended a _____ prison term.

A.   longer; longer

B.   shorter; shorter

C.   longer; shorter

D.   shorter; longer

Answer D, Type FAC

80.   Hastie, Penrod, and Pennington showed participants reenactments of an actual murder case, and asked them to deliberate until they agreed on a verdict. Prior to group deliberation, jurors who thought the defendant was guilty preferred a verdict of _____; after deliberation, they preferred a verdict of _____.

A.   second-degree murder; manslaughter

B.   manslaughter; second-degree murder

C.   first-degree murder; second-degree murder

D.   manslaughter; not guilty

Answer B, Type FAC

81.   Research suggests that minorities are most likely to sway the majority

A.   when the minority favors conviction.

B.   when the minority favors acquittal.

C.   when the minority is composed of women.

D.   when the minority is composed of Whites.

Answer B, Type FAC

82.   Research on the effects of group deliberation by a jury suggests that

A. groups do no better at recalling information from a trial than do their individual members.
B. deliberation cancels out some of the biases that contaminate individual judgments.
C. deliberation increases the likelihood that jurors will use inadmissible evidence.
D. All of the above are true.
Answer B, Type FAC

83. Research indicates that six-member juries
A. are more likely to have hung verdicts.
B. allow less participation per juror.
C. encourage less balanced participation among jurors.
D. are less likely to embody a community's diversity.
Answer D, Type FAC

84. The fact that juries not required to reach consensus discuss minority views superficially illustrates
A. groupthink.
B. social loafing.
C. the fundamental attribution error.
D. the fact that we are cognitive misers.
Answer D, Type CON

85. In order to close the gap between real courtroom processes and laboratory studies, researchers are using _____ as participants and having them view _____.
A. university students; videotapes of courtroom trials
B. real jurors; dramas based on real-life cases
C. members of real jury pools; enactments of actual trials
D. real jurors; ongoing courtroom trials
Answer C, Type FAC

The following items also appear in the Study Guide:

86. From the text, which of the following is a true statement regarding social psychology and the courtroom?
A. Most of the government research funds available to social psychologists have been designated for the study of courtroom procedures.
B. The courtroom is a miniature social world where people think about and influence each other.
C. The study of criminal cases can provide important new insight into the causes of aggression and conflict.
D. Social psychology had its roots in the study of the courtroom.
Answer B, Type FAC

87. Which of the following is not part of the literature discussed in the text on social psychology and the courtroom?
A. how the defendant's characteristics can influence jurors' judgments
B. how the jurors' own characteristics can influence their judgments
C. how the physical environment of the jury room influences jurors' judgments
D. how the judge's instructions influence jurors' judgments
Answer C, Type FAC

88. Research on memory construction indicates that suggestive questioning can lead people to believe that
A. a yield sign was actually a stop sign.

B.   a red light was actually green.

C.   a robber had a moustache when he did not.

D.   All of the above.

Answer D, Type FAC

89.   Research indicates that having eyewitnesses rehearse their answers to questions before taking the witness stand

A.   raises uncertainty in the minds of eyewitnesses as to what they actually saw.

B.   increases their confidence about what they saw.

C.   increases their confidence but also heightens their anxiety about appearing in court.

D.   invariably leads them to give a much more detailed and accurate account of what they saw.

Answer B, Type FAC

90.   Survey researchers sometimes assist defense attorneys by using "scientific jury selection" to eliminate potential jurors likely to be unsympathetic. Results indicated that in the first nine important trials in which the defense relied on such methods, it

A.   won all nine.

B.   won two.

C.   won seven.

D.   lost all nine.

Answer C, Type FAC

91.   In 1986 the U.S. Supreme Court in a split decision

A.   ruled that death-qualified jurors are a biased sample.

B.   overturned a lower court ruling that death-qualified jurors are a biased sample.

C.   ruled that Georgia's five-member juries were as reliable and accurate as twelve-member juries.

D.   overturned a lower court decision that six-member juries could decide cases involving the death penalty.

Answer B, Type FAC

92.   Someone accused of a crime is judged more sympathetically

A.   by females than by males.

B.   if he or she appears to have personality characteristics that are complementary to the one who judges.

C.   if he or she appears similar to the one who judges.

D.   if there was a bystander who watched and did not intervene.

Answer C, Type FAC

93.   What is meant by the "two-thirds-majority" scheme?

A.   Two-thirds of all people asked refuse to serve on a jury.

B.   Two out of three times judges agree with the jury's decision.

C.   A two-thirds majority is a better rule than consensus for a jury to follow in reaching a verdict.

D.   The jury verdict is usually the alternative favored by at least two-thirds of the jurors at the outset.

Answer D, Type DEF

94.   According to the text, simulated juries

A.   can help us formulate theories we can use to interpret the more complex world.

B.   are almost identical to real juries so that we can readily generalize from one to the other.

C. have been viewed by the majority of Supreme Court judges as valuable in predicting the behavior of actual juries.

D. have mundane but not experimental realism.

Answer A, Type FAC

95. Whose eyewitness testimony is probably the most reliable?

A. Thressa's report immediately after a bank robbery. She was simply asked by police to tell in her own words what happened.

B. Sheryl's testimony about a grocery store holdup. She has been interviewed eight times by the prosecuting attorney before appearing in court.

C. David's testimony about a car accident. He has been interviewed three times by the defense attorney before his court appearance.

D. Susan's report immediately after observing an attempted rape. She was asked very specific questions by the police, who believed they already had a suspect in custody.

Answer A, Type CON

96. Attorney Johnson will be defending James S., who is accused of raping a 22-year-old woman. Who among the following jurors is likely to be least sympathetic to his client's case?

A. John, a 40-year-old plumber who once served a sentence for burglary

B. Todd, a 22-year-old college student who is a political liberal

C. Wilma, a 42-year-old mother of two who tends to be authoritarian

D. Rita, a 32-year-old television executive who opposes the death penalty

Answer C, Type CON

97. Attorney Miller is defending Mary, a 20-year-old college student, who is being tried for failing to pay income tax. What should she do to boost Mary's chances of being acquitted?

A. select Bill and Philip, who are also college students to serve as jurors

B. have Mary appear in court as attractively dressed as possible

C. select jurors who oppose the death penalty

D. All of the above.

Answer D, Type CON

98. You have just been appointed to serve as a new county judge. You are concerned about the effect inadmissible evidence may have on the jury in an upcoming trial of a case involving rape. You anticipate that the defense attorney will seek to introduce evidence regarding the victim's prior sexual history. To minimize the impact of such evidence on the jury, you should

A. say nothing about such inadmissible evidence to the jury.

B. remind the jury before the trial that the victim's previous sexual history is irrelevant.

C. only tell the jury that the evidence is inadmissible after the defense attempts to introduce it.

D. ask the defendant to refute any damaging evidence about her previous sexual history.

Answer B, Type CON

99. A twelve-member jury has heard all the evidence in a child abuse case and is beginning to deliberate. At the outset five jurors favor acquittal of the defendant and seven favor conviction. Based on research in the text, the jury will probably

A. be unable to reach a verdict and be a hung jury.

B. bring in a guilty verdict.

C. vote for acquittal.

D. vote for acquittal if the defendant is female and for conviction if the defendant is male.

Answer A, Type CON

100. After hearing evidence in a murder trial, 12 jurors tend to believe the evidence is insufficient to convict the 25-year-old Black defendant. According to the group polarization hypothesis, after the jurors deliberate,
   A.   they will be more convinced the defendant is guilty.
   B.   they will be more convinced the evidence is insufficient to convict.
   C.   they will be evenly split, with some convinced he is guilty and others convinced he is innocent.
   D.   they will be split, with a minority favoring acquittal and the majority favoring conviction.
   Answer B, Type CON

Critical Thinking Questions

101. Explain the misinformation effect and its implications for eyewitness testimony.

102. The FBI includes the "cognitive interview" procedure in its training program. Describe this procedure and explain why it helps reduce error in eyewitness testimony.

103. What constructive steps can be taken to increase the accuracy and objectivity of jury members?

104. Choose a famous criminal case and discuss the potential impact of pretrial publicity on the outcome of the case.

105. Discuss how groupthink processes might operate in jury deliberations.